Happy Birthday Dad,
~~love kinde~~
1985

Backrooms

Backrooms

A Story of Politics

Colin Thatcher

Western Producer Prairie Books
Saskatoon, Saskatchewan

Cover photograph by Ian Biggar
Cover design by John Luckhurst/GDL

Printed in Canada by Friesen Printers
Altona, Manitoba

Western Producer Prairie Books publications are produced and
manufactured in the middle of western Canada by a unique
publishing venture owned by a group of prairie farmers who are
members of Saskatchewan Wheat Pool. From the first book in 1954, a
reprint of a serial originally carried in the weekly newspaper, *The
Western Producer,* to the book before you now, the tradition of
providing enjoyable and informative reading for all Canadians is
continued.

Canadian Cataloguing in Publication Data

Thatcher, Colin, 1938–
        Backrooms

ISBN 0-88833-173-8

1. Thatcher, Colin, 1938– 2. Politicians —
Saskatchewan — Biography. 3. Saskatchewan —
Politics and government — 1971–1982.* 4. Liberal
Party of Canada (Saskatchewan). I. Title.
FC3527.1.T53A3 1985   971.24′03′0924   C85–091538–4
F1072. T53A3 1985

Contents

Preface

Backrooms was written in longhand over a period of five months after my conviction for the first-degree murder of my ex-wife. As I write this preface, I await the results of my appeal application—a process that has now lasted some four months. Upon my conviction, I was placed in the maximum security wing of the Saskatoon Correctional Centre, where I was virtually cut off from the world.

At the urging of my family and to maintain my sanity, I started to write about my political experiences. I was nicely into the project when I was transferred to the Edmonton institution. This book became my insulation against the long days and the resulting anxieties while my fate was in the hands of God. The manuscript was written with almost total reliance on memory, the only notable exception being a copy of Barry Wilson's *Politics of Defeat* used to recall some events of many years ago. The events described are as I recalled and interpreted them in a partisan political manner. I have attempted to present some insight into the working of politicians' minds and to demonstrate how they react instinctively to various situations. Politicians are not society's best loved animals, with some justification; however, perhaps passages in this book will cause you to reevaluate your assessment, and lower it accordingly.

There are events included that I never believed I would narrate, nor have they ever been described in the past. The content and tone of an exchange in the Saskatchewan Legislative Assembly between the premier and the leader of the opposition the day after my conviction led me to conclude I was no longer obligated to remain silent on any aspect of my political associations.

I wish to extend my thanks to the warden and officials at the Edmonton institution, who were very fair in allowing me to communicate with the publisher. My thanks also to Leo Saroop and Bob Watson, my superiors at the school in the institution, for the use of their environment, from which the majority of this manuscript was written.

1

A Political Family

Politics has always fascinated my family. As far back as I can remember my family has had a role to play in the Saskatchewan political scene. Sometimes we won; other times we lost. But we were usually there.

My first recollection of my father's entrance into local politics is of a sunny spring day in 1945. I was coming home from grade school, doing whatever grade one students do while coming home, when I saw a poster on a telephone pole with my father's picture on it. I recall the strangeness of seeing my father's picture in such an odd place under a heading that meant nothing to me: CCF. There were other pictures and posters on the various telephone poles which meant just as little to me. I ran home to my mother full of curiosity and questions. What was Dad doing with his picture on a telephone pole?

My entrance into active politics probably coincided with my father's death—about 5:00 A.M., July 23, 1971. Early that morning I answered the phone to hear my mother say the devastating words, "Dad's gone."

The fact that the news was not totally unexpected did not lessen its impact. I was shattered and bitter. Only ten hours earlier my father had been in my backyard, trying out my new swimming pool. As he sipped on a weak rye and water, he talked of what a great day it had been. He was in an excellent humor. His doctor had put him through a thorough medical checkup and the results were in cheerful contrast to the drab news of previous months. In my father's words he had been given "a clean bill of health." His heart was in good shape and he was generally optimistic about everything except his political future. He was a realist and knew the Canadian political rule: never lose an election in office.

At least his last day on earth was a pleasant one. He spent it at the place he loved the most—the ranch—with his Hereford cows. His last evening was spent in the company of two people who had become most important to him: his grandsons, Greg and Regan. As he left later that evening for his home in Regina, no one guessed he was in the final countdown of his life and that within hours his heart would literally burst.

JoAnn was able to summon a babysitter at the bizarre hour of 5:15 A.M., and we left for Regina. The drive gave me some time for reflection. I suddenly realized I was totally on my own. Despite my age, I had never known that feeling before.

My relationship with my father was typical of father-son situations when both are involved in the same business. What minor disagreements we had centered on the degree of authority he would delegate on the ranching operation. It was sometimes a source of friction between us; he would appear at the ranch and make a variety of changes, only to disappear again, saddling me with the results of his decisions. I would then be furious and probably decide to quit, but of course I never did.

It was my father's way. He was never a great delegator of authority even when preparing a government. Perhaps had he been blessed with a stronger cabinet he might have been different, but probably not. He was difficult to work for, but then how many fathers and sons work harmoniously together without incident? I would say my father and I were well above average in this area but this does not mean we did not have some great battles over how a cattle ranch should operate. In any event, I was now on my own in every respect and, much as I grieved for my father and had serious misgivings for the future, I had a positive outlook.

When JoAnn and I arrived in Regina shortly before 6:00 A.M., my father's brother and his wife were already with my mother. Mom was like a rock and would stay like that throughout. The announcement of Dad's death had not yet been made and my mother and I agreed that key members of the Liberal party should be notified before they heard it on the news. I commented to JoAnn that with these phone calls the leadership race would begin and it would be in full swing by the afternoon. My mother phoned Dave Steuart, always the number two man in the government, while I phoned Cy MacDonald, who was favored by many to be my father's successor. The political way demanded that bells and sirens would go off in their heads simultaneously as they received the news.

Later that morning the residence at 58 Academy Park Road was alive with visitors. My father's passing was a shock, and the displays of emotion were genuine from both the political and nonpolitical people gathering. Unquestionably, however, the leadership campaign was underway. Even at this early date conversations were taking place in corners and the participants had "leadership" written across their faces. It was easy to tell by the embarrassed looks as a family member went by. Actually, they should not have been embarrassed because that is how it is in politics. It has always been like that and always will be, regardless of political stripe. The political vocabulary does not include words like compassion, mercy, or sensitivity.

I returned to Moose Jaw that afternoon for a meeting with a bank manager. At this point I knew nothing about what, if anything, I was inheriting, and I had to make arrangements for an operating loan to keep the ranch running. It was my first foray without someone looking over my shoulder to pick up the pieces if I stumbled. The bank I went to see was wonderful in true banking tradition and the bank manager extracted an amount of blood consistent with his position of strength. I agreed to his terms because it was the smart thing to do on that day. It was also a lesson: your bank manager is not your friend, he is your adversary and, make no mistake, the bank wants your farm.

I returned to Regina later that evening to find a huge crowd at my mother's residence. Premier Allan Blakeney and his wife had arrived and handled themselves most professionally in a sea of Liberals. I had a brief conversation with the premier and from some of his comments I gathered things were not very different from one party to the other. It appeared he was being overwhelmed with willing applicants for the patronage jobs available. I had heard a similar story from my father some years earlier and would see the phenomenon repeated some eleven years later.

The 1971 election in Saskatchewan had, of course, been a disaster for the Liberal party, which had governed since 1964. Certainly one of the decisive factors had to be my father's health and the restrictions it placed on him. He was only the shell of the person I had seen campaign on so many other occasions as he led the party through this campaign. He was sick and looked it, and the precise organizational genius was not there. He had told me numerous times that he did not want to lead the party through another election. The main reason he stayed on was because there was no obvious successor to lead the party to victory. Such a statement, of course, brings up the name of Davey Steuart, his long-time number two man and most trusted minister and confidant. I know the high regard he had for Davey and there was no question of his ability.

However, late in 1969, at almost the precise time my father was considering retirement and was probably about to call Davey in to tell him as much, Dave Steuart surprised him. Apparently Davey felt he was in trouble in his Prince Albert riding and, according to my father, he demanded the newly created Albert Park constituency in Regina under threat of leaving politics altogether. My father was floored. Except for Dave's initial by-election win in 1962, Prince Albert had always been a tough Liberal seat; however, Dave had always managed to squeak it. He had already earned the title of "Landslide" Steuart from his narrow wins in double-digit numbers. Dave Steuart was my father's prize connection to northern Saskatchewan and one of the key players in the economic development of the North. His role in attracting industry to Prince Albert in the form of a pulp mill had been invaluable, and I had often heard my father describe him as "my brightest and best minister." The prospect of Davey leaving Prince Albert for a safe Liberal seat in Regina was unthinkable. Obviously any Liberal could win Albert Park; it had been created with the fine hand of Jack Harrington and was as guaranteed as any seat could be. Davey was to continue his insistence over the next several months before giving up. Davey had made up my father's mind—Davey's political judgment was bad and he would lead the party to disaster. My father was right on that count. When Davey ultimately did get the chance that is exactly where he led it.

The election of 1971 saw the NDP under Allan Blakeney returned to power in Saskatchewan with a 45- to 15-seat avalanche. The NDP had skillfully exploited the anti-Trudeau and anti–federal Liberal sentiment that was firmly embedded in the prairie landscape for the duration of the Trudeau years and will probably outlive the man himself. During the campaign, Allan Blakeney coined a phrase at a meeting in Shaunavon that would win him an election. Whether he originated it or borrowed it does not matter. It was devastatingly simple and effective: "A Liberal is a Liberal."

My father had always tried to keep considerable distance between the provincial Liberals and the federal wing of the party. The reasons were basic to Saskatchewan politics and there was nothing new or original in this thinking. There have been very few more successful politicians than the Honorable J. G. (Jimmy) Gardiner and I overheard him on one occasion telling my father that any provincial government in Saskatchewan had to "have a fight with Ottawa at election time." At this stage, in mid-1971, the anti-Trudeau sentiment dictated such a strategy to be a necessity. My father had carefully forged an anti-socialist coalition into the provincial Liberal party and keeping them there was a very difficult balancing act. Federally, the conservatives in this coalition went unquestionably with the Progressive Conservative party but provincially were anti-socialist enough to be "reluctant Liberals." Combine the anti-Trudeauism with Allan Blakeney's "A Liberal is a Liberal" and the time was ripe for the coalition to decay. Moreover, the feeling among the liberal Liberals in Ottawa that strong provincial wings were a detriment to the party led to Ottawa almost blatantly creating a series of minor irritations in Saskatchewan at that time, which contributed to the demise of every provincial Liberal party in Canada, with the exception of the party in Quebec.

The NDP really won the election of 1971 back in the fall of 1967. An accident happened in the constituency of Arm River. The Liberal candidate defeated the incumbent MLA, a Conservative by the name of Martin Pederson who just happened to be the provincial leader of the Progressive Conservative party. Martin Pederson was a strong candidate who had won the constituency of Arm River in the 1964 general election that brought the Liberals to power. Arm River was the old stamping ground of John George Diefenbaker before a federal redistribution of seats caused him to go to Prince Albert. Arm River was usually NDP territory provincially and Conservative territory federally and, as a constituency, was expected to be part of the anti-socialist coalition forged into the Liberal party of 1964. Martin Pederson went to Regina genuinely feeling there was a provincial role for the PCs in Saskatchewan. And why not? At the federal level, Saskatchewan had been Diefenbaker country for almost a decade and no doubt Pederson felt the same would come true provincially. After all, he was the first PC MLA since the Anderson government of the 1930s.

Martin Pederson's dream of a strong Progressive Conservative party on a provincial basis dissipated quickly. Martin soon found that the key Tory fund raisers on a federal basis were simply not available to him provincially. They were fund raisers or key people for the provincial Liberal party and part of the anti-socialist coalition that was now in power in Saskatchewan. They were brutally frank with Martin and told him in no uncertain terms that there was no room in Saskatchewan for two anti-socialist parties and that, even though they were Tories, they were NDP-haters first. The game was simple—Tory federally and Liberal provincially. A strong provincial Tory party meant an NDP government.

At this point, it seems appropriate to stop and draw attention to the fact that there are two distinct kinds of Tories in Saskatchewan: those far right of center anti-socialists who can be Social Credit in British Columbia, Conservative in Alberta, and even Liberal in Saskatchewan in the 1960s; and those at the opposite end of the political spectrum who vote Tory or NDP but under no circumstances Liberal. It is from this latter group that the original CCF spawned, and to this day they exist. The former group was already in the camp of the provincial Liberals so the latter was the only group available to Martin Pederson. Unfortunately, the money necessary to be a political force lay with the first group. Martin was out in the cold financially.

Another politician noted Martin's predicament; namely my father. He knew all about the second category of Tories and the number of seats in which they made a difference. There were well over fifteen seats that were won or lost depending whether the latter class of Tories voted Progressive Conservative or NDP. It was only natural that a loose, unofficial alliance was formed between Martin Pederson and my father. Raising money was no problem for the provincial Liberals and they could easily make some available to Martin for PC activity in selected constituencies where a Tory candidate would be beneficial to the Liberals. The deal was consummated when Jim Whiteside, executive assistant to my father, delivered an envelope to Martin in the lobby of a Saskatoon hotel. The arrangement worked well and played a role in the Liberal's reelection in 1967. Unfortunately for the Liberals, Arm River decided to reject Martin Pederson in 1967 and the Liberal control of the provincial wing of the Conservative party was gone for good.

These were some of the factors that played a prominent role in the Liberal election disaster of 1971. I must also add that the NDP ran an excellent campaign. They had done their homework well and were in tune with the mood of the times. The state of the economy was poor, and four-bushel wheat quotas and low potash prices (down to thirteen dollars U.S. per ton from a high of forty-five dollars) had certainly not put the Saskatchewan electorate in a heady frame of mind. In fact, they joined the trend of six other provinces and changed governments.

The fifteen Liberal MLAs who survived the onslaught were a varied group. Some were older cabinet ministers who would rather have lost than sit in opposition but were stuck there now. Several others were backbenchers in the former government who now had to turn their efforts to opposition, which is a real contrast to the government side. There were also three very talented newcomers to the Liberal MLA ranks. These were Dr. Don MacDonald, a veterinarian from Moose Jaw who had won the tough Moose Jaw North seat, which had always been NDP; Gary Lane, who took over Attorney General Darrel Heald's Qu'Appelle constituency; and Ken MacLeod, a bright and ambitious Regina lawyer who had won the Albert Park seat formerly coveted by Davey Steuart. These three were certainly the one ray of hope for a comeback of the Liberal party.

The new MLA for Moose Jaw North, Don MacDonald, was the object of one of my first forays into politics. He was one of my closest friends, partly because he was our ranch veterinarian. An anti-socialist conservative, he supported the Liberals provincially. The constituency of Moose Jaw North was held by the NDP and I had always felt that it could and should be won by the Liberals with the right candidate. I went to work on Don and, after reflecting on it for some time, he agreed to be a candidate. I helped him put together an organization for the nominating convention and he won in a breeze. He was to win comfortably in the general election of 1971. He was a real enigma in politics. He was an excellent opposition MLA and getting better, yet politics turned him off and affected his home life in a way that alarmed him. He turned his back on a promising political career in 1975 and did not seek reelection. As close as we were, I felt he never told me the whole story.

Gary Lane was a young attorney who had served his apprenticeship as executive assistant to Attorney General Darrel Heald, who had retired to go to heaven—known as the bench or the judiciary. Somehow, Heald convinced the Liberals in his old constituency of Qu'Appelle to accept Gary Lane as his replacement. It was certainly not a unanimous decision and a very bitter nominating convention at Lumsden took place. Lane won narrowly and skillfully healed the breach before going on to win the constituency in the election. Lane was a good politician and would be on the scene for some time. His arrival was noted, as well as his obvious ambition.

Ken MacLeod was not welcomed by all. He had not been my father's choice for the Albert Park seat and, in fact, my father had encouraged his executive assistant Ken Sundquist to contest the nomination. MacLeod was a torrid worker and simply sold sufficient memberships to those committed to him to make him virtually untouchable. His hard work was reflected in the election results when he easily won Albert Park. Granted it was a safe seat, but the provincial trend was away from the Liberals and still he did very, very well. Ken was a personable, aggressive Regina lawyer who made no bones of the fact he expected to be the attorney general if the Liberals were reelected. The fact that they were not had only raised his sights to the position of party leader.

As the arrangements for my father's funeral were being made, the first signs of jockeying for the leadership surfaced. My mother and I decided that the pallbearers would consist of his executive assistants and various people from the livestock industry. (It was a toss-up whether my father loved politics or cattle the most.) The protest was immediate from Davey Steuart, who rushed to see my mother. Davey brought heavy pressure to bear on her, arguing that he should be a pallbearer because of his relationship and loyalty to my father. He was right, and we knew it. However, new leadership was being discussed openly and it had been our decision to stay out of it. In the end, my mother yielded to Davey and the matter was settled.

We had also received word that Prime Minister Pierre Elliott Trudeau was going to attend. I was personally very upset. I had never been a fan of the prime minister and felt his government had gone out of its way to sandbag my father's government. My father did not feel that way and, in fact, was quite taken with Mr. Trudeau. Mr. Trudeau's obvious gifts were not lost on my father, who genuinely respected his talents. I know he was disappointed when he did not hear from the prime minister after the election defeat. I was not at all enthusiastic about his attendance but I knew my mother was.

The inevitable leadership race was the topic of conversation among the Liberals already. The big unknowns were the three newcomers. Would there be a candidate from among them? Ken MacLeod and Gary Lane were sharks and had their respective feelers out. No question, if either of them thought they could win, they would go. The obvious combatants were Davey Steuart and the personable Cy MacDonald. Both were strong Roman Catholics, great speakers, and commanded loyal followings. Davey had an edge because of his long-term role as the loyal number two man. As an after-dinner speaker and teller of stories, he was as good as they came. There was little doubt that these two would be the headliners but both were looking over their shoulders at the newcomers.

Even though I was preoccupied with family matters, already I was picking up gossip as to how the Liberal party should be orientating itself. The old guard was preparing to support either Davey Steuart or Cy MacDonald. Another faction, composed mainly of federal Liberals, was looking for someone who would carry the provincial party philosophically more in line with Ottawa. The candidate for this faction would be Ken MacLeod, if he chose to run. It was already assumed by many that Ken MacLeod would be in the race probably more because of his aggressive nature than any array of facts. Ken wanted to run, but at this point he was cagily assessing potential support. Gary Lane was in a similar situation. He was considering being a young candidate advocating change in the party, which in 1971 was a popular slogan for anyone. Lane wanted to go. He just didn't know if the timing was right.

Another factor troubling the younger candidates was, of course, the party's prospects in the next general election. After all, the NDP had won a solid majority and inherited a virtually debt-free province by today's standards. Also, Saskatchewan voters rarely deny a new government a second term, which led to the question of whether the new leader would be a true leader or a sacrificial lamb. In other words, should the party go with the easiest person to get rid of after the anticipated loss to the NDP the next time around? It should be pointed out that nobody was giving the remotest consideration to the possible rise of the Conservative party and it was assumed by all that ensuing elections would be the Liberal-NDP fights. Very rapidly, the smart infighters were coming to the conclusion that the next election was a write-off and were focusing their thinking on post-1975. This school of thought was to favor Davey Steuart.

My father's funeral service was held on July 27, 1971, at St. Andrew's United Church in Moose Jaw where he had been a lifelong member. The service was conducted by his long-time friend, the Rev. Allan Martin, who delivered a powerful sermon highly appropriate for someone like my father. Among those in attendance was the Right Honorable John Diefenbaker, who was particularly kind to my mother. Prime Minister Trudeau and Premier Allan Blakeney were also in attendance. Otto Lang had accompanied the prime minister from Ottawa. The entire area around the church was overflowing for at least a block in each direction. The turnout was a moving testament to someone who had served the area for so many years. Virtually the whole Liberal party was there, but for some it was for expediency in the upcoming leadership campaign.

After the service there was the traditional procession to the cemetery and the graveside ceremony. The reception was to be held at my residence in Moose Jaw. As the family was about to depart Prime Minister Trudeau approached my mother and expressed his condolences. He spoke gently to my son Greg, who was only six. I was reserved, almost cool, as we spoke briefly. I thought, whatever it is, he has it in abundance. No question he is a charmer. He indicated that he was returning directly to Ottawa from the Moose Jaw air base and expressed his regrets that he would not be coming to my place.

We returned immediately to my house where several guests had already arrived. The bar was open in my backyard, the weather was gorgeous, and my recently finished swimming pool looked more than presentable. Relatives, friends, and politicians relaxed and mingled in the July sunshine. Many of the people present were provincial Liberals and not necessarily federal ones. Some of them had openly expressed bitterness toward the federal government and the perceived manner it had sandbagged my father's government. Pierre Elliott Trudeau was not the man of the hour. With most of our guests well into their second or third drink, I was informed that an unexpected guest had appeared at the front door. I rushed into the house in time to see my mother greeting Mr. Trudeau and Otto Lang and what seemed like a score of security agents. Where all the security agents came from is a mystery but in no time my street was virtually blocked off and the alley behind my house was closed. One of my neighbors told me later that he had to "choose his words carefully" in order to get home. My quiet neighborhood in Moose Jaw was just not used to heavy stuff like this.

Mr. Trudeau, after explaining that the reason for delaying his return to Ottawa was that he wished to meet the balance of the family, left for the backyard. He politely declined my offer to accompany him for some initial introductions, explaining he would just quietly "visit with some people." I watched the prime minister work the famed Trudeau magic. It will long be debated whether he governed Canada effectively but his individual charm and obvious intellect are unassailable. The comment Mr. Trudeau made in the fall of 1984 after the Tory government had destroyed the Liberal government that he could have won for the Liberals, is not that far out.

The prime minister and Otto Lang left to return to Ottawa and my neighbors were allowed the unrestricted use of their street once again. By now, many of the remaining guests had enjoyed several cocktails and the main subject of conversation in the various groups was pure politics and, specifically, the leadership of the party. The surviving caucus had met the previous day and had elected Davey Steuart interim leader, an advantage that Davey ultimately used to propel himself into the position of permanent leader. Into the fourth or fifth (or sixth or seventh) drink the political talk was becoming more uninhibited, especially since my mother had left to make an appearance at St. Andrew's church at a reception for those who were not politically ordained. I didn't take offense at the talk, nor would my father have—it was the political way. It was something akin to "The king is dead, long live the king." The question of course was, who is the new king and when do we crown him?

Every person who ever enters partisan party politics harbors a desire, no matter how deeply concealed, of some day leading the party of his or her choice. Now many get over it quickly but any politician who pretends that he has never entertained leadership aspirations is one not to be trusted. There are many reasons for abandoning such thoughts but, believe me, every politician experiences them. Such was the case in my backyard this beautiful July 27 afternoon. There were a multitude, each of whom believed he was the messiah who would rebuild the party to be a serious contender in four years. There is a mystique about the leadership of a political party as well as the challenge of a leadership convention that one not politically involved cannot appreciate or understand. A leadership convention has to be the most grueling undertaking known to political man but in a strange way it is also fun. The infighting is horrendous, the miles covered in various forms exhausting, and the rewards questionable, but still a leadership convention is a difficult maiden to turn down. That was exactly what the prospective candidates were experiencing. All wanted the leadership badly but were still grappling with the two major questions a candidate must ask: can I win a convention? and, have I got a shot at the marbles in four years?

Politics is a question of timing and blind luck. Some of the ablest people simply cannot win elective office; conversely, some of the most incompetent jerks win in a landslide. For documentary proof, check the roster of the House of Commons or any provincial legislature on any random date. Back in 1971 in my backyard, Gary Lane was quietly revealing to anyone who chose to converse in his corner that my father had told him that he was to be groomed to be the next leader. Now, if you knew Gary Lane in 1971, or for that matter in 1985, that was a difficult one for even the most ardent Liberal to swallow. However, it was a good political tactic and one that Lane would hone to perfection in the ensuing years. Flying a kite to test the political wind is an art, and Lane mastered it. He wanted to run for the leadership—no question about it. He just didn't think he could win, at least not at that point. However, he was flying all the kites he could and would continue to do so for the next couple of months before deciding to support Dave Steuart. Why? Because Dave was the oldest and would be done after losing the next election. In some respects this sounds like realistic political thinking. In fact, Gary Lane was to play a role in the next four years when the provincial Liberal party lost its identity and moved sharply to the left, leaving a vacuum that few in the Liberal party thought could be filled. The provincial Liberal party became a drugstore version of a left-of-center party, a spot that was more than amply filled by the NDP. And one of their leaders into this never-never land was Gary Lane. Lane was a political chameleon. He possessed no philosophy or principles and the issue in his mind was clear—which side had more votes. In short, being unhampered by any philosophical code or principle he had all the attributes necessary to be a successful politician.

Ken MacLeod was assessing the terrain with what Davey Steuart termed the "lean and hungry look." Ken was not good at disguising his ambitions, although he was an engaging individual with genuine talent. He was well known as one of Otto Lang's boys and had been, and probably still was, a member of what was known in Regina as the "Silver Seven." This was a group of seven Regina lawyers, all of whom were contemporaries or former students of Otto Lang. Basically, they controlled federal patronage and the federal Liberal scene in Saskatchewan. Many people originally wanted Ken to be a candidate, but beneath a perhaps too aggressive exterior was a very keen analytic mind. Ken MacLeod was shrewd enough not to just want to be the leader of the Liberal party, he wanted to be premier. He was enough of a realist to know he would not enter the race as the front runner but, more important, he wanted to win a general election and at this point in 1971 things did not look bright for the Liberals four years down the road.

As the reception was drawing to a close I was approached by our family attorney, Ed Odishaw, who wanted to set up a meeting with me in Regina as soon as possible. When I didn't turn up in the next few days, he called to suggest that I make it sooner rather than later. He didn't want to go into the matter on the telephone but indicated it had to do with the party and he had received several calls from Dave Steuart.

I went to Ed Odishaw's office the following day and we got down to what Dave Steuart wanted. He was looking for the party reserves—the money from fund raising that had been put away for a rainy day. No question, the rainy days were here but apparently Davey did not know where the funds were. Neither did I. However, I did know that a large fund did exist and I knew that a great deal of it was in the form of corporate bonds. I agreed to look through my father's personal effects and went up to the legislative buildings to clean out his office. I was furious to find out it had already been done, apparently by party treasurer Bob Pierce. I assumed they couldn't wait but felt their actions were slightly more than presumptuous. At least they should have what they were looking for. They didn't.

Ed phoned that night to see how I had made out. He said Dave Steuart was really pressuring him and he persuaded me to return to his office the following afternoon to meet Bob Pierce. I had always liked Bob with his dry, cynical wit and he had been invaluable and loyal to my father. Bob was trusted implicitly by my father and he was one of his very best corporate fund raisers. As he had been party treasurer I found it surprising that he could not lay his hands on the funds in whatever form they existed. Bob was not a popular figure in all quarters of the party, but he could not have cared less. He was his own man, although I often wondered if he was a happy one. No doubt it was Bob Pierce's obvious ability, coupled with his cynicism and straightforwardness, that would catch the eye of Bob Blair and propel him upward to the highest echelons of Nova Corporation.

Bob Pierce, as was his nature, got to the point quickly. He knew there was a great deal of money in the form of corporate bonds somewhere. He acknowledged cleaning out my father's desk and said by way of explanation that he had assumed my mother and I had enough to occupy ourselves and as someone was going to do it, it was best that it be a confidant of my father's. In my father's desk he had found a typewritten list of corporate bonds. Beside each corporate name was an amount that we all assumed to be a dollar value. There were no serial numbers or any indication of how the bonds were registered and in what name. The figures added up to just under one million dollars. And it was missing. One million dollars in bonds was missing. Both Ed Odishaw and Bob Pierce urged me to help them find the money before anyone else got wind of the situation. I agreed.

It was not to be nearly as easy as I had anticipated. I went through my father's papers and personal effects with a fine-tooth comb and found nothing. I went through the house on Academy Park Road and came up with nothing. My mother could not help me other than to verify the existence of the bonds. She didn't know the precise form they were in but was aware that no one else in the party knew either. I phoned Ed Odishaw to tell him that I had not found them yet. He said that Dave Steuart was badgering him and wanted to talk to my mother about them. I told him to tell Davey to go to hell. I was doing the best I could without having much to go on.

I was at a dead end as far as my father's personal effects were concerned. The next day I reluctantly started to search in Regina at every bank and trust company. The procedure was the same at all of them. I would see the manager and ask him if my father had an account there, either in his name or in the name of the Saskatchewan Liberal party. At this point, I had no choice but to consider the possibility that my father might have seen fit to convert the corporate bonds to an account because of the election. However, no matter where I went the answer was the same: there was no account in either name and never had been. By now I was sure that it was all over Regina that I was searching and coming up with nothing. I had attempted some form of cover story at each place but it was shallow and in retrospect I am certain it was not believed.

I phoned Ed and said I had to return to the ranch and get some work done. I was at a loss and perhaps some time off to think would be beneficial. Ed said that he had promised to call Bob Pierce that night and that he and Dave Steuart would not be happy. My reply was that they could be as unhappy as they wanted, there was nothing I could do that night.

Ed called me in Moose Jaw that evening and urged me to come to his office and meet with Pierce and Steuart the next morning. I told him there was no point and wanted to postpone the meeting for several days. Ed replied that Dave Steuart was again talking about going to see my mother, to which I replied that if he did my cooperation was at an end. Why Davey thought my mother was privy to something was beyond me, but I was adamant that she would not be bothered with this. She was having enough trouble adjusting to her new reality. I reluctantly agreed to be at Ed's office the next day.

Needless to say, the relationship between Steuart, Pierce, and me was deteriorating sharply. Although they certainly never expressed it in words, I was left with the clear impression they thought I was not being candid with them. Davey talked in circles about the pressures he was under and expressed concern as to how he was going to account to the caucus and the party executive when it met. Pierce interjected with typical Pierce cynicism that the caucus had never been told anything in the past so why set a precedent. That was not what Davey was looking for. I again told them I was doing the best I could and would sooner or later find what we were all looking for. It was then that Pierce dropped the one they had been fencing around for: was the money part of my father's estate?

I was upset that they even asked the question and probably showed it. They had been as close to my father as anyone and knew the answer. The question was asked out of frustration, but I have often wondered if I would have asked it if our positions had been reversed. I hope not. That moment had a lasting impact on me—more than it should have. There would be a day when recollection of it would make my departure from the Liberal party a much less difficult decision. It would also affect my thinking when I met Bob Pierce some dozen years later about a billion-dollar white elephant, or heavy oil upgrader.

At this point Ed Odishaw came out with some soothing words that kept the lid on everything. I was incensed and all three knew it. I angrily told them that it was impossible. Pierce asked how I knew, to which I replied that I had looked everywhere. Pierce pointed out that no one had checked my father's safety deposit box. At this time the federal government was still involved in the estate tax field. The will had not yet been probated and of course the safety deposit box had been sealed. I asked Ed if it was possible to check the contents before the will was probated. He indicated it would be difficult but not impossible. I gave him instructions on behalf of the executors of my father's estate to try to arrange it and, if successful, I insisted either Pierce or Steuart be present. I wanted these insinuations ended once and for all. The meeting ended on that note.

It took Ed a couple of days to complete the necessary arrangements. The bank was to open the safety deposit box in the presence of me, Ed Odishaw, Bob Pierce, and a bank employee. Nothing could be removed. I deeply resented this intrusion by the Liberal party into our family affairs; however, it seemed necessary at the time to keep my father's name untarnished. Pierce, Odishaw, and I met at the bank and entered the vault with the manager. I handed the manager our half of the safety deposit keys and held my breath. The box was opened and Ed and I quickly examined the contents. There was nothing remotely connected with the Liberal party. I asked Pierce if he was satisfied. For the first time I detected a little sheepishness in Bob's voice as he quickly said he was.

The three of us walked back to Ed's office in silence, although we were all probably thinking the same thing: where do we go from here? Pierce broke the silence, "If it's gone, it's gone," he said. I was adamant it would turn up. I asked Pierce if there was any chance the bonds had been cashed for use in the election. He replied that was extremely unlikely without his knowledge and was unnecessary anyway because fund raising had gone well. By this time I had been around Pierce too long and was becoming cynical myself. I commented that they had apparently been purchased out of party funds without his knowledge and could probably have been cashed in the same way. Regardless, I told Pierce I would keep looking, but told him to stop pressuring me.

On the drive back to Moose Jaw that evening I did some serious reflection. My father was not a secretive person, in fact, he was quite the opposite and many times my mother and I would jump on him for talking too much. For him to have deliberately hidden close to one million dollars in corporate bonds was totally inconsistent with the man I had known. I decided to question his executive assistants and then his personal secretaries, going as far back as it took.

I started the next day with his last personal secretary, Muriel DeCreyenaire. She couldn't tell me much. She did the journal entries for receipts and disbursements but she obviously was not privy to party investments. His two executive assistants, Dave Sheard and Ken Sundquist, had no knowledge of the portfolio but Sundquist dropped something that I found odd. He did a good deal of the driving for my father and he mentioned that once, sometimes twice, a week he would drive him to downtown Regina and drop him off at the entrance to the Midtown Centre. My father would get out and tell Ken to wait for him and then he would disappear for ten or fifteen minutes. I asked Ken if he found that consistent with my father's activity, and he agreed it was not. However, he had no idea where he went after he entered the mall and my father never volunteered any explanation. I immediately went to the mall entrance Ken had described and went in. The Midtown Centre in downtown Regina is just a mall with nothing to distinguish it from hundreds like it. I strolled down the main area seeing nothing that I could visualize my father going to. The only possibility was a branch of the Montreal Trust and for a brief moment I thought I had it. I went in and asked for the manager and proceeded to give him the same story I had given so many other places in Regina. The answer was the same: they had not done business with my father in any capacity nor had he ever come in. Another dead end. I went back into the mall and covered it again. Nothing registered that would bring my father there once a week for ten or fifteen minutes.

I called Bonnie Donison who had been my father's secretary up to 1969 and was now a producer at CBC. At least with her I didn't need any cover stories. She knew the political game well and, more important, she knew what I was looking for. However, Bonnie was able to provide no clue as to where I might find the bonds. My father had done all the transactions personally and she had not been privy to them. She had no idea what would take him to the Midtown Centre either. Another dead end. I next went to the only two brokerage houses in Regina where corporate bonds could be purchased. At both Houston Willoughby and James Richardson I drew a blank.

Needless to say, I found the drive back to Moose Jaw frustrating. This was not my problem and I wondered why I was bothering. I phoned to see how my mother was and she mentioned that Davey Steuart was coming to see her the next morning. I phoned Ed and told him to tell Davey I had other things to do if he went to see my mother and upset her. I spent the next day at the ranch and felt better. It took a day away from Regina to find out how thoroughly fed up I was with the Liberal party, their problems and innuendoes. Upon my return home I had a message to call my mother. Davey Steuart had done a great job in upsetting her. Oh, they had had a nice visit but Davey had got onto the subject of party funds. I could have wrung Dave Steuart's neck. I promised my mother I would be back in Regina tomorrow to continue the search.

That night I phoned Jim Whiteside, a former executive assistant to my father who was now in Vancouver. Jim, I knew well—JoAnn and I had introduced him to his wife—and I trusted him implicitly. I told him about the situation and my disgust with Davey Steuart. Jim was not surprised. Apparently he had never shared my father's high opinion of Davey; however, on what was important, he was of little help. He knew of the existence of the "rainy day fund" but not its form or substance. Jim's only suggestion was to return to the obvious because my father was not a devious person. He was not the sort to have an account in Calgary or Toronto or a safety deposit box in Vancouver. His feeling was I would find the bonds in some innocuous place I had overlooked and would wonder why I hadn't looked there sooner.

I went back to Regina the next day and started the task of going through everything all over again. My mother helped me at the house but we drew a blank. I went back to the Midtown Centre and entered the same way my father supposedly had done once a week. Again, other than Montreal Trust there was nothing that made any sense. I even went to other exits to see if anything within eyesight would register. Nothing. Yet something had brought him into this very ordinary shopping mall to do something that he apparently would not trust to someone else. I went and had a coffee to kill a few minutes and think about what I was sure was staring me in the face. Upon finishing my coffee I went back and retraced my steps. I was certain I was missing something. However, I was never to know what it was. My father's weekly visits to the mall remain a mystery.

In total frustration I gave up and walked to Ed Odishaw's office. While waiting to see him I phoned my mother and suggested she come back to Moose Jaw for the weekend. That day, a Thursday, I wanted to leave Regina right away, hopefully never to return. She took some persuading but finally I talked her into it. When I saw Ed I got the usual rundown of the daily calls from Pierce and Steuart and the familiar expressions of concern. I went over everything I knew and had done. Ed could do little but offer encouragement and try to keep Steuart and Pierce at bay.

By now it was late afternoon and I left to pick up my mother. Since my father's death she had become more and more reclusive and this trip to Moose Jaw was more of an effort to humor me rather than something she wanted to do. Her state of mind was a real concern and Davey Steuart's total disregard for her feelings made me livid when I thought of it. She was not quite ready so I went up to the second-floor den where my father spent most of his time when at home. I sat down in the chair across the room from his favorite recliner and stared at it. The den was full of momentoes and pictures of various occasions with him as the central figure. Where are they? I asked the pictures and the empty chair over and over again. I became so intense that I was aware of a strange feeling almost as if someone else were in the room. For a brief moment it seemed as if the recliner moved slightly. I noticed a small closet behind the recliner. Strange how many times I had been in that den and never spotted it before. The furniture was arranged in such a way as to prevent usage. To get to the door a table with a lamp had to be moved, as well as the recliner. I stared at the closet door, crossed the room, moved the chair and the table, and opened it. The closet was empty. Then I noticed a shoe box in the farthest corner of the top shelf. I reached up and brought it out into the den. I was excited that this might be what I had been looking for. Instead I found a pouch of the kind insurance companies give their customers to store their policies. Inside the first envelope was an insurance policy for Marge Guy who had been a long-time employee of the party—long before my father's time even—and for several years his personal secretary. The next envelope contained a policy for Jack Harrington, a party organizer and chief electoral officer of the former government. The next envelope contained much more than single policies. As I emptied the contents onto the floor I saw corporate names on what were obviously various types of bonds and they were all registered in one name: the Saskatchewan Liberal Federation.

Only someone who has experienced the removal of a ten-ton load from their shoulders can appreciate the relief I was feeling as I quickly leafed through the bonds. The amounts were dizzying as page after page of five-digit numbers flipped by. They were all there, they had to be. Even though I didn't count them I knew they were all there. I yelled the great news to my mother, poured myself a scotch—I had earned it—and phoned Ed. I told him we were off to Moose Jaw with the bonds and I would talk to him on the weekend to arrange the transfer to Steuart and Pierce. The drive to Moose Jaw was a short one for a change.

Now that this business was resolved I could again turn my thoughts to where they should have been all along; namely to running a ranch and to numerous other tasks such as earning a living. I was looking forward to my mother having a relaxing weekend with her grandchildren. However, upon arriving home there was a message to call Ed Odishaw, which I immediately did. I regretted it since I was only to learn that my new-found friend Davey Steuart had made his daily phone call to Ed and had learned that I had found the bonds. He wanted them now or at the latest tomorrow. I told Ed to tell Davey to relax. The bonds would be turned over to the party early next week and they would be kept in a safe place. As far as I was concerned there was nothing more to discuss. There was no way that I was not going to take the time to go through everything carefully and be very certain of exactly what I was turning over. Ed agreed to stall Steuart.

That evening I leafed through the corporate bonds and ran a total. It came to $965,000. That amount of money in 1971 dollars was a tidy sum. It should have been enough to take the Liberal party through a couple of elections, but that was not to be the case. In any event, the despicable suggestions of the last ten days were over and I intended to be certain they would never be raised again. No one was ever going to be able to say, "All we got from Ross was an empty envelope."

In politics one never signs anything or prepares financial records that are not essential or required by law and even then not always. However, I was determined to protect my father's name for perpetuity. The last ten days had been a prime example of the vultures descending when the target can no longer defend itself. I was going to turn the bonds to the party, but not until a carefully prepared receipt documenting everything was signed by Pierce and Steuart and, of course, after I had made copies of everything. They wouldn't like it but they were responsible for my thinking in this fashion.

The next day brought a barrage of phone calls from Steuart and Pierce that poor JoAnn had to handle. No matter how often she told them I would not be home until evening they would call back within a couple of hours. I came in the door as Davey was calling again and I took the phone. He was sweetness and light and I was ice cold. It was his intention to come down that night and pick up the bonds, to which I said no, it was inconvenient. I told him they would be turned over to the party the first part of the week in Ed Odishaw's office but did not mention my intention of a signed receipt for them. The edge in Davey's voice began to grow as I told him that was the way things were and he was welcome to arrange a time with Ed and I would be there. He insisted on coming down that night and I told him it was out of the question and hung up. I really believe he thought I was going to pass him the one million dollars in bonds without any record of the transaction. I had had enough of Davey Steuart to last quite some time.

The next evening Bob Pierce phoned to see if we could do the transaction in the morning in Moose Jaw. I repeated what I had told Davey and then told him about the receipt I wanted. His immediate response was that my father wouldn't want it and he elaborated on the dangers of such a document to the party. I pointed out the dangers to my father's reputation without one and that he as a lawyer should know that no one passed that kind of money to anyone without some kind of documentation. The conversation did not end on a particularly friendly note and I knew I could expect to hear from Davey Steuart. I wasn't in the mood for that so I removed the phone from the hook for the balance of the evening.

Saturday brought several phone calls from Dave Steuart while I was out at the ranch. I took one of his calls that evening and listened to one of his increasingly monotonous monologues explaining that in politics one simply did not record matters like this and if my father were here he would tell me the same thing. At this point, I was so fed up with Davey Steuart that he could have told me the sun would set in the west this evening and I would have had to look before I would have accepted it. I again told Davey what he had already heard from Pierce—there would be a receipt signed by him and Pierce that described each and every bond down to its serial number and face amount. I went on to say—which I should not have—that after he had found some way to blow that money, he was never going to be able to suggest that he had inherited a blank envelope from my father. The conversation ended on that note. The next day I made duplicate copies of each and every bond. As I looked at each bond registered properly in the name of the Saskatchewan Liberal Federation I thought about the innuendoes that all this could be part of my father's estate. Those bastards, I thought. Even in death my father had left the party a vehicle that, used properly, could make the stay in opposition a short one. I phoned Ed and asked him to arrange the meeting for Monday. It was agreed I would come to his office an hour earlier and we would draw up a satisfactory receipt that would fully describe the transaction. The whole business could not be concluded fast enough for me.

Monday morning I was in Ed's office and we drew up a receipt. Davey Steuart and Bob Pierce arrived and examined the document. Pierce gave me a brief legal speech, which consisted of an argument that the bonds belonged to the party and I had no right to hold them even over the weekend. Davey then launched into one of his monologues about how upset my father would be and the unwritten political rule that matters such as this are simply not recorded. After what I had listened to the past couple of weeks their arguments might as well have been made to the lamp post outside with similar results. I replied as coldly as I could that if they wanted the bonds they were to sign the document that indicated they had received them. If not the meeting was over and I would deliver them some other way. Exasperated and beaten, they examined the bonds, compared the serial numbers, and reluctantly signed. They took the bonds and left with each side sick and tired of the other.

The balance of the summer was spent adjusting to the absence of my father. Politics was out of our lives and we didn't miss it one iota. My close friendship with Don MacDonald kept me informed of what was happening in the party. The NDP government had called a summer session with the intention of repealing two pieces of legislation: the Essential Services Act and the deterrent fees on medicine. The Essential Services Act was introduced in 1967 in response to a strike at Sask Power. Regardless of political stripe every government should have an act of this sort in one form or the other. Under heavy pressure from labor, the NDP repealed the act with great fanfare and during the life of their government preferred to deal with strikes in the essential services sector on an individual basis. They won points with labor on a short-term basis but lost them in the long run as they frequently had to legislate an end to essential service strikes. While they were going through first, second, and third readings, the group being legislated back to work was

invariably picketing or demonstrating outside while their leaders looked on in the galleries as the NDP did their dirty deed.

The other piece of legislation they wanted to repeal were the
deterrent fees on medicare. Under existing legislation a patient
was charged $1.50 per doctor's visit and $2.50 per day in hospital. Everyone hated the fees. Patients hated paying them, doc-
tors hated collecting them, and the government hated the political flak. They made great cannon fodder for the NDP and they
used it well in the election campaign of 1971. There was a
lesson for all parties in the future: it is political suicide to tam-
per with medicare. It is an emotional issue which to this day
cannot be discussed rationally. The people of Saskatchewan
have always made it very clear that they are willing to have
third- and fourth-rate medicare as long as the illusion is there
that it is free. Anyone who disputes that statement is either an
opposition politician or a person who has never had medical
care in the United States.

One can certainly understand the NDP's thinking but the
rationale of Her Majesty's loyal opposition is a different matter.
They voted with the NDP in the repeal of these two pieces of
legislation. It was unbelievable that Davey Steuart, Cy Mac-
Donald, and others voted with the government on these issues.
The first test of the fresh new Liberal party was a disaster. The
party looked ridiculous and the NDP wiped the floor with
them. Their credibility factor was down to nothing already and
was only to get worse.

The summer of 1971 passed and the main political event of
interest was the Liberal leadership race. For Davey Steuart, it
was now or never. He was fifty-five years old and there was no
tomorrow for him politically. As for Cy MacDonald, he could
run or bide his time. Cy thought he could win and decided to
go. The newly elected MLAs and potential candidates Gary
Lane and Ken MacLeod decided not to go and instead supported Davey Steuart. Their logic was Machiavellian, pure and
simple. They had written off a Liberal win in 1975 and were
looking at 1978–79. A surprise entry in the race was George
Leith. He was a genuine liberal, which put him on the left wing
of the party and was perhaps one reason why my father
ignored him for a cabinet post. He had lost what should have
been a safe seat in the general election for the most inexcusable

of reasons—he simply did not work. George had taken two weeks off in the campaign to do his summerfallowing. And good old George wondered why he had lost and, even funnier, thought he could lead the party back to power.

Against the backdrop of the leadership race was the inevitable by-election in Morse constituency to replace my father. To my regret, I had never really gotten involved in constituency work in Morse. My father had put together a superb executive and had turned what had once been a CCF stronghold into a relatively safe Liberal seat. Being the premier had helped him immeasurably but the quality of the people on the executive had also played a strong role. The president of the constituency was Jack Wiebe, a Mennonite from Main Centre. Jack had been an excellent president and had done a superb job for my father in the additional role of campaign manager. If there was an obvious choice as a successor, it had to be Jack Wiebe. The executive had already endorsed him and all that remained was to have a convention to rubber-stamp the nomination.

At this point I had no desire or intention to become involved in politics. It had been mentioned by the odd person that I should consider replacing my father in Morse but I did not plan to do so. One hot August afternoon, I was driving our stackliner hauling hay in at the ranch when Jack Wiebe and two members of the Morse constituency executive came in the yard. I suppose they had heard that I was a potential candidate, probably because it is commonplace for sons to replace their fathers. Jack was very proper and to the point. If I wasn't a candidate, he asked, then would I support him? I replied that I would certainly support him and had given no thought to being a candidate myself. Jack was a truly nice person and I remember thinking at that time that he would make a superb politician. As they left my yard I went back to stacking hay and forgot about politics.

No doubt everyone who has seen or heard a politician justifying why he or she is going to be a candidate remembers the words, "I have been urged by many supporters," or, "I am gratified by the level of encouragement . . ." The impression the potential candidate attempts to create is that his phone is ringing off the hook or that his door is being beaten down by frantic supporters adamant that he allow his name to be presented so the country can be saved forthwith. In other words, the impression is usually given that the candidate was asked, urged, or whatever and upon reflection and consultation with higher authority reluctantly came forward. Show me a politician who says he was "asked" to run and I will show you a liar, or a jock, or someone with a hyperactive imagination.

Virtually no one is asked to enter politics. Now politicians may very well have arranged for someone to make it appear as if they were asked, invited, or whatever, but the truth is, if you wait around for someone to ask you, you will wait a long time. If you have made up your mind to run for elective office then get on with it. The first step any candidate must take is to surround himself with a core of people who heavily support him. With all this in mind, I started to think seriously about making an attempt for the nomination in Morse. I was a realist and knew Jack Wiebe had a lock on the nomination and, perhaps more importantly, had earned the chance to be a candidate. However, politics is the roughest game in the world and there are no rules of etiquette. I decided to check the waters. I got in my three-quarter-ton truck and went out into Morse constituency to make some carefully selected calls.

Morse was a large constituency that lay between Moose Jaw and Swift Current. The predominating group were the Mennonites, of whom Jack Wiebe was one. As a group, the Mennonites are excellent farmers and citizens. Their political history was Social Credit if they had their preference, and my father had spent many hours on the backroads and farms to gain their support as a Liberal. Once acquired the support seemed to grow and by my father's third term Morse had become a Liberal stronghold. I had heard via the grapevine that Jack Wiebe could be undercut among the Mennonites and that it would be worthwhile taking a look. Before getting that far, I made some stops in the cattle country to get the ranchers' reactions to my becoming a candidate. I had represented the area on various livestock boards including the Canadian Cattlemen's Association. The reaction I got was pretty good and I began to pick up some support. There was no question Jack Wiebe's presence was there, and the odd key person said bluntly that Jack deserved the nomination and I should not run; however, by this time an upset seemed possible and I had almost decided to go. Then I decided to test the Morse-Herbert country, which was Jack's area, to see if the grapevine was accurate. It wasn't. Jack was as solid as a rock in the Mennonite areas and there was absolutely no chance of an upset. I returned to the ranch and proceeded to try to give up the whole idea. It just wasn't there and I knew it.

After I had accepted the political reality of the situation and had decided not to run, I started receiving calls and visits from various people I had contacted in the constituency wanting to know how they could help me in the nomination. To this day I don't know why I didn't simply thank them and say that I was out of it. It is certainly not in my nature to be a sacrificial lamb and I knew I had no chance. But for whatever reason, I felt it was something I had to do, something I had to follow through. I was in and I didn't know why. Once I was in, I decided I would at least make a convention of it. I met Jack Wiebe on a country backroad by chance and told him the news. Jack was a shrewd politician. He smiled and said, "Come out smoking." He knew I couldn't hurt him but the competition at the September nominating convention would be great for the turnout. I mustered what forces I could and went to work to prepare a solid speech. I was going to be slaughtered but I had my eyes wide open and was going to put on the best show I could and take the loss graciously.

The night of the nomination came and went as predicted. I was slaughtered but impressed a lot of people with my speech and the manner in which I took the loss. It proved to be a profitable evening in the long run. I thought my political career had come and gone in the same evening; however, that night in Chaplin was to be a useful tool in the next nomination I would fight, in a constituency that did not even exist yet.

The leadership convention for the Liberal party was not slated to be held until December. My good friend Don Mac-Donald, who had been elected in Moose Jaw North, asked me to join his executive, which I did. I did not get involved in the leadership race, which was strictly a two-man race as George Leith was not really in it. Davey Steuart appeared to have the edge; however, Cy had an excellent organization that was doing well. Cy was one of Father Murray's boys from Notre Dame. He was youthful in appearance and a great speaker— one of the best I have ever seen—and had put together a group of hard-bitten political pros mostly with Notre Dame back-grounds. Like most leadership races this one lasted too many months and both sides became battle weary and some hostility did surface. Davey Steuart won comfortably on the dubious strength of being the older candidate and because of his assurances that if he lost he would leave voluntarily with no bloodshed. Pure and simple, that was the mood of the 1971 Liberal leadership convention that replaced my father.

2

The Race Is On

The following year, 1972, was a quiet one for me politically, although not economically. The cattle industry was booming and money was rolling in like I had never seen it before. Jack Wiebe had won Morse constituency in a relatively narrow win. My only role was on the executive of the Moose Jaw North Liberal Association and that was not doing well in my view. There was no question I was sensitive and biased, but it appeared to me the Liberals were doing everything possible to dissociate themselves from their seven years of government almost as though they were ashamed of them. Certainly, the party had suffered a crushing defeat but all governments are defeated and this does not mean that the party should change its philosophy or ideals. The NDP are a classic example. They are probably the most successful political machine of the last forty years; they rarely change and people know exactly what they stand for. The electorate likes them or hates them and

votes for them when so inclined. The Liberal party in Saskatchewan in the early seventies plunged headlong into a credibility
gap with their own people as they moved ever leftward. They
were awed by the new NDP government, who sported some
very capable new ministers, not to mention ideas.

The Land Bank was an example of the government getting
deeply into the ownership of farm land, an idea that was an
anathema to the Liberal party. For reasons I will never understand, the Liberals voted for the Land Bank Act of 1972. It was
their logic to vote for the act in principle but oppose it in
committee under the guise of "political wisdom." Many of their
leftward movements were undertaken with the same rationale
and under the influence of the federal party, which certainly
had far more input than previously.

I believe I was among the first to voice the concern that this
sharp leftward turn would leave a vacuum in the right-of-center
spectrum—a vacuum that would probably be filled by the Conservative party. Now even I didn't believe it to be true at that
time and most Liberals close to the party in Regina scoffed at
the idea. However, out in the country, in the so-called grass
roots, something was beginning to happen. Davey Steuart and
his caucus, except for Don MacDonald, truly believed that the
right-wingers had no place to go and, while they might groan
and be unhappy about specific issues, they would always be
there for the party when it counted. They were not the last to
make a philosophical mistake of this nature during my days in
politics. Given their theory that the right wing had no alternative, they believed they had infinite maneuvering room in their
attempt to pick up the right wing of the NDP and restore the
old coalition with slightly different components. The chief people in the caucus heading this philosophical switch were Gary
Lane and Ken MacLeod. In the case of Ken, he was simply a
liberal and, even worse, a Trudeau liberal. Take your pick with
Gary Lane. He was whatever he felt he had to be on a given
occasion and was not fettered by minor details of principle or
philosophy.

The move to the left was not the only problem the Liberals
were having. The federal minister of justice and, more important, minister in charge of the Canadian Wheat Board, was
heavy stuff among prairie farmers at that time. Otto Lang, the

chief federal Liberal spokesman for Saskatchewan, was not loved, but his obvious intellect and quick grasp of the complexities of the world grain trade had impressed the rural population. Otto had survived the bloop of the LIFT program (Lower Inventories For Tomorrow) of the late sixties when the federal government had literally paid prairie farmers not to produce. The results were horrendous for all concerned but somehow Otto pulled through and by 1972 was rapidly gaining stature. He had a strange relationship with the farmers. They truly believed he was doing a good job for them, but there was no way they were going to reward him in the form of votes or by increased Liberal representation in Saskatchewan. Dave Steuart and the provincial Liberals had no choice but to acknowledge Otto Lang and the high regard in which he was held, and the provincial party moved more and more to the stance of the Trudeau Liberals. After all, they were in opposition with no patronage to dole out and they needed favors from the federal party from time to time. And they had no fear of a challenge from the right. Totally ignored was the almost violent anti-Trudeauism firmly established on the prairies.

In late 1972 I became president of the Moose Jaw North Liberal Association. My good friend Dr. Don MacDonald was already tiring of opposition politics and of voting with the party on matters with which he fundamentally disagreed. I believe he had already made up his mind to get out of politics. He enjoyed having me as his right-wing president who would spout off at conventions all sorts of right-wing rhetoric that got applause but little else. The party hierarchy had no love for me, mainly because of what I knew of their finances. However, at the convention of 1972 I was elected a vice-president of the party and became involved in provincial executive decisions. Only the NDP allowed their provincial executives much input into the running of the party. Both the Conservatives and the Liberals used theirs as a means of keeping the grass roots informed or, better yet, in line. As it turned out, it was a good place to be to see where the party was going and how it hoped to get there. I was regarded as strongly anti-federal and anti-Lang. That was not completely true. I had a great deal of personal respect for Pierre Elliott Trudeau and Otto Lang and their obvious abilities, but I strongly questioned many of their policies. My right-wing views were tolerated as a sop to the party's past in the hope that I would be a short-term annoyance.

As 1973 came on the political stage, the NDP were riding high. Both the national and provincial economies were booming and the new faces in the government were performing well by any political standard. Roy Romanow had the odd scrape but by and large his oratorical abilities always got him out of trouble. The NDP had no fear whatsoever of the Liberals, and they showed it. No doubt they were also buoyed by the news that the Progressive Conservative party was going to have a leadership convention that year. While no one really expected them to become a serious threat, it was good news for the NDP because of the vote splitting that would inevitably result.

The other significant item of early 1973 was the appointment of an independent boundary commission to redistribute electoral boundaries for the next general election. Such a redistribution had my interest mainly for what it would do for or against Don MacDonald's Moose Jaw North seat. Frankly, I wondered why the NDP were bothering. Things were going very much their way and a weak opposition was allowing them a free ride.

Only the most politically naive would suggest that an independent boundary commission operates free from governmental influence. Votes mean three meals a day to most MLAs, as well as a sharp increase in their standard of living, so altering their constituencies has them at their vigilant best. The prize for being the government of the day is to exert heavy pressure on the commission as it is drawing up the map. Judges and upright citizens will dispute this assertion with indignant honesty, perhaps unaware of their manipulation, but it happened and always will in the political process.

One example of how the commission of 1973 was manipulated was in its mandate, which specifically required it to evenly distribute the constituencies on equal population. Now any political novice knows the NDP own the cities in Saskatchewan and are considerably weaker in the rural areas. It is also well known that rural populations are declining. By giving this mandate to the commission the NDP were getting exactly what they wanted—more seats in the cities and fewer in the rural areas. A political scientist will argue this is as it should be: representation by population. Not so, and this works only to a point

anyway. In Saskatchewan the rural constituencies were made
so large that it is almost impossible for an MLA to serve them
adequately. An MLA with an urban area to service can see
many more constituents in a day, in a shorter period of time,
than can his rural counterpart. So the rural area with the same
population suffers a deterioration in the quality of representation simply because of its geography and size. If you were a
Tory government, and politically wise, you would merely
reverse the mandate, which would result in fewer urban seats
and more rural ones. It is merely a question of where your
strength lies and how you wish to exploit it. Among the constituencies created in the 1973 redistribution were several brand-
new urban seats that only by a minor miracle would elect anyone other than an NDP candidate, and a large rural seat called
Thunder Creek.

As soon as the new map was out the grapevine was hum-
ming and the rumor mills were in full swing. The new Morse
constituency was dramatically altered and Jack Wiebe was said
to be looking at Thunder Creek even though he lived in Morse.
Cy MacDonald was also said to be eyeing it because his Milestone constituency had all but disappeared with the majority of
it going into the new constituency of Bengough-Milestone.
Gary Lane had lost some very good territory to Thunder Creek
and had gained the new Glencairn subdivision into his new
Lumsden constituency. Because of the political uncertainty of
Glencairn, a fairly safe rural seat was now up in the air and
Lane felt compelled to test the political waters elsewhere. Allan
Guy represented one of the two large northern constituencies
that had suffered significant changes. Allan was one of the
good members in opposition having made the transition from
government relatively easily. However, he too began casting
about for an easier seat.

Don MacDonald was my close friend and obviously we
talked a lot about politics and the dynamics of the caucus. Don
was disgusted and had already decided to leave politics at the
end of his term. According to Don, Davey Steuart had told his
MLAs they were the people who would make or break the
party and they were "free to go where they wanted as long as
two did not end up in the same constituency." In other words,
it was every man for himself. Don urged me to try for Thunder

Creek, a rectangle around Moose Jaw with significant areas from the old Morse, Qu'Appelle, Milestone, and Assiniboia constituencies and even a small area from Arm River. It was ideal geographically for me and a safe Liberal seat.

The scrambling of MLAs toward the new constituency boundaries played a role in the vulnerability of the Liberal party in the succeeding years. Dave Steuart, to the best of my knowledge, did not consider leaving Prince Albert even though he now had a much tougher seat to win. Jack Wiebe decided to stay in Morse, which was a courageous decision because Thunder Creek was his had he come in. Cy MacDonald decided to go to Indian Head, which Dave Steuart should not have allowed; Bengough-Milestone was tough but winnable in a hard fight. For Cy to leave was to give in to the NDP with no contest. On top of that Cy had to fight a bitter nomination battle with a local candidate, which was bad for the party overall. Gary Lane decided to come to Thunder Creek. However, the worst decision was in Rosthern, a constituency with a high Mennonite population that had been ably represented for many years by Dave Boldt. Dave had served admirably in my father's cabinet and was a respected Mennonite farmer who had decided not to run again. Allan Guy had decided not to run in his northern Athabasca seat and wanted to run in Rosthern. It was an incredibly bad decision that would come back to haunt the Liberal party. Allan was an excellent politician but had two very difficult factors to overcome: he was running away from his former seat and was a divorced Catholic. The latter was dynamite in a Mennonite constituency. How Davey Steuart persuaded a devout Mennonite like Dave Boldt to aid in the change will always be a mystery to me. As good a member as Allan was, he was not worth the price that was ultimately paid due to sheer political stupidity.

In retrospect, it is difficult to say whether the eventual annihilation of the Liberal party would have been averted or even diminished in magnitude if the MLAs had stayed home to fight the next election. There is no question in my mind that seats were conceded to the NDP that perhaps could have been won by an incumbent MLA; in Allan Guy's case it was a double loss as the Liberals lost both Athabasca, which he vacated, and Rosthern, where he was parachuted in. The whole exercise was an indictment against Dave Steuart's leadership.

The word reached me immediately that Gary Lane was coming to Thunder Creek. He had not declared his candidacy but was off and running and seeing the key people to judge their reactions. Gary was a great believer in the theory that in politics if you wait to be asked, you will wait for a lengthy period. Lane went out to the west end of Thunder Creek for several days, staying at Jack Wiebe's farm and even being accompanied by Jack when he visited key Liberals. It was a quick political blitzkrieg in the hope of tying up the nomination before a battle could begin in earnest. Lane was, and still is, a superb politician and was moving fast. My reaction to all this was not positive. I did not look kindly on a Regina lawyer coming carpetbagging to this area when he belonged elsewhere. Lumsden was a seat that an incumbent Liberal with a good campaign could and should win but one a new candidate would probably lose to the NDP.

Lane's move to Thunder Creek is a classic example of how politicians think and react to given situations. The new Lumsden constituency had to be won if the party was going to make any sort of showing in the next election. If the Liberals could not win that one with an incumbent MLA and a politically astute one, they may as well have pulled the plug right then. The simple fact was that Thunder Creek was seen to be a safer seat than Lumsden and Lane wanted it. It is another indictment of Dave Steuart's leadership that he would allow a situation like this to develop; in many respects he was writing off the 1975 election two years before it was to be held.

It was early August in 1973 when I was forced to make a decision about Thunder Creek. Granted, no nominating convention had been called nor had Lane officially declared his candidacy but the race was on and for me it was a basic choice —get at it now or forget it for good. A good portion of Lane's old Qu'Appelle constituency was now in Thunder Creek and there was no question he had total support from that area. What I had to find out was the situation in the Morse and Milestone portions as it pertained to Lane. I phoned Cy MacDonald and told him that I wanted to go and visit some key people from his old constituency and get their reactions to Lane. Cy was his usual charming self and offered encouragement and accurate information as to who his former key people were. I received his assurance that if I ran he would stay out of it and support neither of us. This was the best I could hope for. I knew full well that Lane would be aware of my interest the next day.

I had not decided for sure whether or not I was a candidate as I set off for the west end of the constituency the next day. My wife was pregnant with Stephanie and I knew a major purchase of farm land was imminent. I was probably in if it was only Lane and myself, but if there was another candidate then that would put me on the sidelines. I had heard rumors about Percy Lambert from Parkbeg being interested, so I made him my first stop. Percy had replaced Jack Wiebe as the president of Morse constituency and was typical of the high-caliber people making up the Morse executive. Parkbeg had been an NDP haven for years before Percy became involved with my father. Slowly, by pure hard work and personal respect, he had turned that poll around to where it approached a saw-off. Percy Lambert was respected by voters on both sides of the political fence and it showed in the electoral results. That morning I found him at the breakfast table and when the opportunity presented itself I asked him about the Lane situation—and about his personal plans. He made it plain that he was not happy to have Lane in Thunder Creek and, while he thought highly of him, felt he belonged in Lumsden. On the question of his own candidacy he was quick to say that he was not interested. I did not bring up the possibility of my running at that time as I now knew what I had come for. The reaction to Lane I found interesting. Percy was enough of a party man to accept him if it came to that, but his not liking it meant certain doors were open.

I spent the next couple of days calling on key people at the west end of Thunder Creek, the area I had to have to give Lane a serious challenge. Farmers I had visited a couple of years earlier who had then been solidly behind Jack Wiebe now gave me their commitment of support. There was no denying Lane had some also, but it was certainly not the tidal wave I had walked into a couple of years ago. After that little foray, I phoned Jack Wiebe and told him I was in and since he had spent some time driving around with Lane, he should accord me the same courtesy. I knew I wouldn't get that but I got what

I really called for—a promise of his neutrality.

At this point, I knew it would be tough to take Lane out, but not impossible. The changing of seats was an issue on which he was vulnerable, as well as being a Regina lawyer. Now being a lawyer is an accomplishment and in most places this would be a symbol of respect. Not in Thunder Creek. It was going to be an integral part of my strategy to play heavily on the Regina lawyer label. A swing down into the portion of the constituency coming from Cy MacDonald's Milestone area showed that Lane had been there and certainly gained some support but that I could also pick up a fair amount and probably get at least a split vote from the area. The east end from Qu'Appelle was all Lane's and there was no room there to steal any votes from him. The old Morse area was the one I had to take—and big.

I received an unexpected bonus when Lionel Coderre took me into the portion that had come from the old Gravelbourg constituency. Lionel had been the MLA for Gravelbourg for about fifteen years and had served as minister of labor in my father's government. I picked up the whole area almost uncontested. Lane could be had but it would take a great deal of hard work as well as an abundance of luck. Lionel Coderre gave me the idea that eventually did Lane in. He suggested I send a letter to the Liberal membership announcing my candidacy and explaining why I was running. It was an excellent idea but the content was what was important.

I prepared and sent that letter immediately. Unfortunately, I no longer have a copy of it to quote from directly; however, it was simple and to the point. I broke down the present number of MLAs in the legislature and pointed out how many were lawyers. Then I took the Liberal caucus and did the same. The figure was far higher than the legislative percentage. I did the same calculation for the number of farmers and ranchers. I went to some lengths to show that there was an abundance of legal advice available to solve farm problems but very little agricultural expertise present on the floor of the legislature. The thrust of the letter was clear: we had all the lawyers we needed and then some; we needed farmers in the legislature, particularly when it came to representing a rural, agricultural seat like Thunder Creek.

If I say so myself, it was a pretty good letter and it unquestionably had an impact. When Dave Steuart asked me who had dreamed up this "farmer" business I knew he must have learned of its effect via Lane. I worked at developing the situation and encouraged my supporters to emphasize that "lawyers" against "agriculturalists" was the prime issue in this nomination. For two months Lane and I went at it hammer and tongs. Believe me, it was tough going but I was certainly in with a chance. The question was, could I take the area west of Moose Jaw by a big enough margin to overcome the lead Lane had from his old constituency? At that point in time the answer was probably no. Lane wanted a quick nominating convention and if that was what he wanted, it was obviously not in my best interest. An open annual meeting was going to be held to decide the issue at the end of September 1973 and the lines became firmly drawn with Lane in favor and my people adamantly opposed.

I knew I was making progress but was certainly still in second place. Lane knew it too, which was why he wanted to go quickly. My strategy was to emphasize there was no rush and that because Thunder Creek was a new constituency every chance should be given to new candidates to come forward. What I was really saying was that I wanted the nominating convention held in the winter when Lane was tied down in the legislature and any absences would be noted. Also, he was under far more pressure than I was because the Lumsden seat was in limbo until Thunder Creek was settled. Lane, incidentally, had never made any formal announcement of where he intended to run in order to keep his options open.

At rural gatherings such as that September annual meeting most motions pass unless they are very controversial. At this particular gathering there was to be a banquet and dance with a meeting sandwiched in. Lane was the guest speaker. What I had to do was obvious. I needed someone to propose a quick motion at the outset of the business meeting advocating a winter nomination, followed by a seconder who would eloquently elaborate on the logic and benefits of such a date, followed by several speakers who would support the motion and get it to a vote quickly. Easier said than done, particularly when you must sit there acting as if it is all new to you and is an exercise of the grass roots in action.

In many respects the meeting was going to be a trial balloon testing how the nomination fight was going. Lane was supremely confident that evening as we both worked the large turnout. There is no doubt that he met people more easily than I did. Several MLAs showed up, curious and looking to get a read on the situation. As I checked the crowd I felt Lane had a definite edge and was resigned to a vote for a quick nomination. Then the business portion of the meeting started and Hoot Hyde from Brownlee was on his feet immediately. In his auctioneer's cadence he made a great speech explaining why the nomination should be held in February of 1974 and made a motion to that effect. Immediately Alfred Bryan from Tugaski was up seconding the motion and making a strong speech in support. Like clockwork, six other supporters made their comments known. Lane's people were clearly taken off guard. The effects of several pre-dinner cocktails and a meal meant that no one really wanted a long meeting and when the question was called I held my breath. No one objected and a vote was not even taken. I could hardly contain myself. I had bluffed a full house with a pair of deuces.

It was over that night and Gary Lane knew it. There was no announcement of his intention but Lane never appeared in Thunder Creek again. He simply disappeared and returned to do what he should have done in the first place—win Lumsden. I do not know if I could have beaten Lane at a nominating convention or not. It would have been tough because of the magnitude of his support from the part of his old constituency that was now in Thunder Creek. I had no idea of the extent of his strength until I went in cautiously after the annual meeting to see his key people. Cy MacDonald was to tell me later that his assessment of the people at that meeting was that they were two to one in favor of Lane. Lane obviously read it differently, or perhaps he was a lousy poker player.

By the time the Liberal nomination for Thunder Creek was held in February 1974 two other candidates had entered the race, one of them being the late brother of Grant Devine, Randy Devine. The other was a Parkbeg farmer by the name of Percy Lambert, a former president of Morse constituency and the same Percy Lambert I had questioned about his candidacy the previous summer. Perhaps he changed his mind because Lane had dropped out—I don't know. In any event, it was a clean race but I had too much of a head start and had picked up all of the support from Gary Lane's old Qu'Appelle riding. I won the three-way fight easily on the first ballot and prepared to go about winning the seat.

Before 1973 ended, two events of significance occurred: Dick Collver became the new leader of the Conservative party in a convention that was noteworthy mainly because of the number of supposed Liberal supporters who were delegates, and the Liberal party suffered a setback with the death of "Big" Don McPherson. It was not only a loss for the party but also for the City of Regina. "Big" Don was a highly respected individual who had donated freely of his time and money to charities and a variety of nonprofit organizations. For years he was one of the organizational geniuses behind the Saskatchewan Roughriders in their heyday and his presence gave the Liberal party respectability and fund-raising expertise. His premature death precipitated a by-election in Regina Lakeview. A political newcomer to the public, although not to the party, was the Liberal candidate, Ted Malone, a Regina lawyer. He had won the nomination in a slugfest with another lawyer, John Embury. It had been a battle of the right and left wings of the party. Embury represented what little was left of the Thatcher wing of the party while Malone clearly represented the federal wing. Malone won narrowly, but his success was indicative that the provincial Liberals were now very close to the federal party and, while not totally controlled by Otto Lang, were not far from it if and when he chose. Malone won the by-election from the NDP by a large margin. Dick Collver cleverly chose not to test his strength or his party's popularity in Lakeview by bluntly stating that the Tories were not ready. It was a shrewd move that drew cries of derision from the Liberals. The Liberal party in Saskatchewan would not have anything to laugh about concerning the Tories for many years to come.

It had become party policy that as candidates became nominated they automatically became part of the caucus, instead of earning the right to be there by virtue of winning an election. This was Dave Steuart's idea and apparently was not passed unanimously by the remaining caucus members. I came in later years to understand that attitude. There is a feeling of "this is too much" as some loudmouth, who has as much chance of winning his seat as getting a trip to the moon on the next rocket, comes into your caucus and is an instant expert on everything and willing to share his expertise on all subjects. You just hope that he doesn't like to go to meetings and is from a northern constituency hundreds of miles away. The worst of them are usually ones who love a meeting and will drive anywhere to impart their recently acquired proficiency in all aspects of politics to the caucus, who have obviously learned nothing in their years in politics. My recollection is that I attended the initial caucus meetings and remained silent while another newcomer did enough talking for all the new arrivals. Tony Merchant had been nominated in Regina Wascana and attended all caucuses because of his proximity to the Saskatchewan legislature.

The Liberals at this point were fairly buoyant. They had won the by-election in Lakeview handily and had a new, young showpiece MLA in Ted Malone. The economy was strong and the federal party was held in reasonable esteem—reasonable for a federal Liberal party in Saskatchewan anyway. The true condition of the party financially had never been revealed at any conventions and I assumed that the bulk of the funds I had turned over were still intact and available for the anticipated 1975 election. Dave Steuart did not enjoy having me around with what I knew of the party finances. I believe he expected me to ask embarrassing questions at some inopportune time. I never did and was ultimately to leave the Liberal party without knowing for sure what happened to all that money. It was nothing new for the general membership and even the caucus to be kept in the dark about finances. In all my years in politics, never once did I see a treasurer of a party ever make a report to a convention that truly reflected the financial condition of the party. If it was excellent, they would make it appear slightly more than break-even; if it was seriously bad the financial statement would indicate there was nothing wrong that a good fund-raising drive couldn't fix.

I spent most of 1974 preparing for the anticipated June election of 1975. Despite the fact Thunder Creek was regarded as a safe Liberal seat, I was not inclined to make such an assumption. I was far from a complete novice at campaigning in a rural seat, having spent an entire summer with my father during the federal election campaign in Assiniboia in the late fifties. That was to be the bitterest election I was ever to be involved with; however, it was on this occasion that I learned the campaign techniques I would subsequently use in Thunder Creek. In short, it meant taking the campaign to the farmyard. It was an exhausting way to campaign, but there is no substitute for it in Saskatchewan rural politics.

There were fragments from five old constituencies thrust into Thunder Creek so the people to run a campaign were in place. They just needed to be coordinated into a solid organization. The NDP were not a concern but there was an intangible factor that I could not put my finger on. Then I knew exactly what it was—Tory. The next caucus meeting I went to, I reported the vibes I was getting in Thunder Creek. When asked the name of the Tory candidate I had to confess there was none and I knew of no plans to nominate one. The other MLAs and candidates scoffed at me; I left that caucus not knowing who was out of touch with reality and hoping it was me.

Of all the things I disliked in politics, the one I had absolutely no stomach for was fighting with Tories. My battle was, always has been, and will continue to be with the NDP. I will, of course, get a spirited debate from many when I suggest the NDP and their forerunners, the CCF, have been a curse on the province of Saskatchewan and have unquestionably retarded our economic development, for which our grandchildren will pay. Their "family of Crown corporations" has resulted in expensive duplication and has not provided the economic stimulus envisioned by the socialist planners. But then, these socialist planners said they were going to do these things if they were elected and, quite simply, they did. In my view, the reluctance of the present Tory government to get rid of some of the lesser Crowns is an indictment of that government's resolve and commitment to economic progress. In 1974 I wanted to fight the NDP and I was strongly fearing it was not going to turn out that way. The last thing I had any interest in was being part of the battle for the position of Her Majesty's loyal opposition.

In late 1974 I heard that there would definitely be a Conservative candidate in Thunder Creek. It was going to be an individual from south of Moose Jaw, in the Baildon area, named Don

Swenson. His brother-in-law, an active Liberal on the Thunder Creek Liberal Association, told me that Swenson was going to run. I had no fear of the NDP in a two-way battle but I was bothered by the number of votes a strong Conservative candidate could siphon off.

I was now starting to hear about Dick Collver and his movements in the Moose Jaw–Regina area. He was making frequent forays into Moose Jaw talking to key businessmen and soliciting their support on the basis of a common economic bond. His message to them was simple: the Liberals could not win in Saskatchewan for many years and the province was into a brand-new political cycle. Many of these businessmen were Tories federally and would have liked to be provincially, but they also were not interested in insuring the reelection of the NDP by splitting the anti-socialist vote. They liked what they were hearing but were skeptical about its reality. Collver had a job ahead of him just to gain credibility with his own potential supporters but there was no question he was ambitious, hard working, and a salesman. His moves were not lost on me because a good portion of Thunder Creek was potentially fertile ground for the Tories, even though the Liberals at this point were well in control. To be more precise, many areas of Thunder Creek were philosophically Tory but were conditioned to support the Liberals in the coalition my father had formed many years earlier. My concern was that this coalition could fall apart and open the door for the NDP.

Nineteen seventy-four was simply not a good year for the Liberal party by any standard. They put on an incredibly bad performance in the legislature and only the true faithful were satisfied. Worse, Dave Steuart had allowed the party to become apologists for Otto Lang and the federal Liberals. There was a gnawing feeling among many Liberals, myself included, that Dave Steuart was hedging his bets and setting himself up for the Senate seat many of us believed he had been promised.

The first issue on which the NDP turned Dave Steuart into an apologist for Pierre Elliott Trudeau came as a result of the NDP incursion into the oil industry in 1973 when they tried to cash in on windfall profits by raising royalty levels and controlling the income of oil companies in the province. At the time, world oil prices were soaring and the federal energy policy was perceived in the West as securing Ontario cut-rate oil prices at the expense of the western provinces. Although the provincial Liberals started out well by attacking the NDP's new policy as a war on business and fought the bill effectively in the legislature, the NDP were master politicians and were able to tie the provincial party to the federal government and virtually turn the tables on Dave Steuart and his caucus. The time was clearly ripe for a break with the federal party. But it never came. Instead the provincial Liberals came up with a policy of their own which not even they believed in. It involved setting up a marketing board with power to set lower prices for old oil and higher prices for more expensive, newly discovered oil. There was to be more consultation with oil companies but no power to break leases or nationalize companies. To say the least, it didn't wash. Later at a premiers' conference, Allan Blakeney attempted to get an increase in the per barrel price of oil and failed. Dave Steuart now attacked him for "folding up like a deck of cards," whereas earlier he had been labeling him as "greedy" and gouging eastern consumers. The flip-flop by the caucus was not well received and was exploited to the hilt by the NDP. Unquestionably, the main beneficiary was Dick Collver, who was quickly moving up and down the length and breadth of the province pointing a finger at both sides.

The second, and by far the more damaging, issue was that of the Crowsnest Pass freight rate. As most people in Saskatchewan know if they have any ties at all to the agricultural sector, this is a fixed freight rate on western grain movement legislated in 1897 as a concession to western producers to reduce their dependence on the railways. It gave the federal government the right to regulate freight rates charged by the Canadian Pacific Railway, and it was used to attract agricultural settlement to the prairies. In order to win this concession from the railway, the federal government promised over three million dollars in grants to help finance construction of a rail line from Alberta to southeastern British Columbia through the Crowsnest Pass. The politicians of the day no doubt considered the right to regulate rail freight rates as a masterpiece of maneuvering, but the irony was, and still is, the significant portion of the legislation turned out to be the statutory freight rates, which became a volatile time bomb for any western politician. Legislative changes in the

1920s extended the Crow rate to other railways and included in its scope grain moving to either Thunder Bay or the West Coast. The result has been that over the years the fixed rate has contributed less and less to the cost of moving grain. By 1974 it was suggested that the proportion was down to half, with the shortfall being absorbed by the railways or made up in grants from the federal government. To western farmers this rate is absolutely sacred and dynamite for any politician foolish enough to suggest tampering with it. Otto Lang was such a politician.

There was no question in Lang's mind that the seventy-year-old freight rate was severely retarding development in the West and keeping grain transportation in an antiquated state, and the facts of the international grain trade screamed confirmation of his suppositions. However, there were powerful interests with vast resources that were unalterably opposed to any tampering with the statutory rate and particularly to the introduction of variable rates. They were doing well under the present arrangement and they had a high-power public relations and communications section to regularly inform the farmer that they knew what was best for him. Obviously, I am referring to the Saskatchewan Wheat Pool, who were quite capable of playing their own brand of hardball politics when the situation demanded. Otto Lang was about to precipitate a momentous debate on changing the Crow rate that would drag on for the best part of a decade. It is an example of the naivety prevalent in his logical mind that he believed the issue could be discussed rationally and intelligently by the interested parties; he underestimated the emotionalism and the depth of the opposition that would be unleashed when this Pandora's box was opened. The end result was to be the destruction of the Liberal party in Saskatchewan.

In late 1974, the stage was being set by the NDP government for a provincial election, probably in June of 1975 but if an issue surfaced then they would be prepared to grab it and run. Otto Lang made his speech to the Canada Grains Council in Edmonton in October of 1974 and in it he proposed a debate to see if the benefits of the Crow rate could be passed on to producers in a different way that would better serve their needs in this day and age. The timing could not have been worse and was typical of the way bitter federal-provincial disputes erupted in the Liberal party. The NDP had been handed the classic anti-fed issue that every provincial government prayed for every four years. Dave Steuart was genuinely upset and outraged that Otto Lang refused to delay the speech, which could easily have been delivered six to ten months later.

In Thunder Creek, the issue was a plus or a minus depending on the area. The most vocal group calling for change in the Crow rate was the Palliser Wheat Growers, a relatively young organization comprising top-quality, knowledgeable farmers who had become disenchanted with the Saskatchewan Wheat Pool. Many of the organizers of the Palliser group were in the eastern end of Thunder Creek and among the most politically active constituents. In the western part of the seat the issue was dynamite and a total no-win situation for me. I was personally involved as a farmer and my views reflected those of the Palliser Wheat Growers: I didn't want to pay one cent more for moving my grain than I had to but I knew I was going to have to or risk my grain staying in storage bins on my farm as the transportation system broke down in the near future. Politically, I could say that in certain areas and in the balance I would have to sidestep the issue. I was finding out as a nominated candidate just how heavy the cross of Pierre Elliott Trudeau could be. I resented being saddled with another federal issue to defend, particularly one that was at Otto's whim. At the caucus meeting I argued that we should split with the federal party over this issue because they had shown a callous disregard for our political situation, almost to the point of the conflict appearing to be orchestrated by the NDP. My position did not get much support and the concensus was the party should try to stay uninvolved. Was that a joke? The answer is yes, but the real question was, on whom?

The NDP immediately attacked the Lang speech and accused the Liberals of conspiring to remove the Crow rate costing Saskatchewan farmers hundreds of millions of dollars. The Wheat Pool jumped into the debate using their public relations department to maximum effect in an emotional if not always factual fanning of the political fires. The Pool had never been comfortable with Lang; they viewed his opening up the Crow debate as confirmation of their views and came forth with both barrels.

Davey Steuart was in a political hot seat. He had staked his political career on making peace with the federal Liberals and was now getting a real beating over it. I am sure he must have considered repudiation of the Lang speech, but in the end he decided a show of disunity would be bad for the party and decided to defend Lang and the proposals even though he disagreed with many of them. It was a blunder of epidemic proportions as the NDP lumped the provincial Liberals with the Lang proposals to alter the sacred Crow rate. The NDP loved every minute and confidently geared their election machinery.

In the country Dick Collver was working hard on the theme that it was time for a new approach and the constant bickering between the NDP and the Liberals was not in anyone's interest. His party had come out flat against any change in the Crow rate but other than that his policies were deliberately vague. The Tories did not have a history of political success in the province and the last Conservative government had been the Anderson government of the early thirties. Since that time they had never been a viable political force on the provincial scene despite the success of John Diefenbaker. Their brief flurry of the 1960s was gone and Collver was starting from scratch. Because they had no past they had no enemies, reasoned many would-be Tories. Collver's main difficulty was to convince potential supporters that his party was not just a flash in the pan. The NDP were comfortable with whatever support Collver could muster since they viewed it as being at the expense of the Liberals.

The Liberals in Regina were totally oblivious to what was happening. As I traveled Thunder Creek in early 1975 I began to feel very uncomfortable about the Tory presence. Don Swenson had been nominated as their candidate but was doing no apparent work. At Liberal caucus meetings I was dismissed as paranoid as the party hacks told stories of their "surveys" and their "findings" that confirmed the Tories had less than 10 percent support and in fact we wanted them at 15 percent. I would leave these meetings thoroughly put down and wondering where I had been. When I read accounts of this period and see quotes from Liberals involved saying that no one ever considered the Tories a threat until halfway through the election campaign, it makes me angry. The Tory threat was there a year before the election of 1975 and the Liberal party closed their eyes and refused to take any direct action. They continued their incredible performance in the legislature, moving more to the left in an attempt to attract the right wing of the NDP—a total impossibility. They made peace with the federal party, but on terms imposed by the Ottawa Liberals.

Another big error was made in the constituency of Estevan in the southeast corner of the province where Ian MacDougall was renominated to contest the seat for the Liberals. Ian had been the MLA during the sixties but had lost the seat in 1971. The NDP winner, Russ Brown, died shortly afterwards and a by-election was held in which Ian again ran for the Liberals, losing handily. Ian was a fine individual but his time in politics was over. The mayor of Estevan, a respected former Saskatchewan Roughrider, was interested but knew little of nominations and was easy prey to a veteran politician like Ian. It would have been a difficult and perhaps undemocratic thing to do, but Davey Steuart should have intervened. No doubt he did not want to put a knife to Ian but leading a successful political party leads to tough decisions. Failure to act in this case opened the door to the Tories, who came forth with Bob Larter, a popular and personable implement dealer from Estevan who literally swept away Ian MacDougall in such an avalanche that there was a spillover to the adjoining seats.

By the spring of 1975, the Conservatives were very close to having a full slate of candidates. The Collver style was unsettling to both traditional antagonists because it was different. There was no past to focus on and certainly no substantive policy to attack. The Conservatives extolled strange things as virtues, such as fielding a full slate of candidates and being a brand-new party. The traditional battlers of the NDP and the Liberals could not relate to these claims and so it was easier simply to dismiss them. Fielding a full slate of candidates gave the Conservatives a certain credibility with the press, and they became interested in Collver's view of the issues of the day. In Thunder Creek I now knew who the enemy was but I did not know how to fight him and, even worse, I had no desire to do so.

No doubt part of the refusal to acknowledge the presence of the Conservative party was the assumption that the Tories would disintegrate on command as they had for the last forty years. Also there was the realization that the rise of the Con-

servatives was in many ways an indictment of the Liberal party
and their attempts to "out NDP the NDP." Unlike many of the
Liberals in the caucus I had been in the field and knew full well
what was happening—Collver's full slate of candidates and
now almost equal position with the press was convincing many
federal PC voters they should give the provincial party a chance.

Other than evaluate the threat of the Tories differently, in
retrospect there was really little else the Liberal party in 1975
could have done. They knew the election date of June 11 a
good two weeks before Allan Blakeney dissolved the legislature
so the candidates were active in the field when it was called.
They went into the election with an excellent set of candidates,
undoubtedly the best I was ever to be associated with. Certainly
there were some that I felt were too leftward in their thinking
but part of the political process is internal philosophical difference. When the election was called on May 14, 1975, I was
campaigning in the Coderre area of Thunder Creek. By now I
had been a nominated candidate for almost a year and a half
and I was happy that the race was on.

The timing of this election caused me some problems. Spring
seeding was particularly late that year and the last person farmers wanted to see was a politician. It also meant I would have
difficulty mobilizing volunteers. As it turned out the June date
didn't hurt the government, but I have always wondered why
the NDP would risk alienating the voters by calling an election
at such an inconvenient time.

Twenty of us got together and took out a loan at a local bank
to buy a trailer, the intention being to resell it right after the
election. We leased some space on a lot in downtown Moose
Jaw and we were in business. It is at election time that one
realizes just how big rural constituencies have become. My
game plan called for six-day-a-week campaigning from early
morning to lights out in the farmyard. I felt I needed the one
day off to keep from going overly stale and for just plain rest-
ing. I knew that in order to win Thunder Creek I had to dissociate myself from the federal Liberals privately, but not in such a
way that it would be picked up by the media, and hammer
away at the split vote—a vote for the Tories is a wasted vote, or
even one for the NDP.

I was out on the road immediately. Seeding was now in full

progress and I had made the conscious decision not to bother a farmer in the field. I would be content to talk to his wife unless she were to urge me to go out to the tractor. Stopping a tractor at seeding time was to risk alienating a potential ally, and time was also a factor. You could only go into an area for so long, see as many people as possible, and then you had to move on. I was always in the company of a local person and I relied on his judgment of whom we should see. I did not want to waste time on committed types of any party who were unlikely to change; rather I wanted to visit the floater types—those "up for grabs" or, more discreetly, undecided. It was my guide's job to apologize to the hard-core Liberals for my not stopping and to ask for their understanding.

I started my campaign in the west end of the constituency and worked east. The logic was that the west end of the constituency had lighter land and was further along in seeding. Actually, I found this approach unsatisfactory and in subsequent elections I used the shotgun approach of traveling in any direction starting from Moose Jaw, which, I believe, gave me a better feel for what was happening. In the campaign of 1975 I worked the rural areas and my wife JoAnn did the towns. The vote count shows that I was thrashed where JoAnn had done the campaigning. Although there were reasons for this that were outside her control, the bottom line was that she was not the political asset many people believed her to be and in the other election in which we were still married I did not have her campaign at all.

The *Moose Jaw Times-Herald* published the candidates' daily itineraries. As soon as I found that the Conservative candidate, Don Swenson, was showing up forty-eight hours after I had been in an area I never again gave out accurate information on where I was going or had been. If other candidates were going to learn of my activities they were not going to read about them in the papers.

I am not the male chauvinist many have portrayed me to be but I concede that I have never related well to women. I was uncomfortable that with so many farmers seeding much of the early campaign would be spent talking to the lady of the house. Although this was the heyday of women's lib I was disappointed at the frequency of the statement, "You'll have to talk to my husband. He makes the political decisions here." This is certainly not to be misconstrued, because I did meet many able and intelligent women in Thunder Creek in 1975, but when I analyzed the vote count I realized I might as well have stayed home rather than spend a lot of time with the wives. I do not mean to sound disrespectful but in Thunder Creek it seemed that in the majority of cases the man of the house decided how the household would vote.

The campaign run by central office was strong as long as the Liberals were on the attack. Of course, on the attack very few politicians were better than Dave Steuart. The advertising was done by Foster Advertising in Regina and it was basically pretty good. The NDP advertising was handled by Dunsky and it was superb as usual. A characteristic of the NDP was the quality of people they had in the backrooms where the campaigns were often fought. Nineteen seventy-five was no exception. Times were good economically and Allan Blakeney's image was high and they packaged both factors into a positive campaign while skillfully attacking where necessary. The Liberal party was tied to the Ottawa Liberals and their policies and there was no credible backing away from them by Dave Steuart. By the middle of the campaign it was obvious even to the Liberals that the Tories were coming on strong, yet there was no change in campaign tactics. The central office was frozen, unable to react to what was occurring in front of them. The press were giving Dick Collver more breaks than he deserved but that is part of the process and press coverage tends to equalize over a period of time. The Conservatives had a song they were using in the advertising that was sung by a Western-style country singer. It was superb. I grew to hate it but I had to admit it was catching the mood of the day.

I did my own thing in Thunder Creek and never deviated from a game plan. I ran as a provincial Liberal unhappy with the Ottawa Liberals and anxious to defeat the NDP. I made it clear that I had no quarrel with the Tories and was careful not to be drawn into any exchanges offensive to them. Although I was the front runner I knew I could be had and worked hard from morning to night. I was blessed with a superb organization which is basically why I won Thunder Creek by about three hundred votes from the Conservatives.

3

Tories Rise
As
Liberals Fall

The election in Saskatchewan in 1975 was a watershed in several ways. The NDP, of course, won quite handily with thirty-nine seats to the Liberals' fifteen, with the Conservatives grabbing seven. The NDP's share of the popular vote took a nose-dive from 55 percent in 1971 down to 40 percent. The real story was that the Liberals were down to 32 percent and the Tories had skyrocketed to 28 percent. It was the dawn of a new age in Sasktchewan politics. The Liberal party was past tense and the future belonged to Dick Collver and his Conservatives.

Collver had totally taken over the Liberal bastion in southeastern Saskatchewan with Bob Larter having a landslide in Estevan, which spilled over into Souris-Cannington as Eric Berntson easily took out Tom Wetherald. In Moosomin, John Gardiner, who a few months ago had scoffed at suggestions he was in trouble, was gone at the hands of a dairy farmer named Larry Birkbeck. I recall seeing John Gardiner at a post-election caucus and he still didn't know what had hit him. Even worse, he wondered why he had lost. Allan Guy was obliterated in Rosthern by Ralph Katzman, and Dick Collver had been elected in Nipawin in a gain from the NDP. Roy Bailey won Rosetown easily for the Conservatives.

It was clearly the end of the Liberal party in Saskatchewan, even though there was more talent in the fifteen remaining Liberal MLAs than in any group I have been associated with, including the NDP as I knew them intimately in my political years. I hope I am not unfair to anyone but I believe all of us would have been in my father's cabinet.The caucus was a well-rounded, diversified group that could deal with any area in government. It had some very bright lawyers as well as solid ties to agriculture, a must for a successful opposition in Saskatchewan. The Liberal caucus of 1975, however, never had a chance, despite the expertise they were to bring to the legislature, because the most important political factor of all—timing —was against them. Saskatchewan had moved into a new political cycle and the Liberals had been left behind.

In contrast to the Liberals was the caucus of the brand-new Conservative party, the serene saviors of Saskatchewan. Led by Dick Collver, they looked to be in a state of permanent dismay and shell-shocked fatigue. The first time I saw them in the legislature, I didn't know whether to laugh or cry. Except for Collver and Roy Bailey, the other five had a look of "what happened?"

After the election a caucus was called for the postmortem. Dave Steuart had already announced that he was stepping down but would stay on while the party prepared for a leadership convention. There was no real enthusiasm at the meeting, although there were the usual rah-rahs about a new beginning, the great new MLAs, and the flash-in-the-pan Tories who everyone knew would self-destruct. All wishful thinking. The underlying current was fear of Dick Collver, who was still largely unknown. The fear was such that if it had been reported that he had been seen walking on Lake Wascana, caucus would have been suspended while the sighting was confirmed or denied. There were no recriminations because there was no point. The concensus was that we must turn to more positive policy proposals and forget about finding new labels for socialists.

For the first time I was in a caucus of only elected MLAs and I was genuinely impressed by the level of discussion and the efficiency of the meetings. Of course, how else could it be? Stuart Cameron, Ted Malone, Tony Merchant, and Glen Penner are very bright people. Stuart Cameron was one I was prepared to dislike because of his open federal tendencies. In fact, I found him to be very charming, open, and perhaps a little shy but very, very bright. Tony Merchant was the brat—he would stir the pot and get it boiling and be called back to the office as the fights broke out. I was delighted to find myself with another cowboy in the person of Sonny Anderson from Shaunavon. We may not have been enthusiastic but no one could dispute the fact that the people were here who could do the job.

The lines for a leadership convention were drawn immediately. The three candidates were assumed to be Gary Lane, Stu Cameron, and Ted Malone. The first sign of obvious jockeying occurred in the summer when a proposal from MLA Tony Merchant surfaced called "Liberally," calling for drastic changes in the style of a leadership convention. Quite simply, it would allow any card-carrying Liberal to vote directly for the new leader by means of electronic voting booths around the province. I don't know if the idea was feasible, but for a party in the difficulties the Liberals were in, new ideas were a necessity. Liberally undoubtedly would sell a lot of memberships if the leadership candidates were popular. Of course, there was the question of cost and Tony talked to the pros, perhaps prematurely, before the idea had gone to caucus. When questioned by the press, Dave Steuart commented that he could support the idea. It was the Steuart comment that caused the flurry.

Gary Lane saw Liberally as a direct threat to his leadership ambitions. To Lane, Tony Merchant was fronting for Stu Cameron, whom Lane saw as Otto Lang's man. As far as he was concerned, Liberally was a plot to give the cities of Regina and Saskatoon a disproportionate effect on the outcome of a leadership convention and allow Otto to take firm control of the party. Lane raised the alarms bells with the accusation that the idea was part of Dave Steuart's deal for a Senate seat, and a meeting was held at the Vagabond Motor Inn in Regina to discuss the proposal. Lane, Sonny Anderson, Jack Wiebe, and I met in Wiebe's room and got to talking about the feds taking over the party. In that eventuality Wiebe stated he would not hesitate to go Tory. Lane and I agreed with him. Only Sonny Anderson said he could not change, which surprised me. Sonny was somewhere to the right of Attila the Hun, but he was a Liberal.

We had a caucus within a few days of the meeting at the Vagabond and for the first time I saw Lane bare his fangs at Steuart. Davey breezed in, I believe unaware of the fuss over the concept of Liberally, and he was verbally jumped by Lane, who wanted what amounted to a retraction. Now Dave Steuart is no shrinking violet but he was clearly surprised by the stinging rebuke he received from Lane and a couple of other MLAs. As was usually the case when he had started something, Tony Merchant was elsewhere that day on business and Dave Steuart, because of his vague public endorsement, took the brunt of the assault. The day concluded with Steuart snarling, "You may have a new leader sooner than you think." As far as caucus was concerned the issue died a natural death, quickly if not unfortunately. After all, we all know the rank and file of a party cannot be trusted with a ballot at a leadership convention —it would strike at the heart of our precious democracy.

The fall of 1975 was spent primarily with preoccupation with Collver and his Tories, although there was little that could be done, since they were being very cautious. Virtually all Liberal strategies were discussed in terms of the Tories, particularly in the context of trapping them in some form of political dilemma where either choice would be disastrous. By now we were hearing corridor talk from the NDP that they too were concerned and were uncertain how to handle Collver. It was obvious they were going to come at him like gangbusters given the opportunity. Still, until we got to the legislature and saw him perform, Dick Collver would remain a mysterious figure whom caucus perceived looking over their shoulders, grinning.

By late 1975 I was already disillusioned with politics. I was there to defeat the NDP and not to be part of the battle for first place in Her Majesty's loyal opposition. The calling of the legislature on November 12, 1975, did not thrill me at first; however, as it became clear that the NDP government was planning a major move into the potash industry a dimension of excitement was added to my first legislative session. I had been in the galleries of the legislative chamber on numerous occasions but this was the first time ever as an elected member. I'm sure it was even more of a thrill for me than for the first-timers who had not been involved in politics to the extent that I had been. I got my first look at the Tories and I recall Dick Collver standing out with a look of determination on his face.

The throne speech that day set off the most memorable political battle that I have ever been involved in and clearly illustrated the importance of political timing, much of which is totally beyond the control of the participants. The NDP government of Allan Blakeney announced plans to acquire up to 50 percent of the productive capacity of the potash industry in the province. Even though the Liberals were aware it was coming, we were still shocked at the magnitude of the proposal. I recall the grins and smirks on the faces of the NDP backbenchers as the lieutenant governor read from the text prepared for him. They didn't know the ramifications of what they were doing. In fact, I am not certain those of us who were to oppose it with all we had did either. I know I didn't realize the damage done to our province's credibility until years later as minister of energy and mines when I was attempting to attract private investment. I recall so often, after making my pitch that private investment was welcomed and encouraged again in Saskatchewan, seeing the flicker of doubt in the eyes and the unmistakable shift of the feet meaning, "Yes and when will the rules change again? The price we were to pay for those mines in terms of image and credibility in subsequent years is not measurable in dollars. The throne speech was a tragedy of Shakespearean proportions that could be calculated in terms of jobs and lost opportunities.

Potash had been a political football in the province for years. Many a politician predicted that "potash can do for Saskatchewan what oil did for Alberta." As usual we are still waiting. Potash is one of the essential ingredients in fertilizers used in other parts of the continent and the world. The first deposits were found in the forties, but it was not until the fifties that it became apparent that the richest known deposits were right here in Saskatchewan. However, although the fertilizer industry was expanding in the fifties, the corporate boards were wary that the socialist government of T. C. Douglas would consider going into the mining business itself, until technical problems in two attempted mines in the fifties clearly demonstrated what a tricky business it was. In the early sixties, two American companies negotiated such significant tax concessions that they were able to convince their boards of directors that it was worthwhile to enter the socialist domain of Saskatchewan.

My father's government came to power in 1964 and his invitation to outside investment was readily accepted by the potash industry; by the end of the sixties there were ten mines in production in the province. While not "doing for Sasktchewan what oil had done for Alberta," the potash industry provided capital investment in the hundreds of millions of dollars and thousands of jobs. In the late sixties, a worldwide agricultural slowdown led to a drop in fertilizer requirements. The price of potash plummeted with disastrous repercussions for all concerned, not the least of whom was the provincial government. The world price went below the cost of production and massive layoffs in the industry were imminent. The other main producers in North America were in the state of New Mexico, where reserves that had not been as rich as Saskatchewan's to begin with had already been worked for a good number of years. The cost of mining the product was high and the economic end of the reserves was in sight.

As most of the potash companies had mines in both New Mexico and Saskatchewan, it is not surprising that my father was approached by the industry with "a deal he couldn't refuse." The emissary was one Page Morris of the Potash Corporation of America, a subsidiary of the gigantic Pennzoil Corporation. Although the industry was to deny it later, they obviously had reached agreement among themselves before they made their political approaches. Page Morris, who talked with the support of the industry with the exception of one mine in Saskatchewan, came to Regina to meet with my father, and the concept of prorationing was born. Central Canada Potash, however, wanted no limits on production because they could sell all their production capacity to one of their owners, a fertilizer co-op in Chicago. They threatened a legal challenge to any such legislation. Attorney General Darrel Heald informed my father that legislation regulating the productive capabilities of the industry would be readily struck down, so my father told Page Morris that if it was the intention of Central Canada Potash to challenge in court, the government simply could not move. In the meantime, he phoned the federal minister of justice, Otto Lang, to seek the federal government's reaction. Lang said they would have no choice but to intervene; however, they certainly would not move any faster than the minimum required by the legalities of the case and the appeal process could be stretched to the limit. Since prorationing was to be a short-term measure lasting less than two years, Lang's assurances were all my father needed. Central Canada Potash was taken care of by the industry. The same intense lobbying was going on in New Mexico and eventually prorationing was agreed upon by both governments, with voluntary industry participation. For political purposes an exchange of visits was proposed.

I was delighted to accompany my father to New Mexico as one of his executive assistants, a role I enjoyed playing on an infrequent basis. Page Morris was our host on the Pennzoil executive jet and on the trip down I heard him make reference to the cooperation of European producers through people in Amsterdam. My father mentioned that a powerful individual in the potash trade (a charming, unassuming little man who once visited me in Moose Jaw) had a strong enough rapport with the Russians to persuade them to cooperate by lowering their exports for a short time. Russia was the one country that could render all these elaborately laid plans obsolete by increasing exports. Prorationing in Saskatchewan and New Mexico was to receive major attention in subsequent American anti-trust action and the conversation on the plane that day and the subsequent dramatic rise of potash prices certainly lend credence to the theory that the price-fixing conspiracy was worldwide.

The Pennzoil jet landed in the early evening in Santa Fe, where we were met both by people involved in the industry and by aides to the governor. That night we learned about some of the intricacies of New Mexico politics. The Republican governor of New Mexico, David Cargo, was in his second term. Since by law he could not run for a third term, he was casting a covetous eye on a Senate seat. I had already gathered that the potash industry did not regard the incumbent, Democratic Senator Montoya, as a friend, and Cargo's handling of potash prorationing would probably determine his political future.

The next day a meeting was held at the governor's mansion in Santa Fe that included representatives of the potash companies, officials of the New Mexico state government, and officials of the provincial government of Saskatchewan. I sat in behind my father. Page Morris was the unofficial chairman, which surprised me, since I was expecting it to be the governor. I recall that Cargo appeared nervous and left the meeting several times, explaining that he had other business to attend to. That struck me as odd because the potash business was not exactly small change. In retrospect, the answer might be probably that the governor, a lawyer, knew the anti-trust implications of this meeting and was aware that some day he might well have to recount what went on in that room. If that was the explanation for his actions, then he was quite right. Some time after our visit the United States government did file an anti-trust action against the potash industry and David Cargo was indeed on the stand. I was questioned by the lawyers defending the potash producers about the New Mexico meeting; however, I was never called as a witness and the potash producers defended themselves successfully against the charge.

Distasteful as it was to all concerned, prorationing at that time accomplished the objectives of the industry and the two governments involved. Layoffs were generally averted, the life of the New Mexico industry was extended by a few years, and, most important, prices stabilized. The cantankerous Central Canada Potash was unhappy but was kept in line by industry pressure, whatever form that may have taken. My father's government was attacked by the NDP as "catering to its corporate friends" and they pledged to do away with prorationing. As is so often the case in politics, when they had the chance to do away with it, they did the opposite—they kept it in place. Prorationing had been successful and Allan Blakeney knew it. As the NDP assumed power the potash industry was moving into an expansionary phase almost to the exact timetable envisioned by my father, who had intended to remove prorationing after the election of 1971. The NDP had different ideas. They hated the private sector but privately they acknowledged the success of prorationing, which they decided to keep as a hook to control the industry. They first used the hook in 1972 with a prorationing fee, which they followed with a complex new taxation plan that dramatically raised tax revenue. Central Canada Potash had had enough. They refused to pay the prorationing fee and filed in court that prorationing was unconstitutional. Other companies followed suit and refused to open their books to the government, arguing that the government was a potential competitor. I'm sure they had no idea just how prophetic they were. The stakes were high because the price of potash had soared and the companies were now recapturing their initial investments after years of losing money.

The throne speech of 1975 was an opportunity for the Liberal caucus to demonstrate clearly who the official opposition was in this legislature. One look at the Tories, most of whom had that "how did I get here?" look about them, told us that it would be our show and we would make them look bad by sheer weight of talent. We made a caucus decision to attack the government's intention on hard business sense rather than on ideological grounds. Dave Steuart designated Ted Malone as the "quarterback" on the issue and then more or less stepped back. I'm not certain why Davey removed himself from being front and center. It may have been a conscious effort on his part to allow the leadership hopefuls to emerge.

The actual legislation to enter the potash business, along with the powers of expropriation, was introduced into the House a couple of days later. It was well-written legislation, in fact the best money could buy. Unquestionably poorly written legislation was destined to be challenged in court so Attorney General Roy Romanow was taking no chances. The irony was that a good Tory law firm, for a fee, had written the most damaging socialist legislation in Canadian history virtually free of legal loopholes. Naturally, the potash industry was ready and willing to supply the Liberals with volumes of material to use to block passage of the bill. Ted Malone prepared the ground well and assigned specific areas to the MLAs. However, very early on I perceived an attitude on the part of some producers of "to hell with it. If we can get our money, let us out of this socialist rathole." Over the years the NDP have preached the evils of the multinationals and how they prey on the small person in order to survive. Unfortunately, far too many people in Saskatchewan have listened to this. The fact is there is great competition in the world for the investment dollars of the multinationals. Many of the companies were quite willing to leave quickly with their money in hand to go to the parts of the world where they were welcome, and they would have things to say to the world investment community that would haunt Saskatchewan for years.

Before the debate on the potash expropriation legislation could begin the throne speech had first to be debated. In my later years in the legislature I came to the conclusion that this was an exercise that could readily be dispensed with. The first debate you participate in has some glimmer of excitement solely because you do not yet know the individuals who over the years will become your adversaries. After that the throne speech debate is obviously a vehicle for government backbenchers to blow off steam and serves no useful legislative purpose. However, in this case, the government had something very controversial to do in the next few weeks so the NDP strategists had decided to get the maximum benefit from the debate. While there was the usual parade of backbenchers on their feet, the best cabinet ministers also made an appearance. It was my first chance to see many of them in action; Allan Blakeney undoubtedly had some talent in his cabinet.

Jack Messer was bright, articulate, and tough. In the coming sessions, Messer was one I avoided in question period unless I had something very good to go with. I always had the feeling after tangling with him of being "beaten up." He came at you with knees, elbows, and anything else he could muster. He was merciless with his adversaries. To this day, I don't classify Jack Messer as a socialist and privately I don't think he would either.

Elwood Cowley was a scoundrel; however, he was a likable scoundrel and an able one. Elwood was the key strategist for the NDP and he lived and died politics. From the opposition benches, it appeared that Elwood carried a great deal of influence with Allan Blakeney. Elwood was a real believer in the effective use of opinion polls and various NDP ministers told me that he had a computer at home that he had programmed to predict voting patterns. In some respects, he was the party's troubleshooter—if an important portfolio needed sorting out, Elwood Cowley would soon become the minister. In addition, he was no more a socialist than I am.

Gordon MacMurchy was a farmer from the constituency of Last Mountain who was a powerful, almost vitriolic, speaker. Like Cowley, he slept politics. He was a faction all by himself on the left wing of the party, yet it was often very difficult to discern from the opposition side exactly where he stood. It appeared he was often at odds with Cowley, Messer, and Romanow but it was obvious he had significant support from the backbenchers.

The attorney general, Roy Romanow, was a classic politician and undoubtedly one of the best orators I have known. A superb debater, he had a strange relationship with the NDP. They would fall back and depend on him to bail them out of a tight spot, yet they obviously enjoyed it when he was taking his lumps. Roy had always wanted to be a Liberal. He was within an ace of joining the Liberals of my father's era. Attorney General Darrel Heald conducted the negotiations. Apparently, Roy had agreed to cross the floor when Woodrow Lloyd surprised the party and resigned as leader of the NDP. Roy decided to stay and contest the leadership of the party, losing in a close fight to Allan Blakeney. Roy did not have the inherent political ruthlessness of Jack Messer but when he got wound up he could be a stinging debater and he had a real political infighter's sense. I soon learned from observing the forays at the start of the session to be very careful when tangling with Roy Romanow and when doing so to make certain that five o'clock or ten o'clock was not far away and to be certain to kill the clock so he couldn't come back. Roy's great strength was his ability to raise the morale of the NDP troops with one of his fiery speeches. He had the talent to take a day that had not gone well for the government and in the last fifteen minutes jump into the debate and kick the blazes out of the opposition while his troops, who may have been downtrodden all day, would bang and cheer and leave with big smiles on their faces. As I write this, Roy Romanow is out of politics but he will be back—most likely as premier.

Along with Allan Blakeney, these were the four heavies in the NDP cabinet. They had others who were competent; however, these four would certainly have stood out in any cabinet. My father did not have a comparable quartet, nor did Grant

Devine even with a mass of fifty-six to choose from. Only the Liberal caucus of 1975 could have matched or exceeded the NDP of that vintage in overall political expertise. However, at that time all attention was focused on the somber little band seated in the corner with looks of dismay. For several of them, I would not be far out in suggesting they were wearing the first suit they had ever owned. It was undeniable, much as we did not like it, that the man of the hour was Dick Collver and all eyes were on him as he prepared for his maiden speech. I am sure he felt the pressure, and would continue to feel it for the next three years, of the vulture squad composed of press, NDP, and Liberals waiting to pounce on him at the first sign of a mistake.

On the afternoon of Collver's maiden speech, the public gallery and the press row were jammed. Both the NDP and the Liberals attempted to feign disinterest, without success. I recall deliberately turning my back and reading a newspaper, although I was taking in every single word. Collver's speech was very ordinary and run-of-the-mill. His delivery style was only mediocre for one who had been on the campaign trail. He clearly intended his remarks to be uncontroversial and was determined not to make any enemies other than the obvious partisans in the chamber. He admonished both sides of the House for traditional practices such as heckling and banging on the desks. He clearly intended to take it straight to the NDP as he continually stressed the Conservatives were the party of the "little people" and they were there to learn and intended to learn well before the next election. He stressed they were the new party and the Liberals and the NDP had had their day. When he was finished both the Liberals and the NDP told themselves he had bombed and jumped to lay that on the press in the hopes that it would be the story of the day. It wasn't completely true and the press didn't buy it, despite snow jobs from the press secretaries of both parties. Certainly Collver had not been great, but he had been adequate and that was all he had strived for. He won the first round simply by being mediocre and, by the size of the grin on his face as he left the assembly, he knew it.

The throne speech debate was interrupted by an all-party agreement to allow the government to present the potash legislation in second reading. Only the government speech moving the legislation would be given and the opposition would not respond. The NDP made it clear they wanted the legislation passed by Christmas and other than that were prepared to be conciliatory to the opposition. Since the legislation was through the attorney general's department, Roy Romanow took the bills into second reading. First reading is merely the presentation of the legislation in the assembly, while second reading is the formal debate and agreement in principle. Third reading is a clause-by-clause study in an informal atmosphere and this is when most amendments or changes are made. There were two bills in this case, one to enable the government of Saskatchewan to enter the potash business as a Crown corporation and the second to legalize expropriation. This was the first time I had seen Roy Romanow on his feet and he was good. He eloquently presented the scenario from a socialist point of view that essentially did not differ from the traditional arguments of the last hundred years.

The potash debate was a blessing for our troubled caucus. Apart from paranoia about the Tories, we had just been through an exhausting convention. The party president had stepped down and a battle royal erupted between the federal and provincial wings when Otto Lang's former campaign manager, Tom Malloy, decided to contest the position. Gary Lane came close to having a heart attack and went searching for a candidate. He found one, a good one, in Terry Jensen, a Saskatoon businessman. However, a month prior to the convention a plane carrying Terry and three others crashed in northern Saskatchewan leaving no trace. When it was obvious Terry could not have survived, the search was on for another candidate. John Embury, a prominent party man, came forward and a bitter federal-provincial fight took place that fortunately went unnoticed by the diligent press corps in attendance at the convention. It has been my experience that when one wishes to mute the press, it is a cardinal rule to have the press room close to a bar with lots of food and, as long as it is free, the reporters will rarely venture out into the corridors except to go home to bed, and sometimes not even then. In any event, the intensity of the battle went over their heads. John Embury won but Otto Lang was quite right when he said later that the party should keep its enemies in perspective.

When the legislature opened the party was divided, tired, and low in morale. The potash situation changed that. We were going to make it "our" show, especially since Dick Collver had decided that although his party would vote against the legislation they would not debate it until the next election. It was not a decision made out of cleverness but rather necessity. Collver knew what a talented caucus the Liberals had and that his MLAs, with the exception of him and Roy Bailey, would be cut to ribbons in debate. He decided to give in to the Liberals this time in order to be able to fight another day.

As the debate on second reading started it was our intention to go at the government hard for about a week and, after it was clear what a great fight we had made, grudgingly let the bill come to a vote. Certainly we had no chance to thwart the legislation—not with the government having a thirty-nine to fifteen to seven edge in seats—however, we hoped to cause some changes by amendment if we could create enough heat. In normal debates both sides readily allow the other to adjourn. When debate is called another day, the same member may rise and continue speaking or, if he is not in the House, another member may keep the first "alive." You can speak only once in a specific debate but you can adjourn as often as the House will allow. These rules are only important in the unlikely event of a filibuster. This debate was not a filibuster at the start, but we were prepared to turn it into one if we could get any mileage out of it.

At the start the NDP put up an array of backbenchers speaking in favor of the potash expropriation. I can well recall their favorite line: "I'll put our Saskatchewan civil servants up against the best of private enterprise." What always made that one ring hollow was the implication that they were putting up something of their own, when in fact it was the old story of politicians talking and the taxpayers taking the risk. The public were not enthused and even NDP supporters were less than lukewarm. Collver entered the debate and put his token opposition on the record. There was little doubt that the public were looking to us to provide the opposition, which we took as a signal that even though they might flirt with the Tories they considered us the true alternative.

The NDP no longer wore smirks on their faces and were obviously getting flak from their ridings. We were hammering at the uncertainty of the total cost, the source of the funds, and the damage to the province in lost jobs and revenues; and were scoring well with the argument that a more conciliatory approach to the industry with a fair taxation policy would bring in far more revenue at no risk to the taxpayer. The debate was going better than we had ever hoped and we ridiculed the Tories for laying down on an important issue, which clearly stung them. The press was on our bandwagon and mail and encouragement were coming in from all over the province. Most important, the adrenalin was running in our caucus and what originally had been just opposition was turning into a crusade or, in legislative terms, a filibuster. The nature of the issue, the inherent bad-guy stance of the NDP, and the chance to show up the incompetence of the Tories were all factors that brought us together as a fighting caucus.

Suddenly we were socializing together, which we had not done to that point, and everyone was more supportive of everyone else. We were effective in question period and had the NDP backpedaling on all fronts. The fact that Dave Steuart was a lame-duck leader did not seem to matter. While he was not the driving force, he was doing what he did best—attack. The internal caucus direction was handled by Ted Malone, who was using the rules skillfully to prolong the debate.

When it became obvious that this was no longer a debate but a filibuster, the NDP stopped cooperating. They would not put any more speakers into the debate and refused to allow our speakers to adjourn. They accused us of wasting the legislature's time and Collver, who obviously had received some heat about his passive role, was saying this was an issue for the next election. Everything told us the NDP were on shaky ground and if we could force any significant political win we could perhaps push the Tories into the category of a splinter group permanently. All kinds of encouragement was flowing in and by using every trick in the book we were able to get to Christmas without the second reading coming to a vote. The NDP were obviously concerned about their own people's reaction because they started an ad campaign on television to explain the legislation. The winning party doing political advertising six months after an election was unheard of.

We returned to session right after the first of the year with some good credible material every day, even though we were running out of gas. The Conservatives felt compelled to put up two or three speakers, which briefly fired us up, and we intensified our scorn and ridicule of the Tories. Now one of the basics in politics is the utilization of the press and they were definitely becoming bored. The most important things to remember when dealing with the press, I believe, are to keep matters simple and direct and, above all, not to make the press person expend any effort. Other than two or three veteran reporters who knew what was happening, the press gallery in Regina was laden with kids fresh out of whatever, probably high school. Their perception and grasp of the issues were not legendary.

We decided to let the bill go to committee where we could involve ourselves one on one with the NDP. The minister on the hot seat was Roy Romanow, and he was ready for a long, protracted battle. Obviously he was pacing himself as he carefully controlled his responses to the heavy questioning, much of it based on material provided by the industry. It was obvious at the outset that the government had no areas where they were willing to make concessions. They had spent a great deal of money to get their legislation well drafted and they had no intention of interfering with the expertise of their Toronto law firm.

The politics of the exercise were starting to change mainly due to the press. For example, one day as I was driving to Regina I was listening to a local talk-show host who announced he would no longer carry news of the potash legislation debate on his show. Certainly we have fought wars for him to have the right to determine the content of his own show. But where does his right end and his responsibility begin? It was the biggest issue in Saskatchewan since World War II, with ramifications affecting the next generation; yet this little nobody, who had never set foot inside the legislature to check on the atmosphere or the issue, arbitrarily decided it was no longer important. The press took the NDP off the hook by removing the spotlight from them and almost cast an accusing finger at us for fighting the legislation. With press coverage becoming inaccurate we started to wind down the committee study. After forty days, on January 28, 1976, the legislation passed.

In retrospect, I probably enjoyed those forty days as much as any I was to have in politics. Our caucus went from a group of greenhorns with some potential to a cohesive, smooth-working opposition. Granted, we changed nothing but I recall with pride my association with those fourteen men and women and the effort we made and the enjoyment of working together. We had outclassed the Tories and exposed them as incompetent, and the province had turned to us to lead the fight against the legislation. Yet the Tories lost no credibility at all and those who had turned to us were not going to support us in future years. The fifteen of us were doomed as a caucus, not because of anything we had done but because of events far beyond our control. That big unknown factor called timing had decided that the Tory moon was rising and the Liberal sun was setting, and that, pure and simple, is the way it was.

After the session was over, attempts were made to keep the potash issue alive but the press were now disinterested and preoccupied with the Conservatives. In the potash battle, I believe Dave Steuart deliberately allowed other people to lead the charge as a prelude to a leadership convention. Ted Malone did an excellent job of coordinating the effort and funneling new material into the hands of the MLAs. Newcomer Stu Cameron excelled in the debate and unquestionably built up a following in the party and within the caucus. Tony Merchant had always been effective so he did not gain the way some did. If there was a loser among the leadership hopefuls, it was Gary Lane. I would not go so far as to say that he bombed, but he definitely did not gain stature within the party. In the session interval it still was assumed the three leadership candidates would be Ted Malone, Stu Cameron, and Gary Lane.

From a personal point of view there were several things that were gnawing me around this time. It was becoming clear that the next election was going to shape up as a fight for second place and the NDP were relishing the prospect of playing off one opposition party against the other for the next three years. Despite our performance in the House we were losing the battle with the Tories for the role of opposition. Dick Collver was not perceived as any savior but he was being tolerated by the electorate and clearly we were not. We were now hearing about potential legal action from Dick Collver's former employers for mismanagement, and many in caucus hoped this would be the start of the predicted demise of the Conservative party.

The vague distinctions between Liberals and Tories were beginning to make no sense to me. Conservative Roy Bailey held the same philosophical views I did, yet Roy Nelson, probably the most right-wing MLA in the whole assembly, was a dedicated Liberal and fervent Tory-hater. I was finding it more and more difficult to reconcile the fact that both opposition parties were playing right into Allan Blakeney's, or more accurately Elwood Cowley's, hands.

In many ways I was becoming envious of the Tories, who seemed to have everything going for them and were not burdened with the onus of being expected to perform, and I was having trouble with the Liberals' tight relationship to the federal party. I am probably colored in my assessment of Davey Steuart by events after my father's death and I concede that is unfair to him; however, I strongly believed, and still do, that the price of our close cooperation with the feds was his Senate seat. As individuals, I had nothing but respect for Pierre Elliott Trudeau and Otto Lang but politically in Saskatchewan they were the kiss of death.

I was basically happy with my personal performance in the first session of the legislature. I was getting over my nervousness in question period and did a five-hour stint of killing time in the potash debate, which really was not that easy. My name was mentioned as leadership material but that was on the strength of my name not on my performance in the legislature. I was still a long way off the top end. The session was prorogued and in the interlude I decided to carve out a right-wing constituency of my own and follow my political instincts. I was going to make a fiercely anti–federal government speech during the budget debate when the House resumed. I was sick and tired of carrying the millstone of Pierre Elliott Trudeau around my neck and was weary of the party being apologists for the federal government. I had no quarrel with Otto Lang but he wasn't going out of his way to do us any favors so I felt it was only fair that I make it clear I was my own person and prepared to call a spade a spade. I gave that speech a fair degree of thought and I mentioned it to Dave Steuart, who said he had no objection to what I proposed to say as long as I was not going to include Otto Lang.

The session resumed in early March with the NDP bringing in its usual budget—balanced as the finance minister read it and in the red when the actual figures were in a year later. My turn to speak came in an almost deserted assembly at about twenty to five in the afternoon. Davey asked me if I was still going to give it to the feds. I replied that I was doing exactly what I had told him, and he smiled and said he was looking forward to it. It was a courtesy in opposition that, if possible, all caucus members were to be in the assembly whenever we had a speaker up, so most of the Liberals were present. The press gallery and the government benches were sparsely populated, and only one Tory was present. Within five minutes, after the thrust of my speech and its anti–federal government tone were apparent, the press gallery was suddenly populated and the assembly was full. Even the premier was there, and I was conscious that both he and Roy Romanow were staring at me intently, taking in every word and wondering what was happening to the Liberal party. The assembly was in silence as I delivered a blistering attack on the federal Liberals and their economic policies. As I was delivering the speech I became aware of Davey Steuart, sitting a couple of rows in front of me, turned completely around and staring blankly at me. I could tell he was not pleased but he wasn't giving me the sign to sit down either. Obviously, the Tories loved it and I could hear the odd phrase like "Come on over now." I finished the speech and left immediately for Moose Jaw.

The next day the press was full of my attacks on the federal government, although the fact that I had been equally vitriolic about the NDP government did not seem to merit attention. I really don't know why everyone was so shocked—my father attacked the feds with regularity. Once, on national television, he told the then-minister of finance, Edgar Benson, to wipe the smile off his face. I arrived at caucus late to hear Davey Steuart saying that he knew about the speech in advance. There was no particular animosity from the caucus, in fact I had said some of the things they would have liked to say. What mattered to me was that my constituency loved it. Immediately, some of the press began to speculate that I was going to defect to the Tories. I never gave a flat, outright denial to the rumors and was vague and oblique when questioned. I had no intention of going Tory but I had no interest in telling anyone that. I preferred my caucus counterparts to think of me as erratic.

In Thunder Creek I was now being looked on as Colin Thatcher and not the son of the former premier. I was proud of my father but everyone wants their own identity and there are two strikes against you in politics when you have a successful political father. I had been successful in my attempts to carve out a right-wing constituency. If things didn't work out with the Liberal party no doubt I had options elsewhere. For the moment I was happy I had served notice that I was not going to carry the cross of Pierre Elliott Trudeau and the federal Liberals indefinitely.

The balance of that legislative session did not go particularly well for the Liberals. It had become only a question of time until Davey Steuart went to the Senate. The only certain leadership candidate was Ted Malone. Talk was beginning to circulate that Stu Cameron was interested only if it was to be a "coronation." Gary Lane was unofficially in and had at least three MLAs with him, of whom Sonny Anderson was the most active. Dick Collver was getting better in the legislature, which was unnerving to the Liberal caucus. By now I knew Dick quite well and he used to delight in saying, "You people can have your games in here; I'll play mine where it counts."

Interestingly the Tories were having problems also. I had become friendly with Roy Bailey and we talked a great deal. Roy Bailey had lost to Dick Collver in the 1973 Conservative leadership campaign. He was an excellent speaker and well respected, but he hated Dick Collver. We must have been a funny pair sitting behind the rail in the legislature with Bailey complaining about the Tories and me complaining about the Liberals. As the session went on we were often joined by one Roy Romanow, and we had some intriguing off-the-record conversations.

I confess to enjoying Roy Romanow's company, although for obvious reasons I did not completely trust him. On one occasion in that session I found myself in a jam with the Speaker and I was facing the prospect of expulsion over a relatively minor issue. (Eventually, being expelled from the assembly became old hat but that was not yet the case.) When it was obvious I was going to have to withdraw or leave, a note arrived that read: "Colin: Withdraw now. I was in the same position in my first session and your father sent me a note which said 'withdraw.' Do it now. I did. R.R." Roy Romanow has the worst handwriting in the world, even worse than mine, yet it is authoritative. I decided to withdraw.

Roy was a shrewd politician in every sense. One evening in the legislature we were doing private members' bills and Stu Cameron was speaking on one he obviously considered important because several members of his constituency executive, his family, and a few friends were seated in the gallery. The subject was related to Roy Romanow's department and Stu was hitting Roy fairly hard and showing off a little for his guests. I saw Roy watching Stu's people during the speech and then look at his watch. Stu finished at about 8:45 and was obviously pleased with his performance. Roy got up without a note as usual and launched into a counterattack on Stu. He was intense, deadly, and devastating. He would look up to the gallery to check the reaction of Stu's guests and, as their expressions began to show concern for Stu, Romanow stepped into high gear and just wiped the floor with him. By now Stu was mad and ready to get back up. Instead Roy gave it to him, all the time watching his supporters in the gallery, until he decided enough was enough when he calmly adjourned debate and sat down. Stu was furious but could do nothing. I learned a lesson I was never to forget—if you are going to tackle Roy Romanow then you had better be prepared to kill the clock, which means keep talking until adjournment. If you give him a chance to get up, he'll kill you the same way he did Stu that night.

Stu Cameron did not run for the leadership of the party as it was widely assumed he would. Well into late spring Tony Merchant was in the Ted Malone camp and was assumed to be his campaign manager. In late May, I received a call from Tony Merchant that floored me. He said that after a great deal of reflection he had decided to run for the leadership and he asked me what I thought. I was taken completely by surprise and was noncommittal, as I was always to be in any leadership race. Obviously Stu Cameron was out if Tony was in.

That weekend Tony contacted all the MLAs who were at home for the long weekend. It was typical of Tony's flair for the dramatic that he could not wait until we were all back in Regina but rather choose to hire a plane and drop in on us at home for maximum effect. I recall Jack Wiebe describing Tony's visit to his hog farm. Nothing reeks quite like pig manure—it permeates your hair, your clothes, and literally sticks to you. Jack had just finished spreading manure on a field when Tony's plane touched down in hot pursuit of Jack's manure spreader. The two of them talked about the leadership campaign in the midst of what had to be, at the very least, a fragrant atmosphere. When you know Tony and know how immaculately dressed he always is, talking in the midst of a field blessed with a fresh covering of pig manure just is not his style. Jack Wiebe was later to relate the whole conversation "stunk." Sonny Anderson was heard to comment, "It was still stinking in Shaunavon," which was the next target in Tony's aerial blitz.

Davey Steuart officially announced that he was stepping down at a fund-raising banquet in Regina in June of 1976. He told a gathering of the faithful in the Centre of the Arts that a good, long battle for the leadership of the party was the most healthy thing he could prescribe for the revitalization of the organization. He also warned the party was now in a battle of simple survival and could no longer afford to ignore the Tories. Sage words considering the situation. Davey Steuart had made some horrible tactical decisions, which had left lots of room for the Tories to be born. On the other hand, he had played a key role in the building of the party in the late fifties and early sixties and his expertise as a number two man is unquestioned. Indeed, I believe he would have made a very competent premier. However, the biggest political factor of all—timing—was against him and with that liability in your corner all your assets pale in comparison.

The leadership race was now officially on even though the convention was not going to be held for six months. The thinking was that a protracted leadership race would give the candidates lots of exposure and in the process of organizing the campaign delegates would automatically be rebuilding the party at the constituency level. In addition, Dick Collver and the Tories would be pushed into the background for six months while the spotlight was exclusively on the Liberals. Obviously, someone in the backroom of the party perceived the candidates as being cast in an indestructible cast-iron mold. The prolonged race was insanity all the way; it was destined to make the end result more frustating and bitter and everyone, including the party and the candidates, tired of it long before the convention date. In many ways it put the final nail in the coffin of the party.

At this time I had not decided whom I was going to support although I knew it would not be Ted Malone. Tony Merchant was obviously the candidate of the federal wing. This did not bother me because I knew Tony was his own person and would do what had to be done to make things happen; however, many perceived him differently. Gary Lane was perhaps the best politician but, as such, he had no philosophy other than votes, and he was not trusted in many quarters within the party. Malone was to play the middle-of-the-road role, neither federally nor provincially orientated. I had no intention of running myself but I did not discourage talk and was probably guilty of even encouraging it. I hoped to "freeze" the right wing of the party until a solid right-of-center candidate appeared. This thinking on my part was complete fantasyland as it turned out; however, I played the game for several months and was flattered by the encouragement I received.

The race had hardly begun when we all received a jolt. In late June, only a couple of weeks into the race, Gary Lane officially withdrew. I think it fair to say in retrospect that some games were being played and Dave Steuart was one of those playing them. Dave Steuart could not stand Gary Lane—nor could any leader Lane was ever to work under—and Lane had played enough dirty tricks on Steuart over the years that he should have assumed that one of the last acts of the outgoing leader would be to ensure that he would not win. We were notified of a very important caucus meeting for the end of June and the word was the date of the convention was going to be altered, as well as the format. Between the notice and the actual meeting, Lane withdrew as a candidate. When we arrived for caucus it was just a normal meeting with nothing of substance brought up. There is no doubt something was in the wind and, whatever it was, it was certainly intended for Gary Lane. Meanwhile, Gary Lane vanished.

The two remaining candidates, Tony Merchant and Ted Malone, were at it almost full time. They were running into problems because many people were refusing to commit themselves so early in the campaign. A commitment for a political convention is generally taken seriously by most people because it is embarrassing to change your mind, and it is very difficult to entice a delegate to break his commitment once he has pledged his support. There is nothing more frustrating than a noncommittal delegate, yet not to see delegates early is to risk another candidate stealing their support. Both candidates spent the summer putting their organizations together. Sonny Anderson joined Tony Merchant as his campaign manager and this camp appeared to have the edge organizationally. Tony had better fund raisers than Ted Malone and was visibly more elaborate. Both candidates went at it as though there was no tomorrow. They closed down their law practices and went on the campaign trail for the balance of the year. In terms of dollars and cents, the party was asking a great deal. In addition to day-to-day expenses, the lost income from their law practices must have been formidable.

I have no doubt that Tony's decision to run after being involved in the setting up of Malone's campaign was a factor in the open animosity that emerged between the two; however, the absurd length of the campaign and the heavy financial commitment had to be contributing factors. The friction became intense. I recall a function given by Tony Merchant for potential delegates after a Roughrider football game. I was shocked to see Ted Malone and his wife there because it did not strike me as part of the "rules of the game," in a game that has no rules. The unwritten law that you do not interfere with a rival candidate's promotions did not seem to deter Malone as he drank Merchant's liquor, ate his food, and searched for delegates at Tony's gathering. His actions spoke for themselves.

Ted Malone was playing the role of the safe candidate. He had won Regina Lakeview in the by-election following the death of Don McPherson. The first time I heard him address a gathering I thought he was a terrible speaker, but as the leadership race progressed he improved dramatically. He would play to the right wing of the party by pointing out that his grandfather was a Tory in the Anderson government of the thirties. He had never made any secret of his dislike for my father and I suspect that I fell into the same category. It didn't matter because I knew I would not work for him for long if he won.

Tony Merchant had been a radical for as long as I could remember. The first time I saw him was when he was barefoot with a pretty young lady (probably his wife) at a Roughrider football game. Now you don't see very many people barefoot at a football game, and when the only person you ever saw like that turns into the epitome of Mr. Conservative in his dress and general decorum, you remember it. Tony became a senior partner in a large Regina law firm and won the Regina Wascana seat easily in a well-orchestrated campaign in 1975. He had a capacity for work unequalled by any politician I have known. His desk was a disaster area with daily newspapers from the *Los Angeles Times* to the Toronto *Globe and Mail* to the Regina *Leader Post* covering all available space. But it really was not chaos because there was organization there—Tony could simply do more things at one time than most people can think of. Time and sleep meant nothing to him if there was work to do. Tony had a mixed following: there were those who loved him and those who hated him. While doing an open-line show for a Regina radio station he had drawn the ire of the Law Society of Saskatchewan for dispensing legal advice over the airwaves. No doubt he had planned the ploy because the society looked ridiculous and Tony became a folk hero.

Tony was Otto Lang's brother-in-law and every move he made was scrutinized in anticipation of Otto being behind the next tree. Nowhere did I see any evidence of Otto involving himself in the campaign, which he had every right to do if he so chose. His wife, of course, was an active worker for her brother. Tony was always the radical or perhaps the purveyor of change. In the campaign he was to make some bold creative suggestions for the revitalization of the party, as well as some strategy moves for delegates that were to take the party by complete surprise. There was no question I would support Merchant if all things stayed equal. The reasoning was simple. Merchant wanted to win and would do what he had to in order to accomplish that objective and no one would be able to control him, and that included Otto Lang and the federal party.

The first of several tactical moves by Tony Merchant came in late July. He proposed the party should separate into federal and provincial wings so the provincial party would be free to divorce itself from the federal party when necessary on localized issues. There was nothing radical in this suggestion at all. Quite the contrary, it was a return to the basic political tactic of Saskatchewan politicians known as "fed bashing." The proposal was viewed by many as a shallow attempt by Merchant to put some distance between himself and his brother-in-law. I didn't agree with that assessment at all because Tony was a fighter and I had no doubt that included Otto Lang if it was politically necessary. Unfortunately for Tony, he was to suffer a credibility gap that was to dog him the entire campaign. Deliberately, he chose a strategy that would portray him as the one who would shake up the party, and to that end he was successful—perhaps too much so. The establishment in a political party is generally cautious and the establishment in this race was no exception. Ted Malone became the "safe" candidate, the one who wasn't going to take the party anywhere but could perhaps hold on to what we had. The problem with that logic was the party was having less and less to hold on to every day, and it was still a long way to December and the convention.

As summer passed into fall, I became aware that I had not encountered Gary Lane anywhere. At first I assumed he was just licking his political wounds, but it was uncharacteristic of him not to be in the midst of a leadership race if for no other reason than to be a kingmaker. When I did meet him briefly at the Centre of the Arts in Regina in the latter part of September, he was unusually cool. Late in October, Party President John Embury and his wife stopped at my house in Moose Jaw. Over a drink, Embury asked me a point-blank question. He had a report that a Liberal MLA was joining the Tories next week and he wanted to know if it was me. I was shocked and denied it and the reports that I was having discussions with the Tories. The next evening Dave Steuart called to tell me that Lane was joining the Tories in the morning and he was calling an emergency caucus.

The reasons behind Lane's lack of activity in the party were now painfully apparent. Although the party tried to kid itself that it didn't really matter that much, there was no doubt the defection was a very heavy body blow. It was not the number change that was significant but Lane's departure reinforced the public perception of a declining party. The Conservatives now had someone with experience in the legislature who was not a bad speaker into the bargain. I had trouble visualizing Dick Collver and Gary Lane in friendly contact in light of Lane's open contempt for Collver in private. Lane had been one of those who had wanted to put the spotlight on Collver's legal problems—something caucus had rejected, not out of any sense of fair play but because we knew the NDP would ultimately do it for us. Lane had made a calculated political decision based purely on personal ambition, and the procedures he went through, or better did not go through, were questionable by any standards. He had administered an embarrassing situation to the party in the midst of a leadership race and had highlighted his new party in contrast to the one he was leaving. According to President John Embury, he took the confidential party membership list with him, as well as other party documents. That is something you do not do if you have any class at all.

The defection of Lane was regarded by some people in the party, and to a lesser extent in the press, as an indictment of Malone and Merchant. Rumors were rampant that I was following Lane within a few days and the subject was even discussed in caucus. The question was put to me on various occasions by the press and I continued my vagueness, although I did go so far as to say that I had had no discussions with the Tories. I went further than that in caucus, where I assured them that I was not about to follow Lane anywhere.

There were those who would have been happy for me to be somewhere else but we had already lost more than we could afford. The party was being torn apart as the delegate conventions got underway and the inevitable strong feelings, at no time very far beneath the surface, began to boil over. Tony Merchant was at it again. At the first two or three conventions at the constituency level he totally shut Malone out by running a slate, stacking the hall, and walking out with all the delegates. Malone screamed foul and then moved to counterattack. The respective slates faced each other at almost every constituency meeting. Many people were upset at the practice and the idea that some "born-again Liberals" were coming out to the local constituency delegate conventions. I could never understand the logic of a dying party protesting at the infusion of new blood, but this was what was happening in Saskatchewan. Merchant took most of the heat over this "stacking" procedure because he started it; Malone was to say he had no choice but to respond. As a result, some party people looked harder than ever for a third candidate. I know pressure was put on Stu Cameron to run. He speculated and then declined. Again, I received many offers of support but my stance remained unchanged.

In the early part of November 1976 I received my first serious overture from the Tories. I emphasize serious because many had been made during heckling in the House or in casual conversations over a drink. This one came in the form of a visit from one Doug Harlton, who had been the campaign manager for Don Swenson in the last general election in Thunder Creek. Doug brought along Wally Nelson, a highly successful John Deere and GM dealer from Avonlea who had been active in the formation of the Palliser Wheat Growers. Wally was typical of the conservatives who had reluctantly supported my father as part of any anti-socialist coalition and who now had a home with Dick Collver. Wally got to the point quickly and asked if I had any interest in joining the Conservatives. I replied that I intended to see the outcome of the Liberal leadership race and the resulting atmosphere but I was certainly amenable to considering the possibility of a move. Wally said that one of the reasons he was here now was because they felt I might be about to enter the leadership race. The implication was clear— the Tories did not want new converts who were full of sour grapes after losing a leadership bid. It made sense and Gary Lane's actions became crystal clear. It was left that the next move would be up to me and we all agreed that whether or not we talked again this meeting would remain confidential.

Within a few days, the fall session of the provincial legislature opened. I had a strange feeling as JoAnn and I mingled with the other Liberal MLAs and their wives at the opening ceremonies. It was not the feeling of being a Benedict Arnold, because I was not and was never to be, but it was just a general feeling of suddenly being uncomfortable. I had always been basically a loner but I felt even more of one that day—perhaps because I already knew what I was going to do very soon even if I wouldn't admit it to myself.

The caucus was representative of the party in that it was unsure of itself and unclear of the direction the party should go. The delegate conventions at the constituency level were almost over and it depended on whom you talked to as to who was ahead in the leadership race. The Merchant strategy was to sell memberships to anyone he could and get them out to meetings to support the Merchant slate of would-be delegates, who generally were young and new to the party. Although it sounds simple it really is an achievement in organization. You have to find some key people in the constituency who are prepared to push memberships, then you have to get the newcomers out to the meetings. Believe me, all that is no mean accomplishment. Tony was not successful everywhere but it did appear to me from what I could glean from various sources that he was ahead by maybe 10 to 15 percent.

Naturally, not everyone in the party loved him for this approach. Many of the old-line Liberals were denied at the selection meetings, which was a bitter pill to swallow for anyone who had been active for the party in several elections. Initially I was not enthused with Tony's methods. However, the more I thought about them, the more they made sense. The party was dying and this was no time to do things in the old, structured manner. It was clearly time to be different and if it was the wrong approach then it really didn't matter because we were well on our way to going down the tubes anyway. Tony's tactics were polarizing the party. There were many disgruntled Liberal workers, but there were also a lot of brand-new names appearing on the delegate rolls.

I decided to consult with someone whose political judgment I genuinely respected. The problem was that I did not trust the person in question to tell me his true opinion since he was not unbiased. After question period the next day, I strolled across to the other side of the House and sat down in the vacated seat of Allan Blakeney to ask the attorney general of Saskatchewan who his choice was to lead the Liberal party. Now one had to weigh Roy Romanow's answers very carefully. Normally you would assume he was attempting to sandbag you so you would reverse his answer to get the true facts; however, Roy knew you did this so, just to keep things honest, on some occasions he would tell it to you straight. You had to guess what you were getting—the 360-degree shuffle or the 180-degree shaft. This time Roy was fairly candid. They had no fear of us at all but, like the Liberals, the NDP were perplexed by Dick Collver. From the NDP point of view, Ted Malone could never hurt them but they were not certain he would be strong enough to hold the Liberal vote sufficiently to keep the Tories at bay. He appeared to share my view on Tony—it could be a disaster or it could be very interesting. What was clear, however, was that the NDP had no fear of the Liberal party in the immediate future.

The situation at the leadership convention, as I perceived it, was that Ted Malone had the edge in caucus, the party executive, and the overall establishment Liberals but Tony Merchant had more delegates. The question was, could he get them to Regina from all over the province? It soon became obvious that the young delegates elected at the constituency level on Tony's slate system were not appearing. A constituency elects ten voting delegates and ten alternates—the alternates getting a vote only if the elected delegates fail to show. Most of the no-shows were Merchant supporters and generally their replacements were those pushed to the side by the slate system that they felt Merchant had orchestrated. The fact that Ted Malone had been in on the same game did not seem to matter. He was clearly the beneficiary. Malone won by about one hundred votes out of about twelve hundred cast, with approximately four hundred eligible delegates not voting.

When the result was announced Ted Malone and his family were on the stage immediately, as were Tony and Pana Merchant. One of the most bizarre incidents I have ever seen then happened. I was close to the front and reached up and shook Tony's hand and congratulated him on an excellent try. In these circumstances, the losing candidate traditionally makes the selection unanimous by being called to the microphone. Incredibly, the chairman, John Embury, did not call on Tony but instead went straight to Ted Malone for a victory speech. I could not believe it. Embury was to say later he couldn't find Merchant and it wasn't his job to seek him out. The seeking process would have led him ten feet from where he was standing; the gesture was indicative of where the party was heading.

Later that evening JoAnn and I prepared to return to Moose Jaw. As we were getting into the car I had a sudden thought and said, "Let's go and have one drink up in the main hospitality room." She asked why and I replied, "We will never be at another Liberal convention." We went upstairs, had one drink, and left. The Malone years had begun.

4

Go Tory

The next week was a quiet one as the legislature wound down for the Christmas break. While the Liberals had been preoccupied with the bloodletting ritual of electing a leader, the Tories had quietly been becoming the opposition. The Liberal party now faced the prospect of two by-elections in seats they already held and there was a real possibility they might lose both. Malone had discussed the subject with Roy Romanow and the NDP were clearly worried about us. They could not have cared less about the seats and would gladly have passed them back to us if they could but they did not want the Tories winning them both. The fact that they perceived it to their advantage to prop us up was indicative of the contempt the government felt for us. I am not suggesting we had the sole say in the by-election dates but clearly they were not going to be called until the Liberals felt they were ready. Malone wanted them in the early part of the year to capitalize on the residual effects of the leadership campaign—that, of course, was based on the assumption that there were some residual effects and that they were positive.

Ted Malone made a major tactical error early. He did not inspect the constituency organizations personally before telling Roy Romanow he was ready. They were in a shambles. Evelyn Edwards, the very popular MLA of Saskatoon Sutherland, had passed away from cancer and after her tragic death her organization had all but disappeared. In Prince Albert, Davey Steuart had known he would not be running again and had done nothing to keep his organization functioning. The party put on a creditable show in Saskatoon and the Liberal candidate worked very hard; however, the Tories were better all the way and their candidate, Harold Lane, won by about five hundred votes. In Prince Albert it was a disaster as the party ran third and the PCs won easily. Ted Malone was criticized for putting so much of his personal credibility on the line when it was felt he did not have to. I do not agree with that criticism at all. Ted had no choice but to put everything we had into it, as well as to attempt to cash in on his exposure from the leadership convention. The simple fact was that the Tories had done their work well and deserved both seats.

After the debacle of the two by-elections I went out into Thunder Creek to talk to executive members about the future. Many of them urged me to "go Tory." My father had built the Liberal party and I was reluctant to be the one to destroy it, but as I traveled Thunder Creek and heard the anti-Liberal sentiment everywhere it was obvious things were out of our hands. While I was reflecting on the future, Ted Malone came to my home and shocked me. He offered me the position of finance critic in the upcoming session of the legislature and I confess to being truly flattered because that is the number one position in opposition next to leader. I was under no illusions as to his motivations—he was afraid I was going to the Tories and this was a carrot to lock me into the party. If I was going to leave the party I should refuse. The problem was, I wanted the position and Malone knew it. He said he wanted a hard-hitting, right-wing attack on the NDP budget and I would have a free rein, although I was not to go out of my way to start anything with the feds. I knew exactly what Malone was thinking. In addition to keeping me in the party, my promotion was a signal to the right wing not to defect to the Tories. That kind of thinking was about four years too late and one can only speculate what the outcome might have been if the Liberal party of the early seventies had stayed true to the party of the sixties. I told Ted Malone I would do it and give him an honest effort. He replied that was all he was looking for. Despite his reasons, I was honored because he still had formidable talent in his caucus—talent that both the NDP and the Tories would have loved to have had. It was not many days to the opening and I was glad to have something to take my mind off crossing the floor.

I put a fair amount of time and effort into the opposition reply to the throne speech. It is difficult to prepare for this kind of reply because you have no idea what is coming in terms of numbers until you hear them in the legislature, and then you must get to your feet at the conclusion of the speech and wing it for ten minutes or so. Then, in forty-eight hours you give the major reply in which you present an opposition analysis of government figures. Now there are certain things you can prepare for. You can research all the old clichés from previous budget replies and there is usually sufficient corridor talk to enable you to glean the flavor of what will be coming down. However, you don't have the numbers nor do you know anything about new programs or how they will be funded. Also, you get surprisingly little help from your own party. The research people don't understand finances nor do the politicians, and that includes former critics. I found the best way to clarify a point was not to try to play accountant yourself but rather to phone the department of finance and ask them. You were kidding yourself if you thought you were going to find a scandalous error in the government's arithmetic. The department would not volunteer any information but they would provide prompt answers to technical questions. As a matter of fact, as I came to know the department of finance people my respect for them grew immensely. Some of them were dyed-in-the-wool socialists, but bright.

Naturally, in the new session many eyes were going to be on the Tories and specifically on Gary Lane. Lane had been very quiet in the fall session and the rare occasions he was on his feet were strictly token. It was expected he would be far more aggressive this spring. However, it was the other Lane who surprised us all. Harold Lane was a fighter and a scrapper from almost the first day he set foot in the legislature and he had no fear of anyone. He got thumped by several ministers right off the bat but it didn't faze him in the slightest. He would be right back at them the next day in question period. Harold Lane gave the Tories a new dimension; on top of that he was a personable, likable individual who had no hesitation in going for the political jugular if it happened to be exposed.

Collver was clearly getting better. His legal difficulties with his former employers had broken into the news and the public were well aware that he was engaged in civil litigation, although few understood it. The NDP started to use it in their asides in question period and the daily heckling on the floor made constant reference to the fact he was in court. It did not unnerve Collver as many had hoped and perhaps had the opposite effect. The net result was that the battle was over as far as the perceived opposition was concerned and the spotlight was clearly on the Tories. They no longer had the luxury of lying back and they were going to have to perform. The difference was that now they had some people capable of performing, which made it a totally new game.

As the spring session opened, there was talk that Tony Merchant, Stuart Cameron, and Jack Wiebe were going to run federally in the election expected later in the year. Though it was still unconfirmed speculation, Ted Malone was visibly upset and, I'm sure, wondering what he had battled all those months for. He became paranoid with justification. The day before I was to respond to the budget speech he called me into his office, ostensibly to discuss my speech but really to confront me with a report that I was going to use the occasion to defect to the Tories. The report had come from a former cabinet minister in my father's government, according to Malone, and there were to be press conferences in Regina and Saskatoon immediately afterwards. I did not know whether to laugh or cry but in Malone's position I would probably have done exactly the same thing. I told him that the scenario was absurd and if I were ever to leave the party I would do so only after informing my Thunder Creek executive. He accepted that and that was the end of it.

I replied to the budget the next day. Despite the time and effort that goes into these kinds of speeches they receive little press coverage. As a matter of fact, a good question in question period will get you far more press than days and days of research into a well-reasoned speech. Why? Because in my experience the press are inherently lazy and have very short attention spans. As I was to learn quickly, if you want press attention use what I call "Eisler's Rule," in honor of Dale Eisler of the *Leader-Post*. Keep it short, simple, and uncomplicated. Violation of any of these three principles may cause the press to overlook you. In fact, I found that the less they understood an issue, the more coverage they would give you. Dick Collver was also a keen believer in Eisler's Rule and knew how to use it effectively.

Dick Collver was his own finance critic and he replied for the Tories a day or two after me. It was obvious from the tone and length of the speech that he had not troubled himself with a lot of research. He made an allegation that seventy million dollars was missing and left it at that. The NDP were upset at the headlines he got and it was beyond me how he had arrived at the figure. Frankly, I suspected he had just pulled it out of the air. Over the weekend one of my friends let it slip that Collver had outclassed me on the budget reply. He was referring, of course, to the missing seventy million dollars. When I told him there was no missing seventy million dollars he replied, "So what? He got the headlines."

He was right. The next week the government hammered Collver to substantiate the missing seventy million while Dick just sat there and grinned. He loved it. Collver had suckered the NDP into doing the reverse of what they intended and they were now acknowledging the Tories as the alternative. The press were pushing Collver into justifying his statement and he would invite them to his office and throw out columns of figures that supposedly had a seventy million shortfall. I was sitting with Dick behind the rail in the legislature shortly afterwards—an event that by now was causing heart failure in the Liberal ranks—and I commented that I was having trouble finding his missing seventy million. He laughed and said, "So am I." The NDP repudiated the missing seventy million a dozen times over the next week. Nobody cared and, it seemed to me, especially not the press. In my experience, their attention span is limited and they now wanted something else—the seventy million had become too complicated.

Within the Liberal caucus things were not going well. While there had been no announcement, it was almost certain that Stu Cameron and Tony Merchant were going to run federally, although Jack Wiebe was not. The spotlight was on Collver, who was having problems of his own in the Tory caucus. Roy Bailey, perhaps with his nose out of joint with the addition of the two Lanes, was talking vitriolically to anyone who wanted to listen about Dick Collver. He even led some of my Liberal colleagues to believe he was a candidate for crossing the floor. I had always liked Roy Bailey and had a great deal of respect for his abilities and integrity, but his hatred for Collver was so intense that I believe it colored his perspective on other issues. As the rumors surfaced that I was going to join the Tories, he advised me not to. He was convinced Collver's bubble was going to burst and he was basing that assessment on conversations he told me he had had with Collver's former employers. Roy's views were disturbing but I was unhappy in the Liberal caucus. We were now trying to survive as a party and were not remotely in the ball game for the next election. At best, we were the force that could reelect the NDP by splitting the vote, and the caucus knew it. The tone had changed from trying to do a number on the NDP to upstaging the Conservatives.

I truly believe that it would be a difficult question to answer if one were asked to write an essay on the differences between Conservatives and Liberals in Saskatchewan if the federal factor was removed. Now this is not necessarily true in other provinces but in Saskatchewan there is no difference other than political posturing by the respective leaders. The NDP have a hard-core vote of 30 percent with a potential easy fringe of an additional 8 to 10 percent. In the latter category are the left wingers, many of whom in other provinces would probably be Liberals. In Saskatchewan, however, left-wing, Trudeau-type Liberals are usually found in the NDP. The remaining 60 percent of the electorate can go either Conservative or Liberal with little effort. Because the NDP take their left wing, Saskatchewan Liberals are generally to the right of their federal counterparts, which runs them right into the traditional ground of the Tories.

That does not leave a great deal of philosophical room for two parties, going for exactly the same people with very much the same subject matter to argue over. In fact, if the federal parties were removed from the scene, the two parties would have to sit down and find an agenda to dispute. I found it ridiculous that I was part of a splinter party that would divide the vote in the next election and be the prime mechanism to reelect the Blakeney government. In effect I was working for Allan Blakeney and the NDP.

I had a conversation behind the rail in the legislature with Gary Lane in which I questioned him about his situation with the Tories. He appeared to be happy and was obviously playing a bigger role with them than he had with the Liberals. He indicated that his more subdued and less vociferous behavior was part of the overall party strategy. As he put it, "We have to be different from the Liberals." He said that if I wanted to talk to Dick Collver, he would arrange it. I told him that I did but I wanted any meeting to be in the strictest confidence. Lane said probably his condominium would be the safest place but he would talk to Collver and get back to me.

The party was faced with its third by-election in a few months when the NDP MLA for Pelly, one of the safest NDP seats in the province, died suddenly. The Liberals did not have a prayer in Pelly when things were going well for the party much less now. The only thing to be measured in the by-election was the degree to which the Tories were cutting into traditional NDP strength. It was to be the third no-win situation for the Liberals in the last six months.

I met with Dick Collver a few days later at Gary Lane's condominium in south Regina. Dick came in a Mercedes with a driver because, as I learned later, he was such an atrocious driver the party did not trust him behind the wheel. The initial fencing was dispensed with quickly and we got to the nuts and bolts. Collver's frank, businesslike attitude impressed me. He knew what he wanted and he had a plan based on sound logic. He emphasized that he did not want just to defeat the NDP— he wanted to destroy them. And he knew that he would have to destroy the Liberal party in the process.

Saskatchewan, he contended, was naturally a Liberal-hating province and the strong anti-Trudeau sentiment was merely a public expression of what had always been the case. He was adamant that there were people in this province who were lukewarm NDP and available to his party but never to the Liberals. He also believed that he could successfully attack the hard-core support of the NDP. The average working person who had a wife and kids and a mortgage, who paid his bills and his taxes and worked hard at his job, was really a Conservative whether he knew it or not. When I suggested that he was watching too much Archie Bunker he snapped back that there were more Archie Bunkers than bleeding hearts and they would all vote Conservative if properly wooed.

The Diefenbaker sweep of the late fifties was an example of what Collver was talking about. At that time the Tories swept the province on the Chief's coattails with a slate of nonentities as candidates and virtually no organization at the poll level. On the federal scene not very much had changed in the intervening years and Saskatchewan seemed to have settled into being NDP provincially and Tory federally. Collver was in effect saying that he could get the same people as his federal wing. For him to succeed, he said, it was essential that he draw support from both the NDP and the Liberals. He wanted the far right but he also wanted room for the left; he wanted his party to be perceived as the "party of the little guy," a party that fought— genuinely fought—for the man on the street.

Dick had been a salesman all his life and it showed. He was persuasive on a one-to-one basis and he was a likable person when he turned on the charm. He told me how much I would enjoy campaigning as a Conservative and he maintained that people whom I would not even try to reach as a Liberal would be available if I were under the Tory banner. We turned to the local situation in Thunder Creek where I knew my rival in the last election would not be waiting with open arms to greet me. After all, he had not lost by that much and I'm sure he was going to be screaming about being cast aside for a Johnny-come-lately and all of those other wonderful labels reserved for one who changes parties. I made it clear that if I came, I was staying in Thunder Creek and would not even consider shifting into Moose Jaw North. Collver said he would handle Swenson.

We had talked for well over an hour and a half and it was time for us to return to the legislature. The next Sunday was

Easter and we agreed that Dick would drive to Moose Jaw and we would talk further. Afterwards, I wondered what Gary Lane's neighbors thought with my yellow Corvette in his driveway and Dick Collver's Mercedes circling ominously around the block.

I returned to Moose Jaw early that evening and told my wife we were having guests on Easter Sunday. She was not enthused. The meeting with Dick, who was bringing his wife, had been set up for whatever the driving time was from Regina after church. Dick was really into the sanctimonious role and was now an ardent churchgoer as well as a total abstainer. The self-imposed abstinence was the result of what was to become an almost legendary low tolerance for alcohol. Neither of us wanted anyone to be aware of our meeting so it was arranged that my garage door would be up and Dick would drive straight in. I would be watching for him and put the door down immediately. Since his driver was not coming I had some concerns about the safety of my garage with Dick's reputation as a driver, but the best I could do was to be certain the double driveway was totally clear of vehicles and hope that he would stop before he went through my new garage.

Ironically, the next day we had a caucus meeting to discuss the rumored move of Tony Merchant and Stu Cameron into federal politics. Both had always been involved on the federal scene and it was natural they would want to go there. They knew the provincial party was finished and that knowledge, in combination with the testiness of their relationship with Ted Malone, was causing them to make their move. In the balance of the week I did a fair amount of reflection on my own situation. There was no doubt I wanted to go and be where the action was, yet I genuinely did not want to betray my colleagues and especially not my executive in Thunder Creek. I liked my fellow MLAs and, more important, I respected them. The difference between my move and that contemplated by Merchant and Cameron was that when I crossed the floor the Tories and Liberals would have the same number of seats, which would make quite a difference in opposition status. It would also mean a great deal to the Tories in terms of research and staff funding and a little to Collver personally as the leader.

I had no philosophical differences with the Liberals and I

respected the abilities contained within that caucus, which, I will repeat, was easily the most talented I was ever to be personally associated with. Yet here I was, about to go to a vastly inferior caucus solely because of the vagaries of the political cycle. I wanted to be on the receiving end of the NDP wrath and venom. Although there was nothing formal, there was more and more collusion between the NDP and the Liberals through the House leaders. It had started out on minute points but it was steadily increasing. The NDP had no fear of us at all and were now concerned about our potential collapse and the prospect of having to face the Tories one on one.

Even though I was convinced the demise of the Liberal party was inevitable, my conviction did not make the decision any easier. I vividly recalled the events leading up to my father's defection from the old CCF party and compared them to the present situation. They were totally different. My father had become a socialist at Queen's University and his political beliefs were firmly entrenched in him when he went to work for Canada Packers in Toronto, where he opened mail, despite being an honor's graduate, for $22.50 a week. Indeed, he was happy to have such a position in the depth of the Depression. His office overlooked a courtyard where each day one thousand men lined up for work; only two hundred were hired. The looks on the faces of the men not selected as they dejectedly filed out had a traumatic effect on my father. It was obvious to him that the system was wrong and not working. Many years later he became convinced socialism did not have the answers either and he left the CCF party. That, however, was not my situation.

If I had disliked my colleagues in caucus or even had sharp disagreements with them, I could have made the change with no difficulty. I confess to having no personal affinity to Ted Malone but there was no particular hostility either. The federal domination of our provincial wing was probably our only area of disagreement and in many respects that domination was only reflecting the political realities of the day. In my father's time, there were no tax credits or disclosures of identity and you had to raise money any way you could. Now an individual could deduct 75 percent right off his tax payable and there was disclosure of amounts over one hundred dollars. These rules gave the federal party leverage over the finances. I suppose I answered my questions and doubts by asking myself another question: "Why should I be dragged down by the federal party when I don't even agree with how they are running the country?"

Dick and Eleanor Collver came to Moose Jaw about 1:00 P.M. on a beautiful Easter Sunday in April of 1977. I held my breath as Dick unsteadily maneuvered his big Lincoln up my driveway and into the garage, where I prayed he would stop before coming out the other side. He succeeded, barely. Dick had come to get my commitment and he jumped in like the salesman he was. He wanted me to get up in the legislature the following Tuesday and announce I was joining the Conservatives. I told him that was out of the question because, among other things, I wished to inform my executive personally. I owed them too much for them to read about it in the papers. Dick was opposed to them having advance knowledge but I was firm on that point. I pointed out that many of them would follow me to the Tories and that, despite his assurances, I was going to need them when I fought Swenson for the nomination. Dick was adamant it would never come to that and, I think, believed it.

I wanted Dick's personal assurance that if I joined the Conservative party I would be viewed in the same way as anyone else in the caucus and that any advancement I might make would be on the basis of merit and the fact I had been a Liberal would not be a point of discrimination. He readily agreed but wanted me quickly. I wanted to wait until the session was over but he was adamant that I come right away. I told him I would give him my commitment now for the end of the session. I argued the Pelly by-election was no reason for timing we would regret later. If I was going to join him it was to be part of a team that was going to get rid of the NDP, not a flash in the pan. Then I told him the Tories did not have a prayer in Pelly. To my surprise he agreed. However, he said that his troops were on a roll and they thought they did and who was he to tell them differently? I told him that two to three weeks after the Pelly by-election was ideal. I reasoned his people would be a little down because of the ease of the NDP win and my joining them would send them into summer on a high.

I also made clear that all that was coming was me and nothing else. What had been discussed in past or future Liberal caucuses would stay there and no documents or privileged information about the party was going to come with me. In effect, I was walking out one door and into another and there was to be no connection between the rooms. Dick was thinking and remained silent for a moment—obviously thinking about the timing. Suddenly he jumped up and came across the room and said, "Deal," and we shook hands.

Dick and Eleanor Collver left shortly afterwards. I walked them to the garage, opened the door, and returned to the house as Dick was backing down the driveway. I was talking to JoAnn when Dick appeared at the front door with a sheepish look on his face. The party had him pegged dead right on his driving— he was a menace. He had backed down the driveway, across the street, and right into the side of my neighbor's car. So much for our quiet, surreptitious, clandestine meeting. Dick said, "Tell your neighbor to get his car fixed and it will be taken care of." He then left with the sheepish look still on his face. As I was crossing the street to go and tell my neighbor, fortunately a good Tory, about his car, I heard a voice call to me from a couple of houses up. It was another neighbor and former president of the Moose Jaw North Liberals. "What's Dick Collver doing at your place?" The best I could come up with on short notice was, "He just happened to be in town and dropped in." Not very good and I proceeded on to tell my other neighbor about his car. He couldn't stop laughing and didn't inquire further but he knew. If I hadn't seen the sheepish look on Collver's face I would have sworn he did it on purpose.

Even though things had basically been agreed upon with Dick Collver, I was going to complete the session as a Liberal and fulfill my duty as finance critic. There are those who may perceive my staying in the caucus as a form of spying but I did not see it that way at all. I had no contact with the Tories other than incidental meetings in the corridors. I continued to heckle them in question period and received the same treatment from them. About two weeks after Easter, Gary Lane said Collver would like to see me and the two of us went by separate stairways to the Tory third-floor offices. Lane stayed in the meeting and Collver started to pressure me to rise in the assembly and cross the floor the next day. Lane pointed out that if I were to cross the floor in the regular session it would give the Liberal MLAs the chance to take some "hide" off me. He said, "You owe them that much." He was right and I could easily handle that aspect; however, I intended to break the news to my executive in their own farmyards, which meant several days out in the riding. Furthermore, I did not expect the local Tories in Thunder Creek to forgive as quickly as Collver predicted and there was no doubt in my mind that I was going to need all the support I could muster at the next nomination in Thunder Creek. I reminded Collver that we had agreed on the timing. He smiled and asked about my neighbor's car. I replied that Collver had succeeded in making him a Liberal where countless Liberal candidates had failed.

In retrospect, I am not certain exactly what Ted Malone should have done to hold the party together. Certainly, he should have read the riot act to the federal people, both publicly and privately. No caucus can give away two members the caliber of Tony Merchant and Stu Cameron and not be badly injured. Unquestionably, the situation between Ted and Tony was tricky, to say the least, but resolving such problems is one of the things the leader of a party has to do. Both Stu and Tony were bailing out of a sinking ship and Malone, in not dealing with that reality, in many ways wrote his own future. Although he did not know it, their move was the last straw in my own decision to leave the party. The scenario was that both would win the two Regina federal seats and the provincial party would then win the two resulting by-elections on a resurgent wave of Liberal popularity. We all knew this scenario was fantasyland, however, and merely the excuse for Tony and Stu's departure. Once he had dealt with that situation, Malone should have confronted me and demanded that I make a statement ending the speculation on my position. He did not do that until much later.

The balance of that legislative session was uneventful except for one event. The Conservative health critic, Harold Lane, was becoming increasingly embroiled with the NDP health minister over the general condition of hospitals in the province. Both Harold and Herman Rolfes had tempers and they both flared. There had been verbal reports of staphylococcus infections in hospitals but they had never been substantiated. Harold Lane was getting carried away and roared across to Herman that not only were our hospitals providing poor-quality service but they weren't even clean. Herman was on his feet, redfaced and demanding a retraction of the statement on cleanliness. Harold Lane was up roaring, "Not only are they not clean, they are filthy." Pandemonium broke out. The NDP have always regarded health care as their own private domain and they did not appreciate Harold Lane trespassing on their territory. The NDP heavies joined the fray and were almost frothing at the mouth as they poured it onto Harold. Harold Lane was afraid of no one and as he responded to the NDP attacks—which were of a personal nature—the hospitals got filthier and filthier. Dick Collver was not in the House or perhaps the hospitals would not have gotten quite so filthy. A motion asking for a withdrawal was eloquently introduced by Roy Romanow, who was now spearheading the NDP attack. As the bells rang, we returned to our lounge to discuss what we were going to do on the vote.

At this point, we were bystanders and looking to get in on something, whatever it was. Stu Cameron proposed a resolution that the filthy hospital question be dealt with by calling the chairman of the Saskatchewan Hospital Association, Hewritt Helmsing, to the legislature that evening to answer questions about hospital cleanliness. Stu argued that this was a golden opportunity to make the Tories look bad. They couldn't win because no one could say the hospitals were filthy and Harold Lane had used the word so often he could not back off from it. Stu argued he would present the motion and he was sure the NDP would go for it. Then we could sit back and watch someone else chew up the Tories.

We returned to the assembly and, before the vote, Stu asked for special permission to introduce a motion that would resolve the issue to everyone's satisfaction. I am not certain, but I am sure someone had tipped Roy Romanow to our plan. Roy agreed to the introduction of Stu's resolution, which required the NDP to withdraw theirs. Roy Romanow was not that trusting and I will never believe there was not consultation beforehand or he would never have agreed. In any event, Stu's motion was introduced and a subpoena for Hewritt Helmsing was prepared and sent out for that evening.

It was ironic that Hewritt Helmsing should be placed in this unusual situation because he had gone the full 360 degrees in politics. He had been an active Liberal when my father was premier, but somewhere in the shuffle afterwards he had become a close friend of NDP cabinet minister Walter Smishek and had, in fact, managed his campaign. He was now hedging his bets and I had been told he was raising money for the Tories. While the whole thing was really silly, it was going to be a fun evening. The NDP thought Helmsing was going to lower the boom on the Tories, while clearly the Tories thought he was going to hang the NDP out to dry. I'm sure that Mr. Helmsing had some intriguing phone conversations over the supper hour.

That evening was one of the more unusual ones I was to see in the Saskatchewan legislature. The assembly took on a court-room atmosphere and was a trifle intimidating even to those of us who were familiar with the place. Hewritt Helmsing—all four hundred pounds of him—was clearly nervous. It had been a caucus decision that we would stay out of it except for Stuart Cameron and perhaps Ted Malone. Tony Merchant was miffed at the decision and I don't blame him because this kind of atmosphere was made to order for him and he usually excelled in it. As we filed into the House, I could tell the Tories were not happy. Roy Romanow started off the festivities under the gaze of full public and press galleries. Helmsing was very uncomfortable and was trying to walk a tightrope and remain as uncontroversial as possible. It took Romanow a long time to get there but finally he asked Helmsing the question, "Are our hospitals filthy?" To which Helmsing replied, "No, our hospitals are not filthy." That was the supposed factual statement the NDP wanted and Romanow sat down. It was expected that the Tories would attack Helmsing since he was no expert but rather another political appointment. Only Roy Bailey questioned him and in the mildest of forms. Stu Cameron then asked him some summing up questions and he was excused. I found it amazing the Tory strategy was virtual silence.

After Helmsing had left and the assembly was back to normal the avalanche on Harold Lane started. Roy Romanow led off with a condemnation that was as heavy as any I have ever heard and he was followed by everything the NDP had. The Liberals got in a few shots but mostly it was an NDP tirade against the Conservatives, who had clearly made a caucus decision to sit there and take it. It must have killed Harold Lane because they were downright vicious. Dick Collver tried to end it by getting up and proposing a resolution that "this assembly recognizes that our hospitals are not as clean as they should be." He was laughed at and shouted down with hoots of derision. The evening ended with one of the worst political beatings I have ever seen as Romanow just heaped coals on Harold Lane and the House passed a resolution condemning the Tories. The only thing that could have made it worse would have been the Tories voting for condemnation of themselves. Harold Lane took it cheerfully with the comment, "It does one good to get his brains beat out every so often."

By any standard the NDP had handed the Tories a severe beating in both words and action and I was very skeptical about Collver's decision to just sit there and allow them to administer whatever they wanted. Later, Collver was to tell me that his party had won that exchange. His logic, to this day, escapes me. What he did win, however, was a clear acknowledgment from the NDP that his party was the one they regarded as the opposition. Within a day or so, I asked Roy Romanow why they had put on a display that almost amounted to overkill. He said it was a clear opportunity to humiliate the Tories on an issue that the NDP regarded as fundamental to their party and in the process they hoped to shake the Tories' confidence in themselves. I replied that in the process they might have made the Tories the official opposition. Roy said that was a risk they had to take.

A speculative story appeared in the *Leader-Post* in the last few days of the session that identified the Merchant-Cameron situation and guessed at my proposed move to the Tories. Roy Romanow called me behind the rail the day the story ran and lectured me on my father, the Thatcher tradition, and how the Liberals and the Thatchers were completely intertwined. He congratulated me on my "shrewd judgment" in being the anti-fed in the party because it had carved out a constituency for me that transcended party lines and had made me almost "invulnerable" in Thunder Creek. It was vintage Romanow honey and I decided to give it the 180-degree translation. I genuinely respected his advice and he had confirmed I had made the correct decision. Strangely, I had a conversation on the same subject the same day with Roy Bailey, who was still on his anti-Collver trip. He urged me not to make the move.

The session ended, much to my relief, and the Pelly by-election got under way. According to Sonny Anderson it was incredibly bitter and the NDP were operating at their venomous best. The Tory candidate had apparently been picked up for .08, which had made for some juicy politicking. Over a bottle of scotch in my Regina office Sonny described open collusion between the NDP and Liberal organizers as they compared marked voters' lists. The NDP were very concerned about keeping our vote "honest," so when their people found a known Liberal saying he was going to vote Tory they would report it so someone could get out to see the person. "A common enemy" is the term I heard on more than one occasion.

I asked Sonny what his plans were politically and he said he was staying where he was and asked me the same question. I talked in circles but finally told him I was going, although I gave no hint of any details or discussions. I asked for his word that this would remain between us and he agreed. I told him to come with me. It was silly for us to be in separate parties—if anything he was more to the right than I was—and I knew Collver would love to have him. He said he would like to but couldn't. He rationalized that he had a strong Catholic vote in Shaunavon that would never accept his change, to which I suggested the seat was a giveaway to the NDP in a split vote under the present scenario. He had the same disdain for the federal government I did and was keenly aware of what was happening. I again asked him to come and he replied quietly, "I can't but I wish you luck when you go."

As expected, the NDP won the seat in Pelly with ease, but again the main story was the decline of the Liberals, who fell to third place while the Tories, despite losing their deposit in the last general election and operating with what had been termed a "dog" for a candidate, were a solid second. Although there was no firm deal between Collver and myself it was 99 percent certain that I would cross the floor. I had canvased my executive and had prepared them as much as I possibly could. Some were coming, some were not, and some were fed up with politics and politicians. I met again with Collver in Regina and it was agreed that the announcement would be made the last Friday in June at a morning press conference. I would do an open-line show that afternoon and that would be it. There was nothing so crude as a cabinet post promise, although there had been discussion on protection from discrimination which, when it came right down to it, meant nothing. I had not wanted a front-bench seat, I wanted a back bench. We did not even discuss what critic's position I would have and I did not really care.

A day or two later, I received a call from a Regina reporter and I gave her the most provocative interview on the prospect of going to the Tories that I had ever done, although I stopped well short of confirmation. My purpose was simple—to prepare Thunder Creek for the announcement and diminish the shock value. I was going but I was going the proper way, or at least what I perceived to be the proper way. Whatever I may have known about the Liberal party was staying where it was and I was bringing only myself and whatever supporters would follow. I was acutely aware that I was walking into a situation where I would have to beat Don Swenson on his own turf playing his rules. I intended to do this with many of the people I had worked with in the past. I had correctly assumed Swenson would greet me with open arms and then plan to knife me in the back a few months later and it was one of the many reasons I was determined to leave the party with as few enemies as possible. To do that was to be certain that I would not be open to the charge of "sneaking" out as Lane had done. In addition, at the last moment I intended to talk to both Ted Malone and John Embury and inform them.

The story ran in the *Leader-Post* the very next day and Malone went through the roof. I had not seen it when he called me on my mobile phone in my ranch truck and demanded an explanation. At the time he called, I was having trouble in a cow pasture and Ted Malone was the last thing I needed. I told him I would call him when I got home that evening but that did not satisfy him. He was demanding I come to Regina immediately. Now a mobile phone is a party line to anyone who happens to be tuning in on that channel or to some of the more sophisticated CB equipment. I am sure the many who listened in on that conversation got their gossip for the day—and there were many—but Malone settled for a call when I got home. When I called him he announced that all MLAs were ordered to attend an emergency caucus the next day. I had a ranch to run and told him I could not be in Regina on that kind of notice. He demanded that I be there and be prepared to repudiate the news story to the assembled press and end all speculation that I was going to the Tories. If I did not, then I would be suspended from caucus.

That was getting pretty assertive and it would have been interesting to speculate where that would have led us many months ago—not just with me but also with Tony Merchant and Stu Cameron. I mulled over the pros and cons of whether I should go to caucus. I had other commitments the next day at the ranch but they could be altered. Potentially, it could turn into a screaming session because Malone appeared on the verge of becoming very upset. I could pull a "Lane" and simply disappear on the back confines of my ranch for the next two weeks but that would mean badgering and harassment of my family. It sounded as if I was going to be suspended from caucus whether I went or not, because I could not repudiate the press story as Malone was demanding and I was not going to confirm it either. If I was suspended it was just a question of sitting tight for two weeks. If not, the same. The matter needed no more fuel to the fire and the outcome would be the same either way so I decided to go.

As I walked into the legislature the next day, there was a barrage of reporters in front of the room we were using for caucus and the television crews were also there, obviously expecting an announcement of some kind. The meeting lasted about two and a half hours, of which about two hours and fifteen minutes were devoted to rehashing the Merchant-Cameron situation. It was almost as an afterthought that Malone turned to me and asked me what my position was. I said I had nothing to add to what had been talked about today. He interjected that he was referring to last evening's conversation, to which I replied that if he was referring to the threatened suspension, I had nothing to say and he could proceed as he wished. Ted Malone flushed and was visibly angry as he tried to keep the emotion out of his voice. He said that I was not going to provoke him and if getting suspended was the excuse I was looking for, I was not going to get it. I came back with "You are the one who was threatening suspension. If you're going to run this party, idle threats aren't going to make you premier." My recollection is that Stu Cameron got in the middle before it went any further and suggested that Ted Malone, as leader, impose a ban on the caucus of discussion or speculation on their political futures. Ted Malone faced the assembled press late that afternoon and told them he was banning further comment from his MLAs on any aspect of their political futures and he was the only one making any further comments, if in fact there were to be any.

I slipped out of the legislature without talking to the press, quite content with the outcome. I had not wanted to be suspended but if it had come to that, it would not have been serious. Ted Malone did not like me personally and never had. I was indifferent to him. No doubt he would have loved to throw me out of the party that day and clearly he should have but then what would he have done with Tony Merchant and Stu Cameron? In fairness to Ted Malone it had been a long tough year beginning with his leadership race and I am sure he must have wondered when things would start to get better. Over the past year he had become an excellent speaker and met people more easily. In the proper circumstances he might well have gone somewhere in politics. Then Robert Stanfield might also have made a great prime minister. Some things are just not meant to be.

Shortly afterwards, Allan Blakeney was asked in a television interview to speculate on the effect on the Liberal party if I were to go to the Tories and Tony Merchant and Stu Cameron were to run federally. Would it be the end of the Liberals as a provincial force? Allan Blakeney replied, "The political landscape is strewn with political corpses of those who have written off the Liberal party over the years." If there is such a thing as the classic last straw then that reply must at least approach it. To see the party that had been built by my father now reduced to the level of being thrown scraps by its archenemy of the seventies was the final act of denigration. I was doing the right thing.

5

A Game with No Rules

My change to the Conservative party was arranged for the last Friday in June of 1977. My last week as a Liberal was spent in my constituency of Thunder Creek talking to people right down to the poll level. I wanted them to understand that I was not leaving because of differences with the provincial party but rather to play a constructive role in defeating the NDP. I was hoping to leave the Thunder Creek Liberals with a feeling that even if they chose not to come with me, I would still be welcome in their yards. Malone's ban on talking to the press certainly made my life easier from that point of view. I scheduled a meeting for the Thursday evening to make an official announcement to my executive, although by then those at the meeting would know the full picture. Immediately after, I intended to phone Ted Malone and John Embury, as well as a few MLAs.

The details of the public announcement of my change to the

Conservatives had been left entirely to Dick Collver's press secretary, Ken Waschuk, a former president of the Young Liberals. He arranged a press conference for 10:00 A.M. on Friday at the Hotel Saskatchewan. I had prepared a personal statement in which I was careful not to be inflammatory. Quite the contrary, I acknowledged my respect for my former colleagues and made it clear that my differences were with the federal Liberals and their domination of the provincial wing. The tone was positive and I stressed how much I was looking forward to my role in a new party.

It was late Thursday morning when things hit the fan. I was south of Mortlach when my mobile phone sounded. The press had got wind of the news conference. It was going to be a long day. I phoned JoAnn at home to tell her it was out and to brace herself for a barrage of calls. As soon as I could get to a phone that was not on a party line, I phoned Collver's office and asked him who had leaked it. He said he had no idea but he knew several reporters had left for Caron to track me down.

Late in the afternoon I was not surprised to be flagged down by a car full of reporters on Highway 1. It was easier to talk to them then on the side of the road than have them follow me home and harass my executive. I told them I was meeting with my executive that evening to talk about the future and that was all I would say. When asked if I would be at the press conference in Regina the next morning I said they should attend and find out. By now, all news outlets were carrying the story that I was crossing to the Tories the next day. When a reporter whom I knew well called to confirm the rumor I asked him for his source. He said it was Tory press secretary Ken Waschuk. When I asked how they pried it out of him the reporter said Waschuk volunteered the information when he invited them to the press conference. I was furious but I had more important things to do.

My home became a madhouse with executive members arriving and the phone ringing constantly. We were just about to start the executive meeting when I was called to the front door. Ted Malone and President John Embury had arrived uninvited. That really took me by surprise. Malone demanded to sit in on the meeting as leader of the party, a right he clearly had as did John Embury as president; however, I told them I thought their presence was inappropriate and that I wished to meet privately with my executive. Malone repeated his demand and was getting angry. I wanted privacy with my executive and suggested that he and John were welcome for the latter portion of the meeting. They reluctantly agreed.

The meeting with my executive was really quite devoid of emotion. There were some who were very much opposed to my move; however, the majority had no comment and I believe their silence conveyed a message of its own. Finally a motion was passed unanimously which basically said that if I wished to go to the Tories they would not stand in my way in any fashion but they hoped I would reconsider. Before I could respond Ted Malone and John Embury returned. Malone's face was flushed and he insisted on exercising his right to sit in on any meeting of the party he chose. I said fine and invited them in. I then announced I was joining the Conservative party in the morning and that was the end of the meeting.

There is simply nothing fair or sensible about politics and the whims of the electorate. Here I was leaving a group of competent, sound, progressive people who in almost any other situation would have been proclaimed the political saviors of the province. Two short years ago we had been an inexperienced lot and now we were a cohesive, effective unit, yet everything had been downhill. It was that essential ingredient known as timing that had been our enemy from day one. It made no sense to be going from this superior group to a vastly inferior one just because the inferior group was riding the crest of a political wave.

Everyone is aware of the public's disdain for politicians, yet it is interesting to listen to how they decide to vote. Very seldom is it because they think the candidate is competent. They will quickly decide not to support a candidate because of his mustache, because their neighbor doesn't like him, or for the very strangest of reasons. Similarly, their reasons for supporting a candidate usually have nothing to do with whether he will do a good job or not. Some real political talent disappeared because the pendulum had swung against the Liberals and nothing was going to make them viable in the near future.

The next morning the phone rang at 5:03 A.M. It was the morning announcer for the local radio station wanting to know if I was in the category of people who had something special to do today. I confess that he took me totally off guard and whatever my answer was, it was not very good. I was scheduled to have breakfast with Dick Collver and when I arrived at his home I found Ken Waschuk and broadcast reporter Joe Ralko waiting for me. They wanted me to give Ralko an interview before the press conference. If it had been up to me, I would have said no. This was something you do not do or it will come back to haunt you. However, this was the Tories' day and I was prepared to do their bidding. I gave Ralko his interview. Over breakfast I was asked if I had any idea how yesterday's leaks had occurred. I said, looking at Waschuk, "That's easy because you told them." Collver was incensed and demanded to know why. Waschuk, looking like a whipped puppy, whined, "Because they said they wouldn't come to the press conference unless I told them what it was about." For a moment I thought Collver was going to fire him on the spot. He was furious. He should have fired him; in my view, Waschuk was an incompetent press man. Within a week he was asking me, in case I was asked, to deny that I had given Ralko an advance interview. I told him, "You made your own bed on that one. Go and lie in it."

On the way to the press conference Collver told me to go and see Don Swenson. Although Dick believed there would be no confrontation at the nomination, I had come expecting one. In fact, I wanted a fight because in order for the seat to be mine as a Tory, I had to defeat Swenson at a nominating convention or I would forever look over my shoulder. The press conference was easy and uneventful, as was the open-line show I did that afternoon. I returned to Moose Jaw a Tory.

I did not go to see Don Swenson that day because there was nothing to see him about. There was not one reason in the world why he should be happy to see me—quite the opposite. I would go later in the summer to pay my respects but for now it was best to let things lie. I knew there would be some bitterness from the local Conservatives; I could not change that and it would be foolish to try at this point. My strategy was simple. I knew I could help the Conservative caucus noticeably and, given time, I could earn my spurs with the local Tories despite Swenson. I would be vulnerable for the first six months but if they cut my throat politically in that period of time, I was of no value to them so I wasn't concerned. Obviously, I knew many of the key Conservatives already from local connections and I was reasonably certain I could count on a good many of them at nomination time. The further that time was down the road, the easier it would be in my judgment.

The balance of the summer of 1977 was quite uneventful except for one little episode. It had started while I was still a member of the Liberal party. A marketing board for beef cattle had been a dream of the federal minister of agriculture, Eugene Whelan, for years but the politics had never been quite right and the track records of several major marketing boards left a great deal to be desired. As a cattle producer and a former director of the Canadian Cattlemen's Association, marketing boards for cattle were, and still are, an anathema to me. At a gathering in Ontario, the minister got carried away and announced he would debate anyone on the merits of marketing boards and I accepted his challenge. The western press picked up on my statement and confronted Whelan with it on one of his trips to the West. After some pressuring by the media he eventually gave a "sort of" postive indication. I was amazed. I had assumed he would dismiss the possibility of a debate with a mere backbencher out of hand. He had left a bit of an opening so I sent him a letter and suggested that the debate be held in the new Saskatchewan Hereford Centre north of Regina under the sponsorship of the Saskatchewan Stockgrowers' Association.

The Liberal party had mixed feelings. There was no question it would be a media event and some saw it as an opportunity to focus attention on the party; however, there were those who saw it as disruptive to party unity and those who did not want to enhance my stature in the party. Now Eugene Whelan is a capable politician and a good speaker in his own style but I had the research arm of the Canadian Cattlemen's Association at my disposal and with their assistance and with the sorry record of marketing boards in Canada I would have splattered him all over that auction ring, and most in the party knew it. I don't say that to be disrespectful to Eugene Whelan but the deck was stacked and he knew it—but then he had opened his mouth. We had another exchange of letters but ironically his acceptance to debate came about one week before I was changing parties. I tucked it away for use after I crossed the floor.

As soon as I became a Conservative I knew that Malone would not allow the debate to proceed. That would probably be the only thing the provincial Liberals had dictated to the feds in a decade. However, I sent Whelan's letter to the CBC in Regina and they jumped at it. They immediately wrote Whelan and received a reply veiled in vagueness from an executive assistant. That reply told me a debate was clearly out of the question, which it probably had been from the very start. Until he said a categoric no, I still proceeded to milk the issue for all it was worth. He had issued the challenge to all comers and here I was with a letter of acceptance. I neglected to mention the political rules had changed since he had written his letter of acceptance, that was for him to do. Later on in the summer Whelan was in Regina and the CBC reporters jumped him about the debate. He hummed and hawed and finally said no. They read his letter to him and generally raked him over the coals, but of course what could he do? The image of the local boy from Thunder Creek backing down the federal minister of agriculture had not hurt me with the Conservative party.

My reception by the Tories on a provincewide basis was a warm and, I believe, genuine one. I was invited to speak at a number of party functions but declined as many invitations as I could because I did not want to appear presumptuous and I did not want to emerge as a hatchet man on the Liberal party. From the very first moment I felt very much at home. As one of my close friends was to comment, "You felt at home because you were an uncontrollable in a party of uncontrollables."

The Conservative caucus meetings were a marked contrast to those of the Liberals. Whereas the Liberal caucus was structured, businesslike, and forceful, Tory caucus meetings were often called with no clear purpose. They would open with a twenty- to thirty-minute lecture from the leader. Sometimes the lecture was about the issues of the day but usually it was a repeat of decorum and what the party expected. Gary Lane was not the House leader nor the caucus chairman but had an ill-defined role as strategy coordinator. His role seemed to be to teach the young Tory MLAs the political ropes. At the first caucus meeting I attended he was demanding twenty-five written questions for the order paper and twenty-five private members' resolutions within thirty days. After the meeting, I asked him if he was serious and if he was, if that included me. He answered, "Especially you." His logic was that I should do it because it was good for initiation into the party and it would look good to the rest of the caucus. He was right about that. I was the only one who took him seriously and did it.

Roy Bailey clearly resented the Collver lectures and his face showed it. Harold Lane tolerated them and Gary Lane would come in late. Eric Berntson's reaction varied with his mood. Eric was an easygoing individual who didn't really care about anything except beating the "——ing reds." His language was coarse and crude and he gave the impression of a buffoon. He was not. When he wanted to be, he was an articulate, bright, devious politician; when he didn't he was a clown. Bob Larter was likable, easygoing, and funny and never got excited. I found Ralph Katzman absolutely insufferable. His lack of taste was exceeded only by the size of his ego. He was disruptive and I always thought he could work the system better than anyone else when it came to MLA benefits, pensions, and any other perks that went with the job.

The Conservative caucus was nowhere in the league of the Liberal caucus I had just left and yet there was a certain endearing quality about them. In the Liberal party, we had always rated performance in the legislature highly, which was an error. The legislature is where the games are played and many people do not even realize when it is in session and those who do could not care less. The Liberals had the horses to look good in question period but the Tories had the campaigners in the field. Elections are not won in the legislature, although they can be lost there. They are won in the trenches of the countryside and here my new colleagues were as good as they came.

Later in the summer I paid a courtesy call to Don Swenson. He was very proper, although not particularly warm, and I was left with no doubt that I would have the competition I anticipated at a nomination. I had to be careful about the timing of the battle.

An executive meeting of the Thunder Creek Progressive Conservative Association was held shortly afterwards, which was notable only for the incredible tension in the air. Everyone was very polite but they seemed concerned about being too open in front of the Swensons. The Swenson family—Don, Dot, and Rick—were friendly and gave no hint of the strong feelings I knew they must have. Dot Swenson was the constituency secretary and she totally dominated the meeting and nitpicked it to death. Although no special subjects were on the agenda and no new courses of action were decided upon, it dragged on to almost midnight. It was certainly different from my old executive and I was wondering how they got anything done if this was typical. I could tell almost immediately that the majority of the executive were probably going to support Don Swenson and it was obvious that I was going to have to build my own organization until after the nomination.

As the fall session of the legislature approached, Dick Collver became obsessed with gaining official opposition status. Intense pressure was put on Jack Wiebe to cross the floor and there were rumors of the defection of the NDP MLA for Bengough-Milestone, David Lange, although I do not know if there was any substance to the report. As matters now stood, we were tied with Liberals and all the benefits of official opposition status were split down the middle. Tony Merchant and Stu Cameron had been officially nominated as federal candidates in the two Regina seats, but they continued to sit as MLAs. Dick Collver desperately wanted one of those seats, or any seat he could get, to tip the balance in his favor. Actually, I think he vastly overrated the importance of being the official opposition in the public perception. The past twelve months had been very good for his party. He was in an excellent position for a big win in the next election and both the NDP and the Liberals knew it.

Tory executive meetings continued to be tense throughout the fall. The Thunder Creek Tories, in contrast to the Liberals, often held their meetings in conjunction with the two Moose Jaw seats, a practice I was going to eliminate as soon as I had had it out with Swenson. Urban and rural politics do not mix, mainly because of the difference in backgrounds. To this day I do not know for certain what arrangement or enticement Collver gave the Swensons to quietly accept me into the party. Don Swenson was no ordinary defeated candidate. He had been a Tory in the years when it had been tough to be a Conservative. He had been a party president and a strong supporter of Collver in the leadership race. He was a Liberal-hater and one of those strange conservatives who vote NDP if they cannot support a Conservative candidate. The strong right-wing Tory who hated socialism and believed in the rights of the individual and the private initiative system, I could relate to with ease, and, in fact, that is exactly what I was philosophically. It was the quasi-socialist types who dominated the Thunder Creek executive I had difficulty with. They were not doctrinaire socialists by any means. They believed in the rights of the individual and distrusted big government. However, they did not trust the free-market system either, which they saw as too powerful. They were the little guys Collver loved to talk about and he was right about them—they were not available to the Liberals. In a two-way fight between the NDP and the Liberals, their vote was NDP every time. I found them intriguing and was determined to understand them. They were the edge that could win an election and I began to see how Collver thought he could successfully attack the hard core of the NDP.

As I was introduced at my first party convention in early November I received a standing ovation. From what I could see of the Thunder Creek delegates they were joining in the general applause. I was pleased with the way things were going but I was warned by a couple of Moose Jaw delegates that Swenson was up to something, which did not surprise me. I was growing stronger in the party while his position was deteriorating locally and he must have picked up on that. Our annual meeting was in a couple of weeks and I expected something there. As long as it was not a nominating convention, I didn't really care what came out of it. I felt I had something to contribute to the Tory party and I intended to do all they expected of me.

At our pre-legislative caucus, Dick Collver asked us to list our three preferences for critics' positions. Naturally, my first choice was finance because it was the position I had held with the Liberals and was the senior post next to the leader. Collver had been finance critic and I expected him to continue, but I asked for it anyway. I was pleasantly surprised when he gave it to me. Nothing could have been a clearer signal that he was happy to have me and he had a very significant role for me to play. When I told an executive meeting the news before it was made public, Swenson's jaw hit the table. He was most unhappy.

Collver knew what he was doing. He was giving me ammunition for the local battle and was giving Swenson a message. I think Dick had realized he could not control Swenson and wanted to minimize the expected bloodbath. The last thing he could afford was to have me knifed in Thunder Creek. That was hardly the way to entice rank and file Liberals into the party. Yet I still felt he had some arrangement with Swenson that I did not know about. As far as I was concerned, I wanted a year in the party and then I wanted to defeat Swenson soundly at a convention.

My first legislative session as a Tory began on November 16, 1977. Just before we were to go to line up for our entrance to the assembly with our wives, I was called to Dick Collver's office to look at a letter that was going to be hand delivered to the Speaker, John Brockelbank. The letter, signed by Berntson as whip of the party, was taking strong exception to seating arrangements at the opening and later in the session. The Conservatives and Liberals had the same number of seats and, despite their easy win in the Pelly by-election, the NDP were by this time terrified of the Conservatives. They were not inclined to give them any recognition if they did not have to. The opening of the legislature was consistent with this attitude and it was arranged as though it was business as usual with the Liberals as the official opposition. The wives of the Liberals were to be seated on the floor immediately in front of the opposition benches—including the Conservative benches—and the Conservative wives were to be placed somewhere off to the side. It was an obvious slight and showed the class of those who were arranging the ceremonies, but so what. The only people in the province who gave two hoots about the opening of the legislature were those directly involved—and not very many of them. However, Collver felt there was some political mileage to be gained out of the incident and was on the verge of sending the letter he had written for Berntson to sign. Since seating arrangements are decided by the Speaker's office, the letter suggested potential collusion between the NDP and the Liberals and, by implication, the Speaker himself. It was this implication that was to spark the controversy.

By tradition the Speaker is impartial, although in practice he is a partisan politician who sits as a member of the government caucus and is part of that decision-making process. When asked for my reaction to the letter, I said we would be perceived as nitpickers and I saw no advantage in it at all. Gary Lane feared it could turn into a filthy hospital debate if the NDP ever pushed it. Eric Berntson, whom Collver had chosen to be its official author, did not care one way or the other. Collver decided to send the letter anyway.

Early the next week the Speaker, John Brockelbank, reacted. He rose in the assembly to acknowledge the letter and suggested that it was an attack on the Speaker's role and a breach of an MLA's privilege. In essence what he was saying was, "How dare anyone suggest that I, a partisan politician, am not impartial." Immediately the government introduced a motion to refer the matter to a little-used standing committee on procedures and ethics. A debate followed in which the Liberals sided with the NDP and the Conservatives argued that the matter was silly, trivial, and surely the assembly had more important things to do with its time. I stayed out of the debate strictly because of the newness of my position. The motion, of course, passed.

The standing committee had not met for years and the last time it had taken any action was against a member for bootlegging on government time around 1915. Privately we told Berntson he was in proper company and those of us who were members of the committee were going to have to weigh our decisions carefully when deciding what action would be appropriate. Ironically, it was one of the committees I had been appointed to prior to the session. I had agreed only because it never met. The other two Conservative appointments were Bob Larter and Ralph Katzman. Collver was upset by the motion. The Tories had taken a beating over issues in the past—one of them being the filthy hospitals—and he was suddenly fearful of another one. My own view was that we could not get hurt on such a remote issue because people outside the legislature would not understand it and did not care. I argued in caucus that we should go ahead and do our jobs as opposition critics and the matter would die. Several days passed and it was announced that the committee would meet in about a week to deal with what was now known as the "Berntson Letter."

When I think back on the whole episode, I have difficulty

respecting some aspects of our democratic institutions. The whole affair was totally absurd and the public should not allow such silliness to be played out when they are picking up the tab. There was no relevance whatsoever to the many hours of debate that went into the Berntson Letter. There were no issues except whether a partisan politician was partisan and whether two political parties with a common enemy were guilty of a little collusion. Of course they were guilty on both counts. The Speaker is there to control the flow of events and on the issues that count if he keeps coming down the wrong way he is not going to last. If the NDP had not been so alarmed about the Conservatives there would have been no problem.

Collver called Gary Lane and myself into his office prior to a caucus meeting to discuss strategy in the committee. Dick was concerned about the possibility that Eric might be called up under oath and the true authorship of the letter might come to light. He shocked Lane and I by saying that we must go before the committee and talk about the collusion between the NDP and the Liberals. We were to take the line, "I was there ... I saw it ..." Lane was visibly upset and protested that this meant he had wasted a year trying to make people forget he was ever a Liberal. The fact that our statements would be under oath was not even a consideration.

I got around Collver's request by arguing that this talk was silly and a complete overreaction to a situation that could be dealt with much more effectively. There was no way I was going to that committee under oath with a concocted story but I did not want a confrontation with Collver either. I argued that we should fight legitimately in the committee and try to snarl it in its own procedural red tape, which as a member I could probably do. If we were not successful, then we would simply leave the committee, making the whole exercise look ridiculous. Under no circumstances would we allow Eric to be called up under oath—if for no reason than that he might just tell them to "——— off" if he was in one of his indifferent moods. Lane sided with me and Collver relented. Politics is one thing but Collver's request that day brought some of Roy Bailey's statements front and center in my mind. I was troubled but there was never another incident in our political relationship approaching this and it was forgotten.

We formulated our strategy at a caucus meeting the next day. There was no way we were going to lay back and let the "reds," as the NDP were often referred to by the Conservatives, do a number on us. We were going to fight. There was also no way Eric Berntson was going to go in front of the committee. I proposed we attend the committee meetings as part of our obligation as a party in the assembly and oppose the use of the committee for the childish whims of the government. We would then flood the committee with motions about procedure, which, if debated, would bog it down and the press would ultimately lose interest. If the motions were dealt with quickly, for example if the chairman ruled them out of order, we would leave as a group protesting the unfairness of the committee and referring to it as a kangaroo court. The committee would then be composed of only Liberals and NDP and any action against Berntson would appear vindictive and lack credibility. The caucus agreed unanimously.

When the committee met the next day, the press was poised for a courtroom soap opera. The chairman was Murray Koskie, MLA for Quill Lake and an attorney supposedly, although he could have fooled me. As he outlined the procedures it became obvious that the committee had no power to subpoena anyone and could not force Berntson to appear, although if he chose to come before the committee he would be sworn in. While there was no chance of that happening, I made several procedural motions as though Berntson might appear. For example, I moved that he be allowed legal counsel should he desire it, a motion the chairman declared out of order since this was not a court of law. I made seven or eight similar motions, all of which were quickly moved out of order. They were determined to get down to the business of flogging and they were not going to be sidetracked. I noticed Elwood Cowley watching us intently. He knew we were up to something and probably had already guessed what. I whispered to Bob Larter and Ralph Katzman that I would try one more motion and then it was time to walk out. Again, it was ruled out of order. The three of us then rose together and walked out referring to the committee as a kangaroo court. The committee members were startled and Murray Koskie was yelling "Order" as we left in righteous indignation. Outside, in the corridors, I redid the scene for the television cameras and repeated the words "kangaroo court," which of course, by any standard except theirs, it was.

The whole nonsense went off quite well. While I expected some minor flak about a disregard for the rules, I thought everyone would want to drop the matter now. We had won this one easily as we demanded that the government get down to the business of running the province and stop playing games at the taxpayers' expense. The next day I was in my constituency when I caught a news report on the radio quoting an unnamed Conservative source as saying that I had gone too far and would have to face the consequence of yesterday's action. I was furious and phoned the caucus lounge. Gary Lane answered and said he knew nothing about it. I was upset at being knifed in the back on what was clear-cut caucus strategy. I still had Swenson to contend with and I was sensitive to any suggestion that I was not getting along with my new colleagues. Lane agreed fully. He hung up the phone and went out and talked to the press and deliberately made a reference to the kangaroo court of yesterday. It was the news of the day.

The next day in caucus I raised the question of the unnamed caucus source, whom I knew to be Roy Bailey because a number of the press had told me. You would never have guessed it from his demeanor. He sat impassively as Collver delivered a sermon on the subject. I simply could not understand the man. He was a talented individual who was one of the better orators in the assembly and undoubtedly destined for a high cabinet post in a Conservative government, yet he was not loyal. It was not the only time he was to talk to the press as the unnamed party source.

Very little was happening in the legislature so the issue of the Berntson Letter hung around, fueled by the added dimension of the kangaroo court. The plot was original only to those who did not watch *Sesame Street* regularly. The chairman of the standing committee on privilege, Murray Koskie, rose in the House to move a motion of censure against Gary Lane and myself for the references to a kangaroo court, even though they had been made in the corridors. He contended the corridors were an extension of the legislative assembly. They are not. For example, an MLA is immune from libel on statements made in the assembly but immediately outside the assembly door he is on his own. However, now we had the "reds" deciding where the extensions to the legislative assembly were and, on this day, the corridors were included.

The word was they wanted to suspend us for five days if they didn't get an apology from both Lane and myself. Collver called us in and suggested we apologize because he didn't want a day of flogging. He was still touchy over the filthy hospitals. Lane and I argued we had nothing to apologize for. The whole business was silly and the committee was exactly what we said it was. Even if we did apologize, the "reds" were going to spend the rest of the day raking us over the coals. We said we should fight if for no other reason than to prove that the days of being pushed around were over. Lane and I had no qualms about being suspended if it came to that—it was good stuff in your own constituency. Collver agreed unenthusiastically and the rest of the caucus were happy that this time we were going to fight.

The debate went on all afternoon and quickly became what is known in legislative jargon as a "pissing match." This time the Liberals and NDP were on the same side ganging up on the Conservatives. Collver loved it and decided it was a stroke of genius on his part. It showed that as a caucus we could look after ourselves and everyone had a good feeling afterwards. Naturally, Lane and I were suspended for the five days but we didn't care. It was good stuff for us and bad for the Liberals, who had made their own bed on that one. They were now clearly perceived as cooperating with the NDP against the Conservatives.

Dick Collver was a good leader although perhaps a trifle unorthodox. There were times when he had a tendency to over-react but by and large he knew where he was going and what his plan was. There was no doubt as to who was in command. He deliberately kept policy announcements to a minimum to give the other parties less to attack, and it was only when truly forced to that he would expound on specifics. While the other parties muttered about lack of PC policy, Collver skillfully played the roles of spokesman for the little guy and opponent of centralized government. The cornerstone of his politics was the return of power from Regina to local government, whether it be school board, rural, or urban-municipal government. His ideas were attractive and were quietly cutting across party lines. Many NDP supporters had become nervous when the potash takeover was announced—a little socialism was all right but there were limits and the land bank and potash takeovers were more than they had in mind. Collver was quite right. These people were Liberal-haters but the Conservatives had a chance to win them over.

Collver also knew the entire spectrum of the Liberal party was open to him if he played his cards well. The Berntson Letter affair—silly as it was—had played into his hands by making the Malone Liberals look vindictive when they voted to suspend two former Liberal caucus members. Lane and I were gone for five days but we took many quiet Liberal supporters with us. I spent much of the five days in Thunder Creek having coffee with former key Liberal supporters. Why not? I wanted them in the PC party for an upcoming nomination.

Dick Collver had told me that Don Swenson was going to announce his candidacy and move for a quick nomination date at the upcoming annual meeting of the Thunder Creek PCs. We were going to elect a new executive and a strong turnout was expected. I was surprised Swenson hadn't tried that sooner. I was becoming stronger in the party all the time and he had made a mistake in letting things go this far. If the worst came to the worst, I felt I could beat him now; however, I knew that the longer I postponed the convention the better it would be for me.

Ideally I wanted the nomination to take place in October of the following year. I anticipated a general election in June of 1979. June was a good month for the NDP—they had never lost an election held in that month—and unless there was an issue they could not resist or the survey polls were right, that was when they would go. An October nominating convention would also cover the unlikely possibility of a fall vote and would give me time to establish myself as an integral link in the party as their finance critic as well as an MLA. The night before the meeting, Swenson paid me a courtesy call to let me know he was going to announce his candidacy.

As I mentioned earlier, at meetings like this the first motion on a subject usually will pass if there are a couple of speakers fast on their feet. After Swenson announced he was a candidate, it was moved that the new executive, in consultation with the provincial executive, call a nominating convention at a future unspecified date. Swenson didn't know it but whatever chance he had flew out the window as that motion was passed.

George Hill, the newly elected party president, had been sent by Collver to keep the lid on things at the meeting. After it was over he, along with several others, came to my house for a drink. He was relieved by the way things had gone and was surprised how cool I had been. I had not realized that George had come down earlier in the day to try to talk Swenson out of the confrontation. The discussion had been to no avail as Swenson naturally felt that Thunder Creek was his. I suggested to George that he should have told me beforehand about the visit but he replied he had done it that way deliberately and that Swenson was told that I had not sent him. George said that, according to Swenson, when Collver approached him about my move, he said, "Accept him and give me six months with him and then do what you want with him." That was the first I had heard of that one but it did not surprise me. I had come expecting a fight. As far as Swenson was concerned, the six months were up and he wanted to deal with me. It was too late. Collver knew he was scoring well with the Liberals and appreciated the dimension I had brought with me, and he was not about to let Swenson upset anything. He had known six months would be enough for me.

As 1977 ended the Conservative party had good reason to be happy. The Liberals had ceased to matter and the NDP, while still in control, felt they were losing ground partly because of some of their socialist excesses and partly because of the growing strength of the Conservatives. Allan Blakeney was their biggest asset. He was a true leader in every respect. It was not that he was exceptional in the assembly—many times he was not that good in question period—but he was always good enough. Even if he faltered, by the time the issue was redone in the corridors for the television cameras, he had always recovered and seldom were there any points to be won in a skirmish with him. The NDP as a party were vulnerable, but Allan Blakeney's personal image and support never faltered.

As 1978 commenced, it appeared the big news politically would be a federal election. Liberal fortunes had improved sharply in recent months and it was widely assumed the prime minister would go to the people sometime that year. This meant that Tony Merchant and Stu Cameron would have to resign their seats and we would automatically become the official opposition. Collver was determined to have this happen during the session so that television cameras would record us changing offices with the Liberals. If there were to be by-elections in those two seats, we were ready. A provincial election was not considered a serious possibility.

During the winter a story broke that Collver had offered cash to several MLAs to join the Conservatives. David Lange suggested that he had been offered one hundred thousand dollars; Sonny Anderson appeared on television making similar suggestions, although he did not quote an amount; Jack Wiebe was not so definitive but was supportive of the allegations. Now there is nothing wrong in trying to recruit politicians from another party. It has been done for hundreds of years. However, the suggestion that Collver was trying to buy them was damaging both to him and to Lane and me. The implication was, of course, "How much did those guys get?" Although Dick Collver wanted one more member badly and he may well have talked to these MLAs, I am pretty skeptical about the cash involved. The party did not have that kind of cash to throw around and Collver was certainly astute enough to know a bad investment when he saw one.

These stories were only the beginning of what was to be a frontal assault on Dick Collver personally, and the attacks would intensify as the year went by. The rise of the Conservative party was an enigma to both the NDP and the Liberals, both of whom were good at fighting each other but simply could not get a handle on the Tories. As year three of the government's term commenced, they still had not come up with an answer to the steadily rising Tory tide. The only area where the NDP knew they were on safe ground was on the issue of leadership—Blakeney versus anyone else. Both parties had hoped Collver's legal troubles would cause an arrest, or at least a slowdown, in the momentum of the Conservatives. To this point they had not and Collver in fact had won a major victory in an out-of-court settlement. The last thing either the NDP or the Liberals wanted was a by-election in a seat the Conservatives would win easily, and Stu Cameron and Tony Merchant deferred to the pressure in their party to stay as long as possible.

In early 1978, the NDP seemed to have decided that in order to stop the Tories they had to destroy Dick Collver's credibility. When it comes to gutter politics, the NDP are in a class all by themselves. To call them devastatingly effective is an understatement. The battleground of politics is located in an area akin to the gutter of society—that is the nature of the beast. When it comes down to it, there are no rules in politics and ethics are only for what may become public. What one party can successfully do to another is fair game—if they can get away with it. However, personalities are generally kept out of it. Not so for the NDP. At the risk of sounding slightly like them, under the guise of sanctimony, they are far and away the most vicious personal assassinators in Canadian politics. They are gentlemen if they are in control of a situation, but when they are threatened, they have no conception of common decency.

I probably sound bitter as I relate this description of the NDP, and I do not mean to. This is the way they were and how they played the game and the rules were clear: if you didn't like it or couldn't handle it the answer was to go home. Most people who remember my father probably heard at one time or another that he was an alcoholic or, if you missed that one, perhaps you got the drug addict story. The NDP hung both of those labels on him fairly effectively. They strung empty liquor bottles up on his campaign posters in Morse constituency; the fact that he was a serious diabetic and any amount of alcohol would have killed him was irrelevant. The drug addict story originated because he took his insulin by needle. They were now zeroing in on Dick Collver.

By the time the legislature reconvened, ugly, unsubstantiated rumors were springing up about Dick Collver and his dealings with his former employers. Stories of misappropriation of funds and poor management were making the rounds everywhere—source, of course, unknown. They were damaging and we all knew it but we were powerless and so was Dick Collver. Outwardly he was unflappable, but inwardly there was little doubt that the stories were troubling him. Some of the zip was coming out of Dick and the pressure of life in the public eye was getting to him. I told him it came with the job and to get used to it quickly—it would only get worse. It did.

In May Saskatchewan Government Insurance launched a $1.1-million suit against Collver calling in a personal guarantee he had given when he was one of the owners of Buildall Construction. He had long since sold his shares in that company to a group of Calgary businessmen and, according to Collver, his guarantee was terminated as part of the sale. By any standards, SGI was reaching and, despite denials that the action was politically motivated, the suit made provincial headlines. It was politics of the lowest order but devastatingly effective. Obviously Dick had to defend himself, and his statement of defense made even more headlines. It was blatant use of a Crown corporation for outright political warfare, but one of the spoils of winning is that you get to do all these little things that can give you such an edge. In the grass roots the word was spreading—Dick Collver is a crook; Collver cannot be trusted.

6

Her Majesty's Loyal Opposition

The legislature of 1978 was totally bankrupt of originality. The government had done everything they intended to do before an election and now they were just coasting along trying to avoid anything controversial. We had our good days in question period and with the two Lanes and me there were times when our antics got carried away. Harold Lane could be a scream sometimes and he delighted in getting people into trouble. The most memorable occasion was when I supposedly called Speaker John Brockelbank a "son of a bitch." Harold Lane sat in front of me in the assembly and in question period he would sometimes heckle me if my questions were particularly bad. The frequency of my bad questions varies depending on whose version you believe—mine or the government's. Anyway, I thought I had some fair material but things were just not working out as I had planned and both I and the minister I was questioning were getting far off the track. On top of that,

Harold Lane was heckling me instead of the NDP minister. The Speaker got up, justifiably, to put matters to an end and while I was trying to make my point with the Speaker, Harold Lane was needling me unmercilessly. The Speaker was not accepting my case with enthusiasm—in other words I was losing badly—and Lane was continuing his commentary. I looked down at him and whispered, "Shut up you son of a bitch." I said it quietly enough that only Lane heard me. Unfortunately, by the time I got to the key phrase, I was looking directly at the Speaker and the whole assembly saw me mouth the words. John Brockelbank was going to ignore the remark but a little jerk on the NDP side called Billy Allen was up in a flash exposing my transgression to the world. "I saw it . . . I heard him," he kept repeating. It was to be the highlight of his political career. Harold Lane was doubled up with laughter, his head between his knees. I denied, truthfully, that I had referred to Mr. Speaker in those terms. The Speaker rose and said he would take no action until he had reviewed the legislative record. By now Harold Lane, in between fits of laughter, was saying, "Throw him out."

Immediately afterwards, I had to do a television clip on the episode. How do you say, "No, I was not referring to the Speaker as a SOB, I was talking to my colleague Harold Lane. He is the SOB"? I told Lane that was what I was going to do, to which he replied enthusiastically, "That will double my majority." I did the television clip and denied that I had referred to the Speaker in that matter and hoped the House tape had not picked it up. Billy Allen went right on bleating, "I saw him, I heard him," in a staccato rhythm. Later that evening there was a lineup to hear the tape of question period. The girl in charge told me the tape had been played so many times it was probably worn out. It did not matter. I had not been picked up and the matter died.

Despite the lack of any substantive legislation we did well as a caucus and, while not endowed with the experience and poise of the Liberals, we were outgunning them in some areas and holding our own in others. Dick Collver had become a good leader; however, the court battles were wearing him down and negative feedback was coming in. Party President George Hill told me on his return from a fund-raising trip to Calgary that he was asked more than once whether the funds were for politics or legal fees. People were beginning to get nervous about Collver.

It was a good session for me personally. The party played up my speech as finance critic; I had found some good issues for question period—I always did my own research for questions and never waited for a party researcher; and in addition I had had a couple of scrapes with the Speaker that had only helped, not hurt, me at home. I spent a great deal of time in Thunder Creek building an organization for the nominating convention. Some of the people I recruited were former Liberal supporters, many were Conservatives who were going to support me simply because they were pleased with my performance as a Tory, others had never been involved before. Generally, I much preferred going for the younger farmers who had a real stake in changing the government. I did this quietly and by summer I had at least one key person in every poll, except Swenson's, which I was writing off anyway. I was keeping a close watch on the membership lists to be certain there was no sudden movement of memberships I didn't know about. Strangely, there was no sign of Swenson working.

I scheduled some constituency meetings around Thunder Creek where I would simply take another MLA and go to a town for what amounted to a round-table discussion on the issues of the day. They were surprisingly well attended for non-election time and an easy way to answer the perennial complaint that voters never get to see their MLAs. I scheduled one for the town of Briercrest, not far from Swenson's farm, and took Eric Berntson as a guest speaker. The next day Swenson called Berntson to tell him he had no right to take part in a nomination. According to Berntson, he told Swenson he was merely swapping meetings with me and I was to take one for him later. Apparently, Swenson was not happy. At an executive meeting a few days later, Swenson and his wife tried to provoke an argument in front of the other executive members but I refused to take the bait. I was doing my job as an MLA and did not have to consult with anyone as to how I should do it. It was obvious that the bulk of the executive were going to support him and he was counting heavily on them. He seemed unaware there was now a parallel organization in Thunder Creek.

The balance of the legislative session was a drag. Collver was determined to see us the official opposition and insisted we delay everything on the assumption a federal election would be called and we would then replace the Liberals. It was only when it was apparent there was no possibility of this happening that the session ended. In June, at a caucus meeting, Gary Lane reported that the NDP had told the Liberals to be ready for a fall vote.

To this point Dick Collver had done everything right. The rise of his party was remarkable and he stood on the threshold of having an excellent shot at being premier. The NDP had the edge with Blakeney, but if we could clean up Dick's image we could narrow the gap sharply. We talked about a campaign committee, a strategy committee, and some professionals to work on Dick's personal image. Dick had made arrangements for a real pro from Ontario to come out to run the campaign. Like many of us, however, I don't think Dick really believed there would be a fall election despite all the signs.

I spent the summer quietly arranging for memberships to be moved to Thunder Creek for the nomination. The possibility of a fall election made it essential that we hold the convention early in the fall. Besides, I had had enough of the needling an MLA up against a challenge is subjected to, and the NDP had played the issue for all it was worth. While Collver and George Hill were nervous, I was ready and had complete faith in the group I had assembled. We had sold a good number of memberships and were finding very little evidence of people committed to Swenson, except the obvious group, whom we were writing off anyway.

By late summer it was apparent there was not going to be a federal election, which made the possibility of a fall provincial election very real, although I was still skeptical because of the NDP's affinity for June. Then a series of leaks from the government convinced all of us that it was coming and coming soon. It was time for a nomination in Thunder Creek.

The call went out from the provincial office to the Thunder Creek executive for a nominating convention within a week. Swenson wanted more time to get his harvest in, but the NDP were not going to wait for him anymore than anyone else, besides I was in the same situation. The Thunder Creek executive met the next night and the urgency was explained. As a sop to Swenson, the date was put back one day. The memberships of those eligible to vote had to be turned in forty-eight hours prior to the convention. I was in good shape and I had a week to sew it up.

The provincial party were nervous about me but they knew little of my Thunder Creek organization. I did not want to give Swenson an issue he could exploit and I had asked the provincial party to stay completely away. The campaign itself was a trifle bitter but I was able to stay above it. There were a couple of minor procedural wrangles but nothing serious. I worked very hard and so did my organization, and when the deadline for membership sales arrived, I knew it was no contest. The memberships turned in by my organization outnumbered Swenson's by over three to one. It was now a question of getting the vote out.

The main uncertainty was the weather. It had been a very wet September and a great deal of the crop was still in the field, especially in the east end of the seat, which was by far my strongest area. The combines starting up on the day of the nomination could have serious implications for me. The day before the nomination, the skies cleared. I was worried about getting my supporters out until my wife came up with the idea of an advance poll for farmers who could not spend the evening away from their combines. The committee in charge agreed to the proposal and Swenson went along reluctantly. As it turned out, the advance poll was a stroke of genius. Swenson knew he had made a mistake when the results of the advance poll ballot box were in, and afterwards references were made to the unorthodox procedure. I won the nomination easily, in excess of two to one. The ratio would have been higher had the combines not started up that evening. Nevertheless, I was happy with the way things had gone and felt my move to the Conservatives had been vindicated. There were some wounds to heal but that is usually the case after a tough nomination fight.

I took a few days off after the nomination and got the rest of my crop off. The election had been called for October 8. We were now several days into the campaign and the Liberals were struggling to put out a full slate of candidates. They had been so certain that they had until next year because of the federal election that they were caught off guard by the early election call. The nomination and its intensity had served to put the seat in excellent shape organizationally and most of the former key Liberals now held Conservative memberships. The pains I had taken to leave the Liberal party on as amicable a footing as possible had paid off on nomination night and would continue to do so in the election campaign. The NDP vote in Thunder Creek does not change much regardless of the candidate and I had already accomplished what I had to with the former Liberal supporters, so the balance of the campaign was fairly routine.

Things looked pretty good for us on the provincial scene. The NDP were running ads on medicare that seemed as archaic as the dinosaurs. They even had Tommy Douglas on a film clip crying, "Don't let them take it away," in reference to the Tories supposedly wanting to get rid of the entrenched medicare system. It appeared the NDP were searching for an issue and I thought the old medicare scare would fall flat. I could not have been more wrong.

Dave Tkachuk was the executive director of the party and, for practical purposes, was the campaign director. Dick's hotshot professional from the East had not yet arrived and when I inquired about Dick's schedule I was told it was still being prepared. I asked about our ads and was told we had a series of great ads that would change as the campaign went on and the issues became clear. I knew Collver had done the groundwork well and if the campaign was executed in the same way we would be in good shape. All I could do was look after my end in Thunder Creek.

As soon as I got into the field, I realized we had been cleverly sandbagged by the NDP. The medicare commercials were devastatingly effective and hard-core Conservatives were beginning to ask for assurance that we would not take medicare away. On top of that, Dick Collver's personal credibility had suffered far more damage that we had realized. If I was picking this up in Thunder Creek, I could imagine what it was like elsewhere. I phoned campaign headquarters to talk to Dick's hotshot from the East. I was informed that he was "assessing" the situation and was not taking calls. After all, why should he waste time with a candidate in the field phoning in a report? I yelled enough that Tkachuk was put on the phone. Yes, they were aware that the medicare issue was more damaging than we had thought. Yes, it was time we changed our television ads. Yes, it was time we changed our radio ads. Yes, we were running a lousy campaign. But tomorrow everything would be different. We were responding to the medicare issue and a brand-new set of ads would be out. All of this—tomorrow.

That night we had the same story from our workers. Our advertising was bad and we had been hurt badly on medicare. I assured them that things would be better the next day—I was at this point still believing what I got from headquarters—but nothing changed. We were still running the same horrible ads as on day one; however, our reponse to the medicare issue was out. The Tories were going to give voters printed "certificates of guarantee" to reassure them that we would keep medicare. I am sure it was a struggle for the NDP to keep the grins off their faces at that point. We were approached by the two Conservative candidates in Moose Jaw about joining their constituencies in a breakfast featuring Dick Collver. I was agreeable but doubted that Collver could alter his schedule, which I was sure would be fixed until election day. When the request was put to headquarters and they responded, "Sure, what day do you want him?" I knew the writing was on the wall.

By the time we realized how badly we had been hurt on the medicare issue and commenced our stumbling and fumbling to react to it, the NDP had shifted gears and gone on to another issue. This time they moved into provincial versus federal control over resources in the province—always a good one. We were too busy muddling with medicare and printing "certificates of guarantee" to even get involved in that one. The NDP were choosing the issues, using them effectively, and moving on. For us, it was a chess game in which the king was in check from the outset. Our campaign office was frozen and unable to react to the changing situations. There was no plan of attack or, for that matter, of defense. Phone calls from the field were not welcome and they would tell you whatever it took to get you off the phone. The ads—the same ones since day one—were still going to be changed the next day. I finally got to talk to Dick's hotshot three weeks into the campaign and asked what he had in store for the last ten days. He said he was still assessing the situation but he would make his move soon. The only move he made of any significance was to get on a plane for the East before any of us got our hands on him.

I reported to headquarters that Thunder Creek was mine and I was available for other constituencies on two days' notice. Dave Tkachuk said they would like me all over; however, the only place I was sent was into Elwood Cowley's Biggar constituency, which was a write-off for us from the beginning. After that, they forgot I had called so I went on with Thunder Creek.

In the middle of the campaign, the NDP shifted gears for the home stretch. They moved into a positive campaign and heavily promoted Allan Blakeney as the best of the three leaders. They took subtle swipes at Collver by making references to Blakeney's "unquestioned" integrity and trustworthiness. They didn't have to be negative to Dick Collver; the Liberals were doing it for them. The Liberals ran a terrible campaign, which concluded with a rash of ads that were very close to personal attacks on Collver. These helped no one but the NDP and hurt us badly. The Liberals earned their own oblivion.

In the last ten days, the Supreme Court of Canada came down with a decision that iced it for the NDP. The potash prorationing law, which had been introduced by my father in 1969 to give the province the right to regulate production and minimum pricing of potash produced in Saskatchewan, was struck down. My father intended the law as an interim measure only and he knew from the beginning it would not stand up to the test if challenged. It had been defended by the NDP in court over the years and it had taken this long for it to be finally ruled unconstitutional. At first it looked like a potential break for us because of uncertainty among the electorate over its possible implications. However, the NDP used it as an example of an eastern court infringing on provincial rights and promoted Allan Blakeney as the leader who could best look after our resources under attack from central Canada.

Never was a move made to project Dick Collver as a leader with something to offer the electorate. Even Ted Malone, with no party, rated ahead of him. By avoiding the issue we gave credibility to the rumor that Collver was "not to be trusted." Obviously we felt strongly that he was or we would not have had him as leader, but we were afraid to say so as a party.

The NDP ran a near-perfect campaign. They put us on the

defensive at the start and kept us there. Their people were vastly superior to ours and it showed. The question was, how did a man like Collver, who had done virtually everything right up until then, suddenly collapse when the chips were down? Why did his campaign decisions go so incredibly sour? Subsequent conversations with members of the NDP confirmed my view that the NDP were ripe to be defeated until the middle of 1978, when things started to change. I believe the pressure of the protracted court battles got to Collver and the personal attacks scored more than he would ever admit. The regrettable truth is that, regardless of the reason, when it counted, he choked.

The NDP won in a walk garnering 48 percent of the vote to our 38 percent. The sun set on the Liberals in Saskatchewan with 14 percent. The new government was made up of forty-four NDP and seventeen Conservatives, with the Liberals hardly close anywhere. We were going to be a very different caucus with the loss of Harold Lane, Garnet Wipf, and the decision of Roy Bailey not to seek reelection. Most of our gains were at the expense of the Liberals, who lost even Ted Malone. Saskatoon had been a disaster area for us primarily because of the strong anti-Collver sentiment. A promising newcomer, a university professor named Grant Devine, had been soundly defeated by Wes Robbins in a seat that we thought we could win.

What had happened? On paper, the NDP had gained eight points in the popular vote compared to 1975, the Tories had gained ten, and the Liberals had lost eighteen. I think it is an oversimplification to suggest that the lost Liberal votes were split fifty-fifty between the Tories and NDP. My majority in Thunder Creek had more than tripled at the Liberals' expense, yet Dick Collver was nearly defeated in Nipawin by the NDP. I feel strongly that a large majority of former Liberal supporters came to the Conservatives in 1978, perhaps as much as 80 to 90 percent. Where the Conservative party failed was in its apparent inability to hold on to its entire support base from 1975. In other words, the quasi-socialist-conservative types returned to the NDP in 1978. They may have turned their backs on the Conservatives because of fear of Collver, or it may be that the 1975 vote was a fluke and that now the Tories were a threat they were deserted by some of their former supporters. Because no one fully understands the Saskatchewan voter who is available to the NDP or the Conservatives but never to the Liberals—I certainly do not—any provincewide analysis of the results is inconclusive. It was an inglorious ending to the Liberals caucus of 1975, a caucus I still rate highly. Ironically, the man who destroyed them was himself destroyed. Dick Collver could have been a good premier, just as Robert Stanfield could have been a great prime minister. It was not to be.

Despite the magnitude of the NDP win, the Conservative party came out of the 1978 election a vastly improved group. Whether the overall quality of the opposition—with the Liberals annihilated—had improved was dubious. Where the Liberal vote collapsed, we had been the clear beneficiaries; however, we were still a rural-based party and had made no significant inroads into the cities. We had a solid L-shaped core of support starting in the northwestern part of the province and extending south to the Maple Creek area and then east across the entire width of Saskatchewan. The main exceptions were the constituencies of Shaunavon and Gravelbourg, which had both gone NDP due to a Liberal-Tory battle. These two constituencies are classic examples of the fact that there is simply no room for viable Conservative and Liberal parties in Saskatchewan without the end result being an NDP government. Both seats were held by strong Liberal MLAs who could win in a two-way concentration of effort but were easy prey to the NDP the moment the Tories were a credible alternative.

The NDP were elated by the size of their win, particularly in the cities. Shortly after the election, I had occasion to be sipping some of Elwood Cowley's Chivas Regal with both Elwood and Jack Messer in Cowley's office—an office I would claim for myself one day—deep in the bowels of the legislative building. Jack Messer said they had taken the middle-of-the-road, small-business vote away from us and the only way we were going to get it away from them would be to knock them off it. I replied that we would not have to because their own hard-core supporters would not allow them to keep it. I always did like Elwood's brand of scotch and the discussion became more philosophical commensurate with the volume of Chivas. The NDP, in their view, had moved to the right in the eyes of the electorate and taken the middle ground away from the Liberals. It was their intention to keep us well out on the right wing where we could have our few rural seats but could not hurt them in their areas of strength—the cities of Regina and Saskatoon. I told them their left-wingers wouldn't put up with it but Cowley disagreed, saying they had no place to go. That informal conversation turned out to be a rather accurate description of how the NDP were going to do things for the next four years, and I was more prophetic than I could ever have realized at the time about their left wing—they did not stand for it.

The party had a meeting of both elected and defeated candidates in Regina soon after the election. Naturally, there was great dissatisfaction with the campaign and those who had run it, but the big question in my mind was how hard were they going to come down on Collver? Tories are well known for not being kind to leaders who lose elections. Circle the wagons and shoot inward is their standard reply to a leadership crisis. If there was going to be any of that, Collver diffused it quickly and cleanly. In his opening remarks he took complete responsibility for the way the election had gone and was very straightforward in evaluating the public mood toward him. He did not announce that he would step down as leader but it is fair to say that everyone in the room assumed he would in the near future. The meeting ended with little or no ugliness—highly unusual in the Conservative party.

Within a few days I received a summons from Dick Collver and a disturbing story appeared in the Regina *Leader-Post*, which quoted Gary Lane as saying he was going to demand an explanation from Dick Collver at the next caucus meeting as to "why his personal assets were not placed into a blind trust" as promised. This was in reference to a commitment Collver had made that, if elected, he would turn his personal holdings over to others for management in a businesslike manner with no input from him. It had been a futile attempt by Collver to bolster his personal image in the wake of the SGI lawsuit. Lane was rubbing salt in wounds that were sore enough already and the next time I saw him I asked him why. He shrugged and said, "People out there are wondering." The smugness of the answer upset me and I shot back, "Who are you kidding? This is the same knife job you tried on Steuart. Leave him alone and he's gone in a year." Lane replied as he was moving away, "Can't."

I had not seen Lane when I talked to Collver. We were not that far from the opening of the legislature and I assumed Dick was going to move me to a new critic's position. I was wrong. He wanted me to become House leader. I told him no. Haggling and jockeying with Roy Romanow on a daily basis had no appeal at all. Besides, it was a play to improve my attendance. I suggested Gary Lane on the basis of loyalty, which drew a series of oaths from Dick. He did not want to give the position to Lane under any circumstances and was on the outs with Berntson. He pressured me to take it until spring. As I tried to change the subject I made reference to how we could jam the SGI suit back on the NDP and Dick suddenly interrupted, "Stop kidding me. I'm finished, you know it. I know it." Collver, suddenly a pathetic figure, went on, "I built this party and I am going to leave it in sound financial shape. We are eighty thousand dollars in debt. I am going to raise that money and leave. I want you to look after the party in here while I do it." It was the resignation in his voice that would not let me say no. I didn't want the position of House leader, but I felt I owed Dick the opportunity to withdraw with dignity. As House leader I could cover his back from within: I agreed.

The first session of the new legislature was one of those when you wonder why it was ever called in the first place. Everyone knew that 1979 had to be a federal election year, so in order to help their federal candidates the government had no intention of doing anything controversial. Besides, if my latest conversation with Messer and Cowley meant anything, the NDP were finished with the far-out, left-wing radicalism of the early seventies. They had done what they wanted and now they were going to cruise the waters of middle-of-the-road respectability.

Privately, Romanow would concede the NDP had been fortunate in their win. The number they had done on Collver personally had been more effective than they had ever dreamed —the final crunch being the manner in which the Liberals chose to zero in on Collver in the closing days of the campaign. The private polls of the NDP had shown the government to be vulnerable to the Tory surge and without the issue of Collver's integrity to exploit, the NDP brain trust knew that they would have been on the other side of the House. Both parties had some readjustment coming. We had to get used to carrying all of the load and the NDP were no longer going to be able to bash the federal Liberals for political points. There was little of legislative substance in this session; however, there was a matter to be dealt with that would consume all of the efforts of certain MLAs during their waking hours and that was the question of a pay increase. This meant the resurrection of the "Committee of Human Greed," which met every four years and held most of their meetings in the MLA washrooms. This avaricious little group, made up of MLAs from all parties, would hold furtive gatherings and report back to their respective caucuses. Their mandate was not what was fair and reasonsable but rather, how much can we take without being roasted in public? Everything is agreed to in advance by both sides of the House before legislation is introduced on the last day of the session. By unanimous consent, the legislation receives first, second, and third readings on one sitting day—a very unusual procedure. The logic is simple. The press are preoccupied with the closing of the session and, more important, I always suspected they were hung over from the free liquor the night before. All this contributes to the minimal publicity a pay increase receives.

At the risk of sounding sanctimonious, what has always galled me about pay increases is the sneaky way they are introduced. I certainly cashed my checks and felt I earned them as much as anyone else, and in relation to the rest of the public service MLAs are not overpaid—quite the reverse. However, most public service salary ranges boggle the mind. I once proposed that each legislature, in its third or fourth year, set the salary ranges and benefits for the one after the next election. Then everything would be up front and the public could express their views. I was unable to get a seconder for the proposal.

The argument that higher salaries lead to higher-quality elected people has absolutely no basis in fact and in my time in politics I could argue very forcefully that the reverse was true. You have all heard the classic NDP argument that without reasonably high salaries, only the rich could afford to be in politics. This is utter nonsense. The law adequately protects any elected person against job loss. I am a firm believer that full-time politicians have been a curse on this country and province. Generally, they are full-time only when working to be ree-lected. The move toward full-time politicians has led to an increase in wasted time in the legislature—or House of Commons; much longer sessions; and a dramatic increase in committees, which are little short of a scam for extra income or an opportunity to see the world. The part-time politicians, in contrast, want to get their legislative commitments over with as quickly as possible so they can get home to what they normally do. Some argue that they do not then give their constituents the quality of service they deserve. If that argument had a shred of validity, there would be no second-term politicians. Furthermore, while this may not be universally true, legislatures do not have to meet every year to be functional. The only reason for convening every year is for exposure and to justify MLA salaries. The legislature is an opportunity for the backbenchers to be recognized by the folks back home. As far as the opposition keeping tabs on the government is concerned, this is already done by the press, since they determine what is reported. Anyway, all the opposition needs to scrutinize are the estimates in the committee of finance. The rest is only political grandstanding and is of no economic use whatsoever. I do not even think that we need a budget every year. Those who do have been brainwashed into this mentality by government. Budget planning is big, big stuff and biennial budgets would decrease the need for many highly paid technocrats. Imagine a government having to live on what it takes in for two consecutive years. I know—absurd. For further reference read Bob Andrew's speeches in opposition about the evils of deficit budgeting.

The role of House leader was easy during the fall session because there was little happening. The NDP were confident because of the freshness of their win and most of our people were content to coast. Our new MLAs were feeling their way and the older ones were a trifle disheartened. Collver's interest was now elsewhere and he was away a great deal on what he said was fund raising. While he did not say so, it was obvious this legislative session was going to be his last as leader and he was not going to wait for the traditional ritual of the Conservative party of devouring its leader.

We had some interesting newcomers who were slowly finding their feet. Graham Taylor was one who was certainly going
to improve quickly, as was Paul Rousseau. George McLeod, a
teacher from Meadow Lake, was now our only connection with
northern Saskatchewan. George was a shy individual who did
not appear to really like Regina. He had to be almost pushed to
get him on his feet in question period and throughout that first
year it was an exercise in frustration to get him active at all. We
had the only lady in the legislature, Joan Duncan, representing
the right-wing cattle country of Maple Creek. The wife of a
pharmacist, she had potential and was tough. She quickly made
a surprisingly able health critic. We were not great but good
enough to have Roy Romanow call us the most inept opposition since 1905.

Our procedure for question period was basic. In the caucus
immediately beforehand, we would run through the proposals
each MLA had and, as House leader, I would rank them in
order of importance. If the leader had a question, he went first
automatically, regardless of its merit, but still his question came
to caucus. Dick had always been very good or very bad
depending on his mood and now he was even more unpredict-
able. After caucus was over one day, he came rushing in and
told me he had a devastating question this afternoon and he
asked me to let him in. We were already seated but I passed the
word that everyone was back one. I asked Collver—we were
seatmates now—what his question was. He said he was really
going to nail Allan Blakeney on this one. He got up and pre-
faced his question with the history of a Progressive Conservative riding association in northeastern Saskatchewan that had
been denied permission by the attorney general's department to
hold any form of a lottery or draw. He then brandished an
advertisement from the NDP association in the same constituency, who were holding a draw at a ladies' tea where strawberry shortcake was served. We were all mortified as Dick
roared on that a double standard was being applied because the
Tories had been turned down. Elwood Cowley quipped,
"That's because you don't know how to make strawberry shortcake." The episode became known as the "Strawberry Shortcake Affair" and was an example of Dick's erratic behavior.
Allan Blakeney had difficulty keeping a straight face as he

replied to the question. A note came to me from Roy Romanow, "It is time to talk about shutting this place down when the lead question is strawberry shortcake." I sent back a note, "Yes. At Elwood's." Elwood had the cork off by the time I arrived.

Throughout the winter of 1979, the federal prospects of the Conservative party were improving sharply as the brief surge in popularity for the federal Liberals was subsiding. It was being said that even Transport Minister Otto Lang was in trouble. Collver was committed to providing any aid we could to the federal party, particularly in the area of fund raising. He was still committed to taking the party out of debt before he left but that was a tough order in the aftermath of a provincial election when potential donors knew they were going to be hit shortly by federal fund raisers. Collver was now openly looking for a new career and I think he saw a possibility for something in a Joe Clark win. Much of his time was spent in Phoenix, Arizona, where he was investigating investment opportunities. Relations between him and Gary Lane had never been the best but now they were reduced to the lowest order. Lane was playing the same game he had played with Dave Steuart during his waning days, and Collver commented to me privately that Lane would never lead this party while "he had any breath in him." I was never to understand what game Lane was playing. Collver assumed it was leadership but I saw no evidence of this. Whatever it was, they came to despise each other.

In early spring, Collver was becoming involved with a project to subdivide and develop an old dude ranch in Wickenberg, Arizona, and he became less and less interested in Saskatchewan politics as the legislative session progressed. The Committee of Human Greed was still meeting on a daily basis in the MLA washroom. The NDP backbenchers wanted a hefty pay raise—so did ours for that matter—but whatever it was going to be, there had to be agreement, or at the very least a promise not to oppose the raise, from the opposition. We were very short of office space and, because of the financial state of the party, drastically short of research funds to employ quality people. The NDP felt they were in control and had over twenty restless backbenchers who were disgruntled because they were not in the cabinet and at the least wanted more money. To get us to go along, the government quickly let it be known they were willing to up caucus grants, research funding, and secretarial allowances. To a party that was broke, their offer was quite an enticement. The NDP were proposing to replace the four-year ritual of raising MLA salaries with an automatic annual increase of 7 percent across the board. In addition they were improving the MLA pension program, which was already scandalous, providing office allowances at the constituency level, and incorporating constituency secretaries at half the pay of regular government clerical staff. The provision for constituency secretaries was clearly intended for spouses. Our self-appointed member on the committee, Ralph Katzman, was promoting MLA car and travel allowances and goodness knows what else.

Dick Collver wanted all the money for the party that was available and had very little interest in the other aspects of the committee. We were getting to the stage where the House could prepare to wind down at any time. A federal election had been called for May 22 so there was not much attention paid to the activities in the legislature. We needed funds and the government MLAs wanted more money. It was time to take the matter out of the washrooms and down to where it belonged in the first place: Elwood Cowley's office. Collver and the caucus appointed George McLeod and me to talk formally with the NDP, and we had instructions to make the best deal we could for the party.

The first meeting was held in Elwood's office within a few days. The government was represented by Jack Messer, Roy Romanow, and Elwood Cowley. With George McLeod present in our little group, Elwood's scotch supply took a real beating that evening. As usual, Katzman had balled up what the NDP were prepared to offer for research and caucus grants and it was far from as cut and dried as he had led us to believe. We were a long way apart. Our position was simple. Politically, we could not accept the proposed increases—many of which were very skillfully hidden—without opposing them strongly in public. Without drastic increases in our opposition office funding we were not prepared to take the abuse from our own people that would inevitably follow.

At about this time I met Dick in the corridors and he was in a hurry. He stopped me and said he was going to Arizona and would not be back this session. "Look after things," he said as he breezed out the front door. It was unbelievable. No warning, no briefing, no arrangements.

The Committee of Human Greed continued to meet in Elwood's office and the NDP were gradually moving in the right direction on the issue of research and caucus funding. They were also getting nervous about their pay increases and the meetings in the washroom resumed. Soon it was raised in caucus by Katzman, who claimed to be representing his roommate, that it had been drawn to his attention that I was taking too hard a line with the committee and everything was in jeopardy. I replied that what McLeod and I were doing was totally consistent with instructions agreed to by caucus and the NDP were merely using the gullible Katzman as a negotiating tool. I argued that the NDP would agree to our research and caucus grants because they had to give their backbenchers an increase or they would have trouble. They were playing poker and I felt we should up the ante.

As a group caucus agreed but as individuals they wanted their money and were weakening. I phoned Collver in Arizona and explained what had happened. He agreed with my position and said he would phone some of the other MLAs. I met with Jack Messer later that day and he gave me what he said was their top offer and added, "I advise you to take it. Al won't go any further." Later that day he did go further and it was clear the NDP would ultimately give us our bottom line. However, our MLAs wanted their money and they cracked. In the washroom meetings, which had increased in frequency, the NDP were telling Katzman et al. that I was being far too tough and everything was off if I continued to hold out. The next day when I arrived for caucus I found a meeting already in progress with Romanow, George McLeod, and Bob Andrew. I told them to get a new House leader and left.

Later I was told a deal had been struck and the session would be all over today. The House would conclude and the last order of business would be the salary increase. First, second, and third readings would be given tonight. I asked them what made them think they would get the required unanimous consent. There were some shocked looks as I said that the whole thing was disgusting enough, but to do it in this manner was the height of degradation and could not be justified. The agreed-upon office funding was less than Romanow had presented me with verbally the day before and I was doubly upset at the way the NDP had used the oldest trick in the book. I would not agree to consent to the bill but I did say I would think about it. As you can imagine, I was not very popular for the rest of the afternoon. It was a Friday and everyone wanted to go home for the summer. The Tory caucus had hard feelings about what I was doing and the NDP were threatening not to introduce the legislation unless they knew how heavy I was coming.

This business of salary increases was one of the aspects of being an MLA that I really disliked. Had I not lived within driving distance of Regina, I would never have been one. The lot of those who lived out of motels on a steady diet of booze and politics, I did not envy in the least. You had to wonder why they did it. For some it was the sense of power; for others it was an ego trip. I'm not sure why I was there. I like to think it was for the noble purpose of fighting the socialists and trying to keep some kind of balance in the province, but undoubtedly I was no different from anyone else, except that if it had been up to me I would have had our pay and hours cut in half. No one, especially not our constituents, would have noticed and only those who made more money in politics than they could else-where would have had cause for complaint. During negotia-tions in Elwood's office, he said they were going to put in an opting-out clause for those who voted against the bill. I told him I would be delighted to be the first to take it and then, as a matter of course, the whole assembly would have no choice but to do the same. And if they didn't I would preface every ques-tion or speech with the phrase, "As the lowest paid MLA . . ." or "As the only MLA with a conscience . . ." That point was not raised again.

The NDP did a pretty cute trick that evening. Shortly after ten they arranged to have the bar opened in the area behind the press gallery. Each year after the session closed, we used to get together for a sort of windup party. The front doors of the legislative buildings were locked and the party would go on until the last one left. As soon as the bar opened the press gallery emptied—after all the liquor was free. The legislation for the pay increase and all accoutrements was then introduced under the hollow gaze of an empty gallery. Unanimous consent was given for the bill to proceed to second reading at which point I got up and began to speak. I hit hard at the shoddiness of introducing legislation at 11:15 P.M. on the last night of the session and giving it three readings in a matter of minutes. I was talking about public trust and looked up into the empty press gallery. Nobody cared. Why should I? I wound up quickly and sat down. The press missed it all. They would not know for days what was in that legislation, if in fact they ever knew.

I left the assembly quickly and was going to go straight home when I met Elwood Cowley in the hallway. We had a couple of drinks in his office and then ended up in the opposition lounge. We were joined by George McLeod and additional scotch appeared as if by magic. The House was into its closing stages so the three of us went into the assembly with our cups full of Chivas—the House was in committee so coffee was allowed. We were sitting behind the rail—not being as unobtrusive as we had intended—when the sergeant-at-arms ambled by. He peered into my cup—he did not like me—and said, "That doesn't look like ginger ale, Mac." Indignantly Cowley interjected, "I would hope not. It's quality scotch." We were hustled out of there with Elwood complaining about the poor quality help of today—no class.

7

My Marital Breakdown Becomes Everyone's Business

The federal election of May 1979 saw the defeat of the government of Pierre Elliott Trudeau and the establishment of a minority government by Joe Clark and the Tories. In Saskatchewan, the eradication of the Liberal party was completed with the defeat of Otto Lang, who despite his great intellectual capacity was unable to overcome the politics of the grain industry and the emotional disinformation fed to farmers, and MPs Cliff McIsaac and Ralph Goodale. Tony Merchant, who a year earlier would almost surely have won in his riding, finished third, as did Stu Cameron in his. The election results were a testimony to a two-way lack of understanding: the prime minister did not understand the West, nor did he care to, and the reverse was true here. Reduced to the most redneck proportions, the Liberal party in the eyes of many was French and metric, and Saskatchewan was tired of both.

Dick Collver returned from Arizona the proud owner of a

dude ranch in Wickenburg and he was all bubbly as he prepared to subdivide it. He announced he was stepping down as
leader of the Conservative party but would serve out his term
as the MLA for Nipawin. His decision was secretly welcomed
by all who did not want to see him subjected to the "Tory firing
squad." It was a wise decision for everyone. There was a Senate
seat open and it was widely assumed Joe Clark would appoint
him to it. Many, and I was one of them, were upset when
former MP Jim Balfour was appointed instead. Balfour had not
been one shred of help to the provincial party and had
appeared almost to shun it. Dick, while no doubt he would
have accepted the seat, showed no rancor when it did not work
out. What he wanted, he said, was to be the Canadian trade
representative to Phoenix. It would have been an easy appointment for Joe Clark to have made; however, like so many things
of a political nature during his brief tenure, he never found time
to get it done.

There was no obvious successor as leader of the Conservative
party. Gary Lane, of course, badly wanted to run, but he was
quick to perceive his liabilities—he was an ex-Liberal and the
pro-Collver faction would go after his hide for his perceived
disloyalty to Dick. I could easily have supported Eric Berntson if
he had cleaned up his act. He had the talent but he did not
really care. If he were ever motivated he could be a deadly
political weapon. However, when the spirit moved him he
could be foul mouthed, crude, and drink heavily. When frus-
trated, his reaction was far too often to say, "——— it," and
walk away. Dick Collver tried to get me to run. He promised
me his support, but I was not interested. I was just not willing
to make the personal commitment necessary to make a successful party leader.

During the summer it became obvious that Graham Taylor
was going to be a candidate. In some ways the race was not
dissimilar to the last Liberal leadership campaign—the party
faithful were waiting for the knight on a white charger. I suppose the faithful in any party go through that stage, but having
been through it once before, I was not expecting any miracles.
What we saw was what we were going to get. The name of Dr.
Grant Devine was being tossed around more and more frequently. He was a defeated candidate in a Saskatoon riding we

should have won, a victim of the anti-Collver mood that was more prevalent in Saskatoon than anywhere else. I had met him for the first time at our 1977 convention, when he had indicated to me he was being encouraged to run federally. I took him to Collver immediately, visualizing him as a key candidate in Saskatoon. I knew his family well. In fact, his late brother had contested the Liberal nomination in Thunder Creek in 1975. His father and uncles farmed a few miles north of me and I had spent many a winter afternoon in the rear of George Halstrom's farm machinery business playing "smear" with Don Devine, Grant's father. Grant Devine was promoted from the start by Eric Berntson and Bob Andrew. As an economics professor he had had a unique opportunity to comment without having to enter the political spectrum. The fact he did not have a seat was, to my way of thinking, a benefit and not a liability.

In August of 1979, politics was abruptly shoved to the back burner of my life. My wife vanished with my son Regan and daughter Stephanie, abandoning Greg in the process. Grant Devine was canvassing for support in the early part of September but I was really not interested in getting involved. However, I had no objection to Devine contacting my executive and I volunteered to expedite his meeting potential delegates from Thunder Creek. In mid-September I located my two children and returned them to Moose Jaw, although my wife and I remained separated. I was granted temporary custody of the children pending a custody hearing. In the leadership race, Grant Devine and Graham Taylor became candidates, with Paul Rousseau, by far the most right wing, rumored to follow. Graham avoided soliciting MLAs for support—I have no idea why—and I did not even have a conversation with him on the question of leadership until two or three days before the convention, when he called me and said, "My door is always open." By that time the campaign was essentially over.

The entire fall of 1979 was a write-off for me politically. Other than looking after the day-to-day constituency business, I rarely went near Regina except when either court or constituency matters arose. Up until this point, I really did not have anyone I could truly call "my lawyer." I had only been involved in the most minimal litigation and making a will was probably the most important legal event of my life. All that was obviously changing since only a major miracle was going to resurrect my marriage and my wife and I were on a collision course for custody of the children. I chose Tony Merchant to handle the legalities for several reasons. We had been on opposite ends of the spectrum in the Liberal caucus, yet we had always been friendly. I knew he was very bright and had always envied his capacity for work. He was not going to tell me what I wanted to hear. Quite the contrary, he would be blunt and straightforward. He also understood the political game, although I sincerely hoped my private affairs and politics would not become intertwined.

It is not my intention here to recount my personal troubles as such. I will mention them only as they relate to political decisions I made. In October, an interim hearing was going to be held in Regina for custody of the three children. Tony told me that most of the judges did not want to hear the case. The reasons are clear. There is a close connection between politics and the judiciary, much as the latter is loathe to admit it. The straight fact is that many judges above the provincial court level are appointed by the federal government of the day and most of the appointments are made because of some connection to the governing political party. I exclude the Supreme Court and Federal Court because I have little knowledge of matters there. I do not make the above description to be derogatory, but rather to describe what is an indisputable fact of life. This fact was one of the underlying reasons why members of the judiciary who knew my father or me—which was most of them—were disqualifying themselves. However, Judge M. A. (Sandy) Mac-Pherson was prepared to hear the case.

When Tony Merchant told me Mr. Justice MacPherson was going to hear the case, I was not particularly concerned. To my knowledge I had not met him and I knew very little about him other than that he was from an old Tory family and had been appointed by the Diefenbaker government. Judge MacPherson had been a member of the arts board during the late sixties at the time it came under the provincial government's jurisdiction, and was one of those removed from the board by my father.

Tony Merchant said he felt Mr. Justice MacPherson would be a good judge for this type of case, but pointed out that it was not exactly fashionable to make custody awards to fathers. The first time I saw Mr. Justice M. A. MacPherson in court, I felt I was in trouble, notwithstanding the fact that he awarded me interim custody of the children pending a full hearing.

Paul Rousseau was the last candidate to enter the leadership race. I loved Paul's right-wing thinking and he had come a long way as a speaker. On top of it all, he was a charming gentleman. Unfortunately I was in such a mess I could not actively support him. Grant Devine had accepted my invitation to meet with my executive and potential delegates in Thunder Creek and my constituency was now well on its way to supporting him almost unanimously. He played the right-wing economics professor and the Palliser members loved the refreshing change from the steady diet of left-wing economics they had been fed recently.

At the same time as the leadership candidates were lining up, Gary Lane was battling Harold Lane for the presidency of the party. It was the classic south versus north fight and promised to be more interesting than the leadership race. I felt strongly that the president should be someone outside caucus who could serve as a pipeline to the grass roots. Most of the delegates from Thunder Creek were going to support Gary Lane because they knew him and, for some, he had once been their MLA. It was my intention to support Harold because he was not a caucus member and I felt he would make a far better president.

The final custody hearing took place in early November, and my only concern was that my children could stay together in their home. However, things did not go well and although the decision was reserved Tony was concerned and my mother was convinced I had lost.

I did not get involved in the leadership race the way I should have as a sitting MLA. I had decided I was finished in politics because of my marriage breakup and anyway the result was a foregone conclusion at least six weeks prior to the convention. Losing badly to an aging cabinet minister in the previous general election had not hurt Devine with the delegates. In fact, the idea of electing an outsider had some appeal. While Devine was not a good speaker at the outset, time on the campaign trail quickly changed that and his wife was a definite asset. He won the convention easily and Gary Lane won the presidency over Harold Lane by a surprising margin. It was now a new guard in

Regina all the way around.

Immediately after the convention I left for Moose Jaw to face a judgment awarding custody of Stephanie and Regan to JoAnn, while Greg was allowed to stay in the household in which he had been abandoned. JoAnn came over that night to say she was leaving on a jaunt and would be back to assume the family home in a few days. In that period of time I appealed the decision and was granted interim custody pending appeal. I was taking the children to Palm Springs, California, for Christmas and Dick Collver had insisted we visit him at Wickenburg while we were down there. Just before we left, JoAnn and I exchanged divorce petitions.

Getting away at Christmas was good for all of us—especially the children, who are always the victims in the mindless torment inflicted by their parents on each other. I had a chance to think about where my life was headed. Politically, I believed it was all over. A divorced man was unacceptable in straitlaced, conservative Thunder Creek. My soon-to-be ex-wife had spent much of her time that fall staying in Rouleau with Gerry Weckman, my former Liberal president in Thunder Creek, and his wife. JoAnn was applying the political pressure points as best she could. In California, I decided I would finish my term and groom someone as a replacement. My marriage over and divorce papers filed, I was suddenly on the Palm Springs scene as a bachelor.

We returned to Saskatchewan in January and I felt much better about facing people. Despite all that had happened, and much of it was fairly juicy material by Saskatchewan standards, the press had not become involved, even though I swear everyone in the whole world must have known everything. I was frankly amazed at their compassion. I explained my situation to Grant Devine and requested a lower critic's position, a request to which he readily agreed. He had to heal the breach with Paul Rousseau and Graham Taylor. Rousseau he put into finance, Taylor became House leader, and he gave agriculture to me—it was to be my favorite critic's job. When the House resumed, I was much better than in the fall and managed to make a contribution. Because Devine did not have a seat, Eric Berntson was made the leader of the opposition. There was no real push to get Grant in the House. In fact, many of us wanted to keep him out as long as possible. He was not ready to face the Blakeneys and Romanows of the world. He would have been a lamb in a pack of wolves. Roy Romanow was already proclaiming that the closest Grant Devine would get to the legislature was in a seat in the public galleries.

The night before the legislature was reconvening, I received a call from Eric Berntson. He had just met with Dick Collver, who had told him he was holding a press conference in the morning to announce the formation of a new political party committed to Saskatchewan becoming the fifty-first American state. He was going to indicate that he had a broad base of support across the province and the country as a whole, which cut across party lines. He had also told Eric that he would be joined soon by another MLA. Eric was obviously fearful it was me and I assured him it was not.

Dick had outlined his plans for a new party when I visited him in Arizona over Christmas. He had told me that there was no way he was going to sit as a Conservative in Saskatchewan while that "twit" Devine and the "treacherous" Lane ran the party. He decided to form his new party in order to have some fun for two to three years and be a thorn in the side of the NDP, who, he believed, would be in power forever. He told me I was finished in politics and invited me to join him so that we could raise "hell" for the balance of our terms and then fade away. Collver had been drinking heavily at the time and I decided to forget his invitation.

Dick held his press conference and made his announcement. It created a furor both in and out of the province while Dick laughed all the way to the legislature. Grant Devine was, of course, concerned because there was no way anyone could gauge its impact on the Conservative party. After all, the leader of the party only a few short months ago was now openly advocating what in years gone by would have been viewed as sedition and treason. It was headlines coast to coast. Naturally, the NDP were promoting the theory that Collver was expressing the secret wish of all Conservatives, which was to sell the country out to big business and then join the States. Several days later Dennis Ham, Conservative MLA for Swift Current, joined Collver. His move was damaging to the party and to Devine's leadership. There was speculation that I was next but speculation was all it was. I considered Collver's action totally irresponsible and I would never have joined him under any circumstances.

Dick Collver was to totally dominate the balance of that session of the legislative assembly. He was a thorn in the side of the NDP as he had planned and he would provoke the ire of everyone else by his calls to join the movement. For the first time, he was free of all political constraints and he enjoyed his freedom to the fullest. The topics he covered ranged from free trade to right-to-work legislation to becoming the fifty-first state, and he had compelling, and often valid, arguments for each position. He was enjoying himself immensely. He made little pretense of representing the constituency of Nipawin, but he did voice many truths that could not have been uttered within the framework of normal party politics.

My personal problems became acute when I lost my appeal for custody of Stephanie and Regan. I applied to the Supreme Court of Canada but was turned down. In addition my estranged wife was granted our family house—the same one she had abandoned several months earlier when she left Greg behind. I had lived in that house since 1948 and had bought it from my father when he moved to Regina. I had put the title in JoAnn's name in case something should happen to me. The court gave Greg and me twenty-four hours to leave the only home he had ever known, and we moved to a motel. Subsequently, we purchased a home in Moose Jaw, immediately upon which JoAnn moved to Regina leaving me with two homes. This turmoil made me almost a nonentity in the legislature and it would be fair to say I was a poor-quality MLA at that time. Compounding the problems was the fact that my son Regan was not going to stay with his mother and was returning to Greg and me as fast as someone would return him to JoAnn. A subsequent application to the court led Judge Sirois to grant me interim custody of Regan pending a rehearing. Indirectly, my personal problems led to what was always to be a very chilly relationship with Grant Devine. It has always been incorrectly assumed that I refused to let Devine run in my constituency. That is not true. I was never asked and I did not make the offer.

To his frustration, Devine had been shunted to the back

pages of the newspapers with the return of Dick Collver and his headline-grabbing antics, and the caucus either did not want to or could not pick up the cumbersome committee system Grant had set up when he became leader. One committee reported to another, which then brought the matter to caucus, where nobody had any idea what it meant anyway. Eric Berntson usually dealt with the caucus committees with the exclamation, "—————— it." During this session, Devine was being counseled by those who were urging him to find a seat as soon as possible and those—of whom I was one—who told him there was no rush. After all, it was a long way until election time, and where he was the NDP could only snipe at him from afar.

Through the latter part of the session, I was preparing for the court hearing under the Matrimonial Property Act in which I would be divorced and find out the bill for seventeen years of marriage. As the time got closer, there was a great deal of communication between Tony Merchant's office and my own. Our caucus secretary was a very competent lady named Paula Hosie whose husband, a Regina land appraiser, was hired by my wife's attorneys to evaluate my agricultural assets and to prepare a report for submission to court. It was an awkward situation. While I did not have any concerns about Paula's integrity all my calls had to go through her, as did my correspondence. I went to Devine, explained the situation, and suggested one of us be moved to the Conservative office upstairs. He seemed to appreciate my concerns but did not want me to change offices. He did not want to do anything that might revive the old rumors about my joining Collver. He said he would move Paula.

Several days went by and nothing happened, so I again went to Devine. He apologized and said he would do something about it. Still nothing. I then told him that if he was not going to move her he should say so. He acted surprised and said she would move tomorrow. She did move but the next day she was back. I am sure she had no idea what was going on but now I was incensed. The matter seemed so trivial I could not understand what the difficulty was. I went to Devine's office and demanded to know what kind of a game he was playing and why? He said he would deal with the matter personally. For whatever reason, he fired Paula Hosie. I thought at the time, this guy wants to be the premier and he can't even arrange a simple change of secretarial desks in his own staff.

When caucus questioned the firing, Devine merely said it had been his decision. It was obvious they knew it had something to do with me, although they did not know exactly what. It was the proverbial mountain out of a molehill and I was getting angrier and angrier. Finally I had had enough. I said I was leaving caucus for the balance of the session and they could consider me an independent. I left and took the most important items out of my office. For the balance of the session, I worked out of my desk in the assembly and had my correspondence and phone calls routed through Dick Collver's secretary. Miraculously, the press gallery was never aware of my action. I continued to attend the legislative sessions and took part in the areas I chose completely independently of the party. I did not return to caucus, my office, or the opposition lounge that session.

The next day I spent at my ranch and that evening I was visited by Grant Devine and Gerald Muirhead, the MLA for Arm River. While I was mixing Grant a drink the phone rang. It was the president of the Thunder Creek executive to say that he and some of the executive had just met with Devine and Muirhead and were now on their way up to my place. If there is a political no-no, it is going into an MLA's riding without his knowledge. To meet with his executive without his knowledge is an act of all-out war. As soon as I came off the phone I asked Devine and Muirhead to leave. Gerald, who is a gentleman, headed straight to his car. When Grant hesitated I said, "Please leave before I say something we will both regret later." He left. Almost simultaneously, the executive members from Thunder Creek came in.

The meeting had been arranged by Devine's office, and the executive had been trying to reach me all day. I was fortunate to have an aggressive group of people working for me in Thunder Creek. I had kept them fully informed of my personal difficulties from the outset and they had been most supportive. They had the impression that Grant Devine wanted the constituency and was testing the waters. He had told them I was acting irrationally and was short-tempered in the legislature. He then gave them a quasi description of what had transpired. It was interesting that these people, who a few short months ago had supported Devine's leadership bid, were stating in pretty strong terms that they would bitterly fight any attempt by him to come to Thunder Creek. All this over a secretary. There was no doubt that I was edgy with all the personal turmoil around me but I was amazed how inept the new leader of the Conservative party could be. The rift between Devine and me now included the Thunder Creek executive. Regardless of what happened to me, he could never come to Thunder Creek without facing a pitched battle he would undoubtedly lose.

The fact I was not sitting in on caucus did not seem to affect my relationship with the other MLAs. When I had a question for question period I merely told the House leader, Graham Taylor, and he fitted me in smoothly. No one ever knew. Neither Devine nor I made any attempt at communication although we were both civil in chance meetings. At the end of the session, Eric Berntson caught me in the hallway and said he wanted to run something by me. Bob Larter, the MLA for Estevan, had had enough. His wife was ill and, subject to the party honoring certain commitments, he would resign to create a by-election for Grant Devine in a safe Tory seat. I told Eric I felt Devine should run in Saskatoon, which was a wasteland for us but one we had to improve on if we were ever going to be a viable political force. Also, Devine was no Collver and if he were to walk into the assembly cold with all the attention squarely on him, the NDP would finish him for good. Blakeney, Romanow, Messer, and MacMurchy were a long way from a university economics class and would just love to get at him. Then there would be the inevitable comparison to Collver, who was dominating things totally at his whim. I questioned the parachute factor as well. Bob Larter was immensely popular and drew support from all parties. Estevan was NDP at least 50 percent of the time and it would be a disaster if Devine were to lose it. This was not what Berntson wanted to hear but he said that "it was only thinking out loud at this point." A by-election was held in Estevan later that fall and the Conservative candidate was Grant Devine.

I returned to court on July 2, 1980, for a rehearing of the custody award of Regan to JoAnn. In spite of all efforts for a change of judge, the case was being reheard by Justice M. A.

MacPherson. Tony Merchant gave it his best shot, but about two-thirds of the way through the hearing—it lasted well over a week—Judge MacPherson called the attorneys to his chambers on a technical matter. When Tony Merchant came out, he told me the judge had told him his present inclination was to give custody of Regan to JoAnn: most of the evidence was not yet in. It was a "body blow," as Tony Merchant described it.

My son Greg, who had just turned fourteen, took the stand and gave testimony for about one hour. For the balance of the day he was cross-examined by his mother's counsel, Gerald Gerrand. At first he treated Greg cautiously, then he took off the gloves. Gerrand was no courtroom amateur and, after taking a break to confer with JoAnn, he unloaded heavily on Greg. Greg handled the questioning with ease and in my biased view he was a superb witness, especially considering his age. There was another day of testimony from a psychiatrist designated by Judge MacPherson that highly favored me, but if the conference in the chambers the other day was indicative, it was all over.

The summing up by the trial judge was extraordinary. He referred to Greg as a "monster" and used terminology like "despicable." Even though it was difficult, I forced myself not to react to the comments that were being presented so as not to run the risk of being cited for contempt. Many of the descriptions of Greg made subsequently have been based on the trial judge's comments. Anyone who knows Greg knows the truth about such characterizations.

Upon completion of the rehearing on the custody of Regan, I went straight into a hearing on the division of property under the Matrimonial Property Act. That one lasted about three weeks and when it concluded, I had had enough of courtrooms to last a lifetime. Judgments in both matters were reserved. Despite all the time spent in courtrooms, the press had not yet reported anything, even though they were fully aware of what was happening. I was told a junior reporter filed a story with the Regina *Leader-Post* but it was not published.

Some strange things were happening politically in the late summer of 1980. Two NDP cabinet ministers resigned abruptly and by-elections were called to coincide with the one in Estevan. By far the more shocking departure was that of Jack Messer, one of the real heavyweights in the government.

Obviously the NDP were feeling fairly comfortable if they were willing to risk a hole like this on their front benches. No question they still had lots of talent but the loss of Messer was the start of their downhill slide.

In late August, the decision on the future of my son Regan came down and the world of this eleven year old was needlessly shattered. Mr. Justice M. A. MacPherson awarded custody of Regan to his mother. Both Greg and I were forbidden to have contact with him for one year. Regan Colin Thatcher chose exile.

It had been months since I had seen my daughter, Stephanie. All attempts to see her were refused so I applied in court for the normal access privileges. Tony Merchant filed a normal application for regular court chambers but the file was referred back to Mr. Justice M. A. MacPherson. When the matter came up, the issue of Regan's absence was raised. Judge MacPherson adjourned the matter to another day and told JoAnn's lawyer to notify the press that the matter would come up and to let them know the date of the hearing. Mr. Gerrand agreed to do so.

When the court reconvened some days later, Mr. Justice MacPherson spoke directly to the press. He said he had asked Mr. Gerrand to notify the press that the matter was coming up because he wanted their help. He encouraged them to cover the story, claiming that the publicity would assist in discovering the whereabouts of Regan.

Members of the media had told me and Tony Merchant that there had been some consideration of covering my marital breakdown, but that some of the press corps had discussed the subject and thought it wrong to report my personal troubles. They reasoned that the fact I was a politician did not justify "open season" tactics, such as those used by trash sheets covering Hollywood movie stars.

Although Judge MacPherson actually said, "Ladies and gentlemen of the press, I seek your help...," I think many of the press took his comments as something close to a command from the court, and they felt almost directed to give the absence of Regan some publicity. The story as reported was hardly unbiased, and the press clearly did not understand the legal technicalities. For example, at no time was I ever required to be in a courtroom, but when there was some kind of an application being heard the press would mention that I did not appear in court and make it sound as though I was ignoring a court order. Above all, however, the consequence of Mr. Justice M. A. MacPherson's actions was that my marital breakdown became everyone's business.

Three by-elections were called in the province that fall, of which we should have had an easy win in Estevan, where Devine was running, an outside chance in Jack Messer's Kelsey-Tisdale seat, and no hope at all in North Battleford. Most of the party resources were going to be centered in Estevan, where it quickly became apparent the race was not going to be as cut and dried as we had hoped. The entrance of Ralph Goodale, a recently defeated Liberal MP, as the Liberal candidate, gave the race a brand-new look as a strong Liberal presence had never been anticipated in the strategy planning. It was also becoming increasingly obvious that Bob Larter had not done a good job in clearing the way for Grant Devine with the local Conservatives. Stories were circulating freely about friction with the constituency president and the provincial organization, and there was rumored to be local hostility to a parachute candidate. Devine's campaign was to be almost exclusively handled out of Regina by people who were out of touch with Estevan. The prime advertisement was Grant Devine in a three-piece suit and his wife in an ultra-suede dress walking through a wheat field. They looked very elegant for any place but a wheat field. The NDP loved it.

Meanwhile, up in Jack Messer's old riding of Kelsey-Tisdale, a little-known Conservative candidate named Neal Hardy was quietly working hard on a minimum budget with a group of local people who were not supposed to be campaign experts but were scaring the NDP. I saw Billy Allen in the legislative hallways and asked him what was happening from their view. He said they had Devine beaten in Estevan but things were going wrong in Kelsey-Tisdale, where the Tories were coming on fast.

The NDP won two of the three by-elections but not the combination everyone had anticipated. A strong Liberal vote elected the NDP in Estevan, while Neal Hardy won an upset in Kelsey-Tisdale. North Battleford was an easy win for the NDP. Naturally, the NDP were ecstatic at retaking Estevan, although their jubilation was dulled somewhat because the loss of Kel-

sey-Tisdale prevented them from proclaiming the total annihilation of the Conservative party. The northeastern part of Saskatchewan was considered the exclusive property of the NDP
and Neal Hardy's cracking of that armor had some NDP strategists looking over their shoulders.

By any standard, the Estevan defeat of Grant Devine was a
serious blow to the party and to the credibility of Grant Devine
as leader. Had it not been for the win in Kelsey-Tisdale it would
have been a disaster. Devine took the loss graciously in the face
of NDP ridicule—something that was noted by all concerned—
and wisely said that he was committed to Estevan and would
return in the general election. The Liberal campaign had made
no pretense at being anything but an attack on the Conservatives and to that extent it had been successful. The size of the
Liberal vote made Ralph Goodale think he would be a good
leader of the Liberal party and soon after the by-election he was
elected to the position.

Regan Colin Thatcher's disappearance—if it could be called
that—was now widespread news, and my executive and others
were telling me that the one-sided press reports were doing me
no good. Up until now, I had been coasting along, just trying to
finish my term as an MLA; however, I now decided that if I was
finished that decision would be made by the voters in Thunder
Creek and not by a court of Queen's Bench judge. I phoned
Tony Merchant and said I wanted to hold a press conference.
He was worried about the legalities but said he would think
about it. I asked party press secretary Garf Spetz for his help
and advice. Spetz got along well with the legislative press corps
and, because of the possibility of being cited for contempt of
court, this carefully selected group was the group I wanted to
address. The plan was that no written press release would be
given out. Instead there would be one copy of my statement,
which I would read and make available to any reporter wishing
to make reference notes and then destroy. There were to be no
questions.

Merchant and Spetz helped me prepare the statement, and
we took great care to keep the Conservative party out of it. The
dicey parts were the reference to Mr. Justice MacPherson's
making the whole matter public by involving the press, and the
sequence of events leading to the arrival of the press in his

courtroom and the subsequent publication of the whole affair. What was said in this context was quite accurate and went unchallenged, but the possibility of his reacting like a bull in a china shop could not be discounted beforehand. The *Moose Jaw Times-Herald* gave extensive coverage to my statement and I had their story xeroxed and put in every mailbox in Thunder Creek. By now everything was in the open and my constituents could pass their own judgment. It was a gamble I would rather not have had to take but I was told by others, including Grant Devine, that it turned things around.

Just before the legislature went in, two disturbing things happened. By far the more difficult was the $819,000 award to my estranged wife to be paid within six months. Since I was not carrying that kind of cash around in my jeans, I had little choice but to appeal. The other was the surfacing of an interview I had done months earlier with The Canadian Press at the tail end of which I had answered some questions about Devine in a most unflattering way. Regardless of my feelings at the time—the interview had taken place during the court wrangling over the divorce settlement—my comments were totally out of line. I apologized to Devine but he was never to forgive me. In his position I probably wouldn't have either.

8

Sensing Victory

The opening of the legislature in the fall of 1980 was a tough one for Grant Devine. The NDP heckled him unmercifully because, having lost Estevan, the only way he could get to the floor of the chambers was by invitation. Expect no sympathy in politics when you are down because the only sure thing is that someone will try to kick you on the way by. I knew I had to perform this session. My constituents in Thunder Creek had been tolerant of my personal problems for a year but now they expected me to get down to business. My major court battles were behind me. I intended to do a good job as the agriculture critic and I was going to be an MLA in the manner the party expected and needed. I had decided to run again and I had to return to form.

In the fall of 1980 it appeared the NDP would be in power for perpetuity. Allan Blakeney's image as leader could not have been higher and his stature transcended party lines; our leader did not even have a seat. The size of the Liberal vote in Estevan had to be of comfort to the government because a split vote had always been the NDP's best friend. However, the loss of Jack Messer had greater implications than they had believed initially and the taking of his seat by the Conservatives had more than just normal by-election overtones. The strong support for the Liberals in Estevan was not a good indicator of the direction the party was headed.

Although none of us realized it at the time, a major shift in voter sentiment was commencing in Saskatchewan. The extent of the change would not be known for another two and a half years but it had started already—so subtly it escaped even the sophisticated polling of the government. Meanwhile, as Messer had predicted, the NDP were trying to avoid anything contro- versial and were trying to stay close enough to the center that the small-business types would feel comfortable. The NDP are deadly effective when they are being radical and have a cause to champion. At the end of 1980 they were playing the role of Liberals, and smug ones at that.

Nineteen eighty had seen a large amount of change in the Conservative party. Dick Collver was now a full-time resident of Arizona and had little contact with affairs in Saskatchewan. When he had formed his new party the positions of several staff members with close ties to him became tenuous, to put it lightly, and, of course, a change of leader had to mean a rear- rangement of personnel. The election of a Conservative govern- ment in Ottawa provided an escape hatch and party director Dave Tkachuk headed the list of those who went east. The party organization shrank to the point where virtually the entire organization was contained within the legislative buildings. Only a small office was maintained in downtown Regina and the Saskatoon office was closed because of lack of funds. The three by-elections had been ones the party could ill afford, and the deficiencies in the party machinery were painfully apparent. The losses further demoralized the party and by the end of 1980 we were a pathetic lot.

The party machinery was now under the control of Gary Lane as party president and Tkachuk's replacement—an indi- vidual named Tom Trilovitch supposedly recommended by the Ontario Tories—was his choice. Trilovitch's Ontario background was hardly an asset in Saskatchewan politics. He was a nice guy but really never had a prayer. Lane also recruited Elmer Strumeki from Alberta, whose specialty was fund raising using the most sophisticated of techniques. He implemented a tax advantage plan known as TAPS to draw five dollars a week from donors' bank accounts across the province. This sophisticated bit of financial wizardry did not even raise enough money to pay Strumeki's salary. The Lane presidency was a far cry from the days of George Hill.

The first political event of 1981 was a federal election nobody wanted. The Liberals were starting a leadership campaign, Joe Clark's government was bringing in a budget, and the NDP were in the middle. None of the three parties could afford an election as all of them were still paying their bills from the previous one. However, the Clark government fell on a non-confidence vote and the country was plunged into a general election the Liberals were so sure of winning they kept Pierre Elliott Trudeau as leader. They ran a skillful campaign and kept Pierre Elliott away from the press except in carefully controlled situations. They won in a walk.

On their third attempt my ex-wife's attorneys were successful in placing a contempt of court motion against me because of Regan's so-called disappearance. The contempt of court application was not an attempt to find Regan, however. My ex-wife knew exactly where he was. The reason for the contempt application was that I had declined to give names of potential witnesses, which, I had been advised, was my right. The application was, rather, an attempt to pressure me, politically and otherwise, before the Court of Appeal heard the case about our property settlement. My ex-wife, who by now was a newlywed, seemed to be under the mistaken impression that she was ending my political career. In fact, from a strictly political point of view, the publicity about Regan's disappearance had become an asset. By now there was considerable sympathy for my position in Thunder Creek, and Gary Lane told me I should keep it as a fight for my children and I would have no problem.

There were no particular issues of earthshaking importance in early 1981. As agriculture critic, I had a good session. Of course you must have a good minister in order to be successful personally in opposition. It is like being a rodeo rider—you don't score well if you don't draw a good horse. Gordon Mac-Murchy was a skillful adversary and politician and always made powerful responses to my questions. Grant Devine was out in the country meeting people and speaking to any group that wanted to listen. Without anyone noticing it, he was developing a populist approach. It was not contrived nor was it done with professional help and it was in complete contrast to the cool, demur attitude of Allan Blakeney. Devine was a great admirer of Peter Lougheed and spent some time with those who had taught Lougheed how to handle television so effectively. The previous year he had spent most of his time around the legislature, now he was rarely in. The results a year later were to further demonstrate what we all knew—elections are not won in Regina.

The NDP were still in control, however. Public attention had shifted to the repatriation of the constitution and the wrangling between the provinces and the federal government. Allan Blakeney was the epitome of reasonableness and administrative competency. The national media were obviously enthralled with him and his staff presented him in the best possible image. Roy Romanow also maintained a very high profile as, along with Jean Chrétien, he was co-chairman of the national repatriation committee. The provincial NDP split sharply with their national party over the issue of provincial versus federal control of resources. It was three full years since the last provincial election and the time any government starts to look for an issue. We were in the position of having to be different from the NDP, yet clearly opposed to the federal government. We chose a position identical to the one taken by Peter Lougheed in Alberta. In retrospect, I don't know why on earth Allan Blakeney did not go to the people quickly on the issue of provincial rights not being fully guaranteed in the new constitution. He had every reason to. He must have known our organization was in a shambles and we would have been sitting ducks if he had chosen to call an election any time in 1981.

Gary Lane was our critic on the constitution. Day after day he would question Allan Blakeney and day after day Allan Blakeney would shove his questions down his throat in a businesslike and decisive manner. After two weeks of this I suggested to caucus that we should stay away from Blakeney and the constitution. I argued that Lane's questions were playing on Blakeney's strength and I was tired of the smirks on his executive assistants' faces every time Lane stood up. Lane insisted he was scoring points—he was the only one who thought so—but he did cut back on the questioning. We were more successful when we accused the NDP of siding with the Liberals to bring down the Clark government. If they had not done so then all this constitutional business would not have been necessary. The NDP did not like this tack and our attack may have played a small role in persuading the government not to risk an election on the issue.

In the midst of the session I was found guilty of contempt of court and fined six thousand dollars. I was surprised because even though I had disobeyed a court order prohibiting contact with my son Regan, the reason I was in contempt was for refusing to provide the names of the people who had aided Regan in going to Palm Springs. In other words, I had rightly been found guilty for all the wrong reasons. After seeking Gary Lane's advice, I made a statement to the press that I was fighting for my children and I appealed the decision. The matter had no impact politically.

One day in early May when I was collecting my daughter, Stephanie, from my ex-wife's new home, she and her husband approached me about settling the property matter. At first I was wary of talking to them directly because of previous bad experiences when our conversations on such matters became part of affidavits in a court. However, I agreed to listen and after one meeting I was convinced they were serious. We met at least three more times in early May. On May 16, JoAnn Wilson was shot, wounded, and hospitalized. The whereabouts of Regan became known and I was ordered by the Court of Appeal to place him in school the next day. Sometime later, Regan was officially declared in my custody. Despite the fact JoAnn was hospitalized the negotiations between me and her husband for a settlement continued. We had at last one thing in common— we both hated courts.

The party organization was on the verge of collapse and we were broke. For a while there was grave doubt that we could meet our staff payroll, and even Revenue Canada was threatening us for not forwarding income tax for the previous year.

The staff were receiving no direction from anyone and the party director imported from Ottawa was in the process of leaving. Gary Lane, as president, wanted as little as possible to do with the chaotic situation. Eric Berntson was the picture of frustration. The staff could seldom get direction from Lane or Devine so they would call Berntson instead. He had a frequent colorful commentary on both of them.

Routine party matters and decisions that previously had always been made by the president were being brought to caucus. Very simply, the party was now talking about the disastrous state of affairs and Lane was trying to distribute as much of the responsibility as possible. The caucus as a whole was in a disgruntled state as the spring legislature was concluding with widespread dissatisfaction with Grant Devine's leadership being openly expressed. Devine was aware of the feeling. Rather than meet the growing criticism, his response was to open caucus meetings with a rah-rah speech as though everything were wonderful and then withdraw into as tight a corner as he could muster.

Within the caucus, the lines were rapidly being drawn on the question of Grant Devine's leadership. Perhaps the greatest asset Grant Devine possessed at that time was Gary Lane. Many caucus members feared the removal of Grant Devine would lead to the coronation of Gary Lane as leader and, given the state of disarray the party organization had fallen into under his presidency, this prospect was totally unacceptable to most of them. When I was told by some members of caucus that Lane was going to challenge Devine for the leadership at the fall convention, I scoffed for two reasons: he didn't have the nerve and he wasn't that dumb. I didn't doubt for a second that he was up to his old tricks of checking out the political waters but he had too much savvy to be the one who did the actual knife work. There is no doubt in my mind that if a strong candidate had been at hand, Dr. Grant Devine could not have survived as leader of the Progressive Conservative party.

In many respects, the fate of Grant Devine in 1981 was tied to the mood swings of Eric Berntson. Berntson was a unique individual. He had the capacity to grasp the intricasies of the most complex problems and put them into solvable political form, or he could just as easily say "——— it" and tie into the booze. In mid-1981 Berntson was furious with Devine and Lane and made no secret of it. Shortly after an exchange with Devine—one which I did not witness—he told me, "That little SOB is ——ed if I say so. If I say he's not getting nominated in Estevan, he's not." One never knew what side Berntson would be on, on a given day but in mid-1981 he was definitely not on Grant Devine's team.

The more Devine withdrew, the worse things seemed to get. Devine had hard-core support from Bob Andrew, Jim Garner, Herb Swan, George McLeod, and Bob Pickering. Ralph Katzman and Neal Hardy were out of it by choice. Paul Rousseau, Graham Taylor, Joan Duncan, Larry Birckbeck, Gary Lane, and Eric Berntson wanted a change; and Gerald Muirhead was on both sides. Incidentally, I was for a change if things went smoothly; however, I was not going to participate in a blood-bath. If caucus decided in favor of a change and Devine tried to hang on, sandbagging his nomination in Estevan was the most commonly expressed mode of political execution. Grant Devine did not know how to deal with the situation. Who would? His options were limited and his problems severe. The fact that the NDP election machine did not pick up on what was happening across the floor should have been a signal to us that the machine was not in the fine tune to which we had been accustomed.

A relatively new Mrs. Anthony Wilson was out of the hospital and called a press conference. I was, of course, going to be the subject, and her statement was strictly for political consumption. Security was tight and the conference was by invitation only. I waited a couple of weeks then I had a small survey taken in Thunder Creek to measure the impact of the shooting and JoAnn's well-publicized but vague statements to the press. I found that people were weary of the affair and weren't listening any more. It was no longer a political factor.

In the summer of 1981 speculation was starting that a provincial election would come in the fall. The constitutional talks were still in the news and Allan Blakeney continued to gain stature on the national scene. A few deliberate leaks had led to some interesting stories—such as Saskatchewan being seen as the weak link in western resistance—but basically the NDP were in complete control of their own destiny. In our camp, an election was something to be feared and we could not even afford a survey to find out just how much we should fear it.

A caucus meeting was called for Kenosee Lake in southeastern Saskatchewan. When I asked Berntson what it was about he replied, "We may dump the little ——er." I remarked that we were not ready for that and he said, "You never are." By "you," I assumed he meant the party. Paul Rousseau also felt Devine could fall at the Kenosee caucus. I told him that Lane was looking at us to lower the boom on Devine so that he could emerge as a savior. "That would be over Berntson's dead body," replied Rousseau. A day or two before the scheduled gathering, Gary Lane called to make sure I was going. I asked him frankly what he was going to do on the issue of leadership. He fenced but the message was obvious. He wanted someone to do his hatchet work and he would play the role of the statesman. That was par for the course.

Kenosee is a resort community in southeastern Saskatchewan. The beautiful setting is in sharp contrast to the austerity of the surrounding prairie and Kenosee is used by many people from Saskatchewan and the northern United States as a quiet place to relax away from the rigor and realities of everyday life. The organizers of this caucus saw it as a place where the air could be cleared and things discussed frankly without fear of someone storming out and talking to the press. There was little doubt that this was going to be a plain-speaking session. Grant Devine was going to get a tongue-lashing from several directions and probably so was Lane. Grant Devine well knew what was happening. He had asked a variety of political people throughout the province—not all of them Tories—how he should handle the dissident elements in caucus. Obviously he had heard of the Estevan plot—even though it had never been pursued—because he had taken steps to secure his position with the local executive. He did not plan to step down and obviously hoped to weather the storm by holding the meeting in a remote setting and letting the dissidents blow off some steam.

It is probably my Liberal upbringing, but disloyalty to a leader, in my view, is the absolute bottom of the barrel in politics. A dissident element in any caucus is a fact of life due to the Machiavellian nature of the business and the grossness of the egos involved. The truth is simply that the Liberals wield their knives in private while Tories do so whenever the inclination arises. I did not enjoy what was going on in the summer of 1981 as I had considerable sympathy for Grant Devine. He had become leader without having gone through the "chairs," and it is fair to say that his not yet having won an election had a bearing on the attitudes of some of his detractors.

As I drove to Kenosee for the caucus meeting, I did not really expect there to be a change of leadership. It is one thing to speak out in private and quite another to do so in an open forum. But then something had to happen at this meeting, either a change at the top or affirmations of a sharp change of direction internally. Obviously, with rumors of a fall election in the air, a change was risky but not impossible. Years earlier in Manitoba, when the opposition NDP were in the midst of a leadership campaign, the governing Tories called an election. The NDP merely moved up their convention date and one Edward Shryer became the new premier of Manitoba.

Grant Devine had many qualifications to make him an attractive leader for the Conservative party. In contrast to its perception of Dick Collver, the public's perception of Devine was good. He was a converted Roman Catholic and a devoted family man. If Dick Collver had enjoyed even one of these assets, he would have been premier in 1978. As a speaker, Devine was getting better all the time and hard work did not faze him. Like all of us, he had his frailties. In my view, he did not demand enough from his immediate staff and he surrounded himself with inept executive assistants. He also could not make up his mind and was only too glad to put off decisions. It was these liabilities that had caused the frustration among the party faithful and the majority of the caucus.

When I arrived at Kenosee there was a tenseness in the air. I could see a change in some of the MLAs from a month ago—it was now time to stand up and be counted one way or the other or hold your silence forever. Joan Duncan was the most vocal in favor of a change. Eric Berntson didn't think a change was possible but thought that both Lane and Devine "needed their asses kicked." Paul Rousseau wanted a change, so did Graham Taylor but he also questioned the practicability. Gerald Muirhead was going to wait and see what happened tomorrow. He was still on both sides. Nobody disliked Grant but no one thought he was doing much of a job either.

The next morning we met in a conveniently out of the way building where there were no hotel or party staff to overhear anything. This was to be a meeting between a leader and his disgruntled caucus only. We were seated in circular fashion when someone suggested that Grant should move to the middle of the circle, a suggestion that was met with polite laughter. Devine was the chairman, moderator, and leader and he had obviously given this meeting a great deal of thought. This time there was no attempt to submerge things with a rah-rah speech and he did not pretend there really was no problem that some good old-fashioned dialogue couldn't cure. He said he was here to listen. He was going to take notes and respond the next morning. He wanted to hear from everyone and he wanted to hear it like it was. That was what he got. He got a roasting the like of which I hope I never have to sit in on again and it came from everywhere, even from some of his hard-core support. While Devine had come fully expecting a rough session he was taken aback by the ferocity of some of the MLAs.

Eric Berntson unloaded on both Devine and Lane. However, he pulled no punches, particularly not on Lane whom he termed "incompetent"—a mild adjective by Berntson's standards. He was not that heavy on Devine personally but was disgusted with the downtrodden state of the party. Graham Taylor was not as colorful as Berntson but he was just as forceful. He described the entire state of the party as "disastrous," and said in light of the fact that he had lost the leadership race, he was restraining the magnitude of his comments. He attacked the choice of personnel both in the party office and on Devine's personal staff. The upshot was that he had great respect for Grant Devine as a family man but little for him as a leader of a political party. Gerald Muirhead surprised me by taking a decisive stand. He was gentle but firm and suggested Grant take off his "rose-colored glasses." While Muirhead was not at all vitriolic, the fact he was not strongly in his camp clearly shook Devine.

The harshest attacks on Grant Devine came from Paul Rousseau, Joan Duncan, and me. It was rough and those few words sum it up. I suggested we had to be facing a fall election simply because the NDP must know that we could not have mounted anything resembling a serious campaign, despite having a strong grass roots organization. The blame for the state of the party lay squarely on the shoulders of those in this room. Joan Duncan was equally strong, and Rousseau even more so. The MLAs in Devine's camp had little to say in his defense. Grant Devine knew he had a problem but I don't think he expected the frankness he got. We took a break for lunch and over the noon hour I asked Gary Lane what he was going to say. He changed the subject and I knew it was over then. Grant Devine would survive.

After lunch, we reconvened. When Gary Lane's turn came he spoke with the double weight of being party president and a veteran MLA. He spent most of the time defining staff problems and outlining some of the corrective measures planned. He dwelled on finances and minimized the failures of the past year. This was the MLA who supposedly had been ready to challenge Devine at the fall convention. He was the same Gary Lane who had sniped at the lame-duck Dave Steuart and Dick Collver, and here he was tap dancing a retreat after being at the center of malcontents for the last several months. For some reason, I was not surprised.

The threat to Grant Devine's leadership ended with Lane's sterile comments. Had Lane been consistent with his earlier position in private, Grant Devine could not have survived that caucus meeting. As it was, I don't know how he took the kind of face-to-face criticism he endured that day. If he harbored any animosity afterwards he certainly did not show it. Some of the criticism was not fair; a great deal of it was.

In retrospect, the intensity of the caucus rhetoric had a positive long-term effect in that it got Devine doing things that should have been done long ago and jarred him into starting to think like a leader. He responded the next day with a wooden, almost contrived speech that had been prepared beforehand. We were thanked for our frankness and assured our suggestions had been noted and action would be taken. At the end, and this I am sure was for the benefit of those who had discussed the Estevan conspiracy, he noted there would be a nomination in Estevan in a couple of days. Berntson recoiled at that one as Devine noted dryly, "The date for selling memberships is past."

Translated this meant, "You bastards don't know everything."

Soon after the Kenosee meeting, Devine appointed me to the campaign committee, along with Gary Lane and Bob Andrew. The rest of the group were from outside caucus, which was important. For the balance of the summer we met every Saturday afternoon in Grant Devine's office. I was happy to be on the committee because the tactics used by the NDP in 1978 were still fresh in my mind. I was looking forward to giving them a taste of their own medicine. We all knew our chances in the fall were slim to none, and there were many things we would have liked to do but could not for lack of funds. Two back-to-back federal elections had sapped our donors and it was going to take the dropping of an election writ to get the funds rolling in. We all knew we could raise money after the writ was issued but the advance work had to be done on a shoestring budget. It would not take the NDP long to get wind of the discord at Kenosee Lake and our financial state would soon become known because of the number of outstanding creditors who were either commencing or thinking of legal action. We had to decide on a campaign chairman.

MP Bill McKnight, a former party president, was happy to accept the chairmanship of the campaign committee. This was a major step. McKnight had the personality to do the job and the tenacity to make people respond. After all, he had been president at the start with Collver, which, in his own words, "had to mean I'm a little crazy." We were already further ahead than we had been in 1978.

Our advertising and promotion, which had been horrible in 1978, was the next area to be dealt with. A Toronto woman by the name of Nancy McLean was recommended. She had done much of the work for Bill Davis's Big Blue Machine in Ontario and had worked extensively on Joe Clark's successful federal campaign. Her specialty was personal-image jobs. There was no doubt that after their success in contrasting Allan Blakeney and Dick Collver in 1978, the NDP would be trying a similar strategy with Grant Devine. We agreed to have videotapes of Nancy McLean's work sent out for us to view. When we saw it, particularly the personal touch on Bill Davis, we knew she was what we were looking for. We had her flown out and she impressed everyone with her professionalism. She understood immediately that her job would be to make the untested, untried, not that well-known Grant Devine appear to be the equal of the high profile, highly respected, and polished Allan Blakeney. No easy matter. But McLean had obviously faced these kinds of problems before and she was impressive as she outlined her plans. Had Dick Collver had someone like her in 1978, things could well have been different. We hired her at that meeting.

By now we were into early September and there had been no election called. The constitutional talks were still giving Roy Romanow and Allan Blakeney the opportunity to play the role of statesmen at a perceived monumental moment in history. I suppose every politician likes to think he or she is radically affecting the course the country will take. This certainly seemed to be on the minds of the members of the Trudeau government as almost everything became secondary to the resolution of the constitutional question. This lofty view of things was not shared by the ordinary Canadian citizen and certainly not by the average Saskatchewan resident. In this province the average voter had far more pressing problems on his mind. Interest rates were going out of sight and grain prices were taking a sharp decline. The combination of these two factors was politically volatile given the right touch.

The predictions for the provincial economy in 1982 were not good. The price of gasoline was climbing steadily—an issue the Liberals had used effectively to defeat the Clark government, only to let the price jump dramatically after the election; the real estate market was dropping; and the first signs of serious trouble in agriculture were appearing. Anyone who had a mortgage up for renewal was genuinely concerned. Regardless of when they called the election, the NDP were going to want to divert public attention from the difficulties in the economy to more philosophical matters such as leadership or federal-provincial confrontation. Our task was not to allow them to dictate the terms and pace of the campaign as they had done in 1978. Right at this time, we received reports of a provincewide survey with heavy political overtones. From the questions one could not guess which party was conducting it; however, it was not us and it was not likely to be the Liberals so it had to be the NDP having one last look before they pulled the plug. If only we could see the results.

Nancy McLean was a Tory but she was also well aware of our financial status. She was willing to go so far and then she wanted to be paid. One could hardly blame her. The cash position of the party was critical, yet we had to spend money we did not have. Will Klein of Pioneer Trust was a member of the campaign committee. He had turned down the position of chairman for business reasons; however, his presence opened some important doors for us in the financial world. Klein knew everyone because of his background with the Chamber of Commerce. He enjoyed a strong rapport with the provincial head of the Royal Bank, who had been a Conservative candidate in Winnipeg in the 1960s. Will Klein played a vital role in assisting Grant Devine to negotiate a $450,000 line of credit with the Royal Bank. We could never have gotten into the ball game without it. Once Grant Devine secured that line of credit we knew we could be tough in the election, particularly if we were fortunate enough not to have to fight it this fall.

Whether the election was this fall or next year—at this point we were certain it would be called as soon as the NDP got the results of their survey—we had to set the tone of the campaign and force them to react to us, not the other way around. We had seen how good they were when they had weeks to plan what they were going to do. It would be interesting to see just how good they were if they had to be spontaneous. I proposed that on day one of the campaign Devine announce the elimination of the provincial gas tax, which amounted to thirty cents per gallon. The gas tax is one of the most powerful taxes in the minds of voters. My father won an election in 1964 partially on the promise of the legal use of tax-free purple agricultural gasoline in farm half-tons. In the 1967 election one of his best campaign slogans was a bumper sticker proclaiming "I'm using purple gas." I believed that a reduction like this would be a simple and concise issue that anyone who owned a car would relate to easily. They would be able to see clearly exactly what it meant in dollars and cents. The NDP would have to react immediately. While they were calling us irresponsible and all the other adjectives that don't matter, we would be on to something else. The key was to be the first with a dramatic issue. The campaign committee bought my idea. The next important thing was to keep it quiet, because if the NDP got wind of it they would probably steal it from us—a tactic that was fair ball. I know my father always perused the minutes of NDP conventions for any good ideas. It was of paramount importance that no one be aware of the gas tax proposal until the writ was issued.

We were also discussing a mortgage interest reduction program proposed by Paul Rousseau. Interest rates were going through the ceiling in the fall of 1981 and mortgages at the rate of 20 percent were becoming more and more common. The NDP had made a vague attempt to address the situation by introducing a moratorium on mortgage payments for one year, but this had done nothing for anyone facing a renewal or even a new mortgage. Rousseau proposed we set a figure—12 percent was his choice—and the province would subsidize the difference to the actual rate. This one was an ideal issue to introduce with some fanfare while the NDP were calling us irresponsible for the gas tax. Again, it was one we would have to keep to ourselves or risk seeing it in the NDP platform. We were light years ahead of the pathetic excuse for a campaign we had waged in 1978. As we waited for the election writ, we were under no illusions about our prospects for winning, but we were going to muster a creditable campaign.

Throughout the summer, negotiations with Tony Wilson had continued for a property settlement with my ex-wife. While there was no doubt who was calling the shots, we had general agreement on the major points by fall. The Court of Appeal had said it would hear the case in November and both Wilson and I wished to avoid an appearance if at all possible. The framework was there for an agreement; however, the minor details were becoming frustrating. The nitpicking increased and as points verbally agreed on had to be rehashed I began to wonder what their game was. Wilson wanted to settle and had it been up to us, it could have been done quickly. I had hoped to have it all over before a fall election. My personal difficulties were behind me in Thunder Creek provided nothing new surfaced. I was now beginning to suspect that JoAnn was creating problems in order to raise something in the middle of an election campaign. Wilson said this was not the case and obliquely suggested that there might be others who did not want to see an agreement. This explained some things, and we continued to negotiate.

Politically in September of 1981 strange things were happening. There was no election call. In Saskatchewan there must be a lead time of twenty-eight days and as the days ticked by we were amazed and becoming paranoid. We could be had, there was no question of that. The NDP had conducted an extensive polling survey and it had to be telling them to go. All the economic indicators said the economy was in trouble and that it would be a long winter of unemployment and high interest rates. Yet there was no call.

By the first of October it was obvious there was not going to be a fall election. To have called one in November would have been to risk the perils of an early Saskatchewan winter, which no provincial government had ever done. Only the NDP strategists at the time know why the government did not go, but the decision must rank as one of the great mistakes in Saskatchewan politics. Unmistakably, they had us cold. They must have known about the discord in the party and bits and pieces of the Lake Kenosee meeting must have gotten back to them. Alan Blakeney had never stood higher and Grant Devine was still perceived as the parachute jumper who had blown an easy by-election not that long ago. True, they lacked an issue but with some preparatory work they could have maneuvered the constitutional talks to at least an excuse for seeking a mandate. But they didn't. Clearly, the opinion poll they took must not have given them what they were looking for. Then again, perhaps their election machine was not what it once was and just maybe we were overrating their capabilities. After all, many of their key people from other campaigns had moved on. I think it was a little of both. Time was to demonstrate conclusively that the NDP organization was not the machine it had been in the past, and the smooth-as-silk model of 1978 was to be an inept clunker in 1982.

In retrospect, I think the NDP must either have been unaware of the disrepair in the Conservative party in the fall of 1981, or if they were aware of it then they must not have taken it seriously. The Conservative caucus has never been short of what the press term "informed sources" and I find it difficult to believe that the NDP were in the dark. I have never seen the numbers of their survey in 1981, but we must have shown surprising strength. Of course, the lack of a concise issue may have played a role. Several times in the summer they had tried in vain to drum up the Crow rate issue and they were actively opposing proposed provisions in the constitution for control of provincial resources. The difficulty they were probably having was that most people could not have cared less about the constitution and were far more interested in their mortgage rates, operating loan rates, and the price of gasoline. They then must have concluded they needed an election budget to deal with the relevant concerns just prior to the dropping of a writ. Hindsight is twenty-twenty but it was a horrendous decision.

The NDP's decision to delay the provincial election took some pressure off me as far as concluding a property settlement with my ex-wife was concerned, although I did not want to go to court anymore than Tony Wilson did. It was time to call in a lawyer and have an agreement drawn up. Both sides informed the court we had a settlement and the court date was canceled. Talks broke down as verbal agreements were put to paper and it was not until just before Christmas of 1981 that Wilson and I settled again what had been agreed to a month ago. Our lawyer then went to work to satisfy the concerns of JoAnn's attorney.

As the legislature opened in the fall of 1981 we could smell a big win. We were determined to forget past differences and be a united caucus no matter what the issue. Most important, we were going to be supportive of Grant Devine. We didn't know the extent to which things had turned around, or indeed why, we just knew the fact there had been no election was good for us and bad for the NDP. It showed in the legislature. We were cocky and confident while the "reds" were sullen and defensive. They would react angrily to suggestions they were the western arm of the federal Liberals and we continued to score points by pointing out that they had been the deciding factor in bringing down the Clark government. As the economy tightened the slick NDP advertising campaign became counterproductive as more and more people made the comment, "I wish they would use that money to cut interest rates." As 1981 came to an end, there was little doubt the tide was turning—the question was, how far?

It did not take a degree in political science to figure that 1982 was to be an election year in Saskatchewan. We were looking at April, June, or October; with June the most likely, but April if they got an issue or if the polls were right. Obviously we had to gear ourselves to April. In early January, Will Klein of Pioneer Trust told Devine his company was doing a provincewide survey to acquire data for a project. They offered to include pertinent political questions that would give us some indication of the mood of the electorate, their view of both the NDP and us, and what the most important underlying issues were. It was like a gift from heaven. Even though we now had a line of credit, money was spent cautiously and a survey of this breadth would have been highly costly. After the results were in there was a stampede of fair-weather friends so transparent you could not see their reflections in a mirror, but Will Klein and Pioneer Trust were up-front, genuine allies and the party owed them. We would not have made it without them and the line of credit from the Royal Bank.

The results of the survey conducted by Pioneer Trust confirmed our suspicions. We were only 2 percentage points behind the NDP in the decided vote, with over 35 percent undecided. The economy was front and center in the minds of the electorate and they were not giving much thought to abstracts such as the constitution and families of Crown corporations. Allan Blakeney scored high marks as leader even from those who were not going to vote NDP; however, a whopping 68 percent felt the NDP as a party had lost touch with the people. There is no such thing as an easy win over the NDP, but what the poll told us overall was that a change was in the making. The "reds" were vulnerable on the economy and if we met the voters' concerns, we could pull off the upset. It was not a matter of people flocking to us—they were on the verge of leaving the NDP and the rest was up to us.

In mid-February I signed an agreement with my ex-wife that ended all actions between us. It was a relief to everyone, particularly to the lawyer who acted as our intermediary, whose suave professionalism had been severely tested. Neither of us was completely happy with the agreement but we could both live with it, which, I guess, is what hard bargaining is all about. I had eliminated the possibility of a surprise in the middle of an election campaign. My constituency of Thunder Creek had been most tolerant of my personal problems but I did not care to push it any further. If an opposing candidate attempted to use my personal problems against me, I expected a backlash in my favor; however, when in trouble, the NDP know the art of gutter politics better than anyone and there was now little doubt they were in trouble.

The Conservative nomination in Thunder Creek was another matter. The Swenson family were still bitter and only surfaced at the odd meeting to attempt to cause a problem. The procedure was to listen politely to their complaints and then ignore them. They still had a small core of supporters who were not enthused with me, whom they could undoubtedly muster at a nomination, but I would not have any problem provided I kept my head up. I expected Swenson to try something but it did not appear he was going to run himself. The name I was hearing was that of Don Hill, whom I did not know personally despite the fact that he lived within a few miles of my ranch. This was fine with me because a contested nomination is the way to go on the eve of an election—any politician will tell you that. When a nomination is contested it means lots of memberships are sold, your organization gets a dry run, and as a result is in fighting trim for the election to follow. It also forces the candidate to get out and get some things done that have to be done anyway. I have always enjoyed nominations in Thunder Creek --my president Lyal Stewart referred to them as "spectator sports"—because they made subsequent campaigns relatively simple. I had only one concern this time around. I did not want my personal problems to be recounted off a podium by a Conservative. By an NDP or Liberal I could not have cared less, but not by another Tory.

The legislature reconvened in early 1982 and we all knew it would be a short session that would end with the bringing down of a budget. No doubt the NDP were again running a survey to identify the points of concern, which they would make pretense of dealing with in a budget before calling an election. The economy had worsened since last fall, when they had seriously considered going, and undoubtedly there were words of recrimination in their caucus. With the knowledge we were even for practical purposes, we deliberately became very aggressive and were constantly needling them to call an election. It was a war of nerves and it was bothering them. They were looking at the same numbers we were; they were scared and not disguising it very well. When any kind of vote was held, as the NDP members were polled we would sing "bye-bye" to them.

The session had brought Dick Collver back from Arizona. He, of course, had no intention of running again. His party, which advocated union with the United States, had, at best, been an ego saver for Collver, who had wanted to collect his MLA's salary and allowance yet not suffer the indignity of being an ordinary MLA in a Conservative party he viewed as his personal property. I had again spent New Year's Eve at the Collver ranch in Arizona.

Collver had organized a New Year's Eve reunion of sorts for his original staff going back to pre-1975 days, and I had been invited only because of the proximity of Palm Springs. I had not planned to attend but my son Greg had been invited to a New Year's Eve party in Phoenix and as the logistics of getting him back to Palm Springs were going to be complicated I had arranged to meet him in Wickenburg. I was starting to feel old. One son had been invited to a swish New Year's Eve party in Palm Springs and the other was going to one in Phoenix.

The gathering of the old clan at Wickenburg somehow became a topic of interest in Regina and *Leader-Post* columnist Dale Eisler ran a lead editorial on it. My name was not mentioned. When I arrived early New Year's Eve Dave Tkachuk and only one other member of the old staff had shown up. By now Tkachuk was in charge of Bill Bennett's riding in British Columbia but it was clear he missed Saskatchewan. Dick passed out early and Tkachuk and I talked politics most of the evening. He told me that if the party wished, Bill Bennett would loan him to us for an election. Organizers with expertise were what we desperately needed and it had been worth the trip over for that information. Greg arrived early the next morning and we left for Palm Springs, after Dick Collver, in a terribly hungover state, sold me a golf cart from the factory he owned in Phoenix. Devine was paranoid about Collver and I was hesitant to tell him about my visit—the paranoia was the reason the other expected guests had not arrived; however, I did suggest he contact Bill Bennett. When an election was called Bennett sent us Dave Tkachuk and two additional organizers who knew what they were doing. There was nothing improper about this at all. The socialists support each other vigorously; the anti-socialists had better learn to do so too.

I could see an April general election looming so it was time to nominate a candidate in Thunder Creek. The executive selected a date and from the start the dissident group was up to something. Apparently, they had planned to get 100 people quietly to the convention without my knowledge. They only succeeded in getting 80 and with 350 voting delegates it was by no means a large convention. I don't know where the press got the information that it was close. Bitter yes, but not close.

In the meantime, a different sort of a movement was gaining momentum in Alberta. In a by-election in High River a candidate of a party advocating separation from the rest of Canada won a narrow victory over the established parties. It is not my intention to go into the reasons why it was possible for that to happen. Suffice it to say that the electorate will do things in by-elections they would never do in a general election, especially when the fate of the government is not in jeopardy. Western separatism is as old as Confederation. A most compelling case can be made for the argument this continent should have been divided north-south rather than east-west. There is little doubt western Canada would be considerably better off economically separate and apart from central Canada. You do not need to have a Ph.D. in economics to figure out that when you sell on a world open market but must buy on a tariff-protected market, then your standard of living is suffering. In other words, if we were to buy our cars and televisions the same way we sell our wheat, potash, and oil—on a worldwide, best-price-available basis—we would have little reason to be part of this country.

It is a regrettable fact that for the last twenty years "made in Canada" has signified inferior, higher priced goods. If we were a developing country today I suggest there is no way Canada would emerge as presently structured. For the West, eastern Canada is nothing more than a place to send our taxes, while in return we are a cheap source of raw materials and a captive market for their finished goods. However, regardless of the accuracy of these statements, there is simply no way the West will ever separate and the reasons are probably similar to the reasons why the PQ were unsuccessful in their cause in Quebec— a fear of the unknown. The old-age pensioner fears his pension will be lost and you can explain until the cows come home that it will just come from Calgary or Vancouver instead of Ottawa; he is not going to take the chance. The same is true for those on unemployment. We have become so dependent on government in this country that any change affects far too large a proportion of the population. In political terms, "Separatism is the political wilderness."

The Western Canada Concept, or WCC, was a source of real concern to the Conservative party because most of the organizers were our people and we had far too many supporters poised to join them if they showed any sign of credibility. While no one wanted to see another party to split the anti-NDP vote, there was a great deal of sympathy for their aims and undoubtedly they had the capacity to hurt us badly.

Our survey, which had been conducted courtesy of Pioneer Trust, had not been geared to tell us very much about the WCC. Although the leaders were mostly right-wing Tories, there was evidence the WCC was crossing party lines in a very strange fashion and neither we nor the NDP knew exactly what the pattern was. Actually, many of those involved in the WCC were having economic difficulties and had joined the party to strike out at the system they held responsible for their problems. There is little doubt the WCC evoked a sympathetic response in a large proportion of the electorate and had a charismatic leader emerged at this time who knows how much support they might have garnered. However, they did not have the expertise to translate this sympathy into votes and they proceeded to be caught in the classic squeeze play.

In March of 1982, the NDP government brought in a budget that was not worth the paper it was written on. I can say that with certainty because I was to become part of the government that would operate for many months under its guidelines. It was a document that greatly inflated projected revenues—particularly in the area of personal income tax—and grossly underestimated expenditures. It projected a very modest surplus, which was the biggest fantasy of all. The "reds" had done their homework and they had identified many of the concerns uppermost in the minds of the electorate. I was surprised at the low-key manner in which they chose to deal with them, however. There was some help for people facing problems renewing their mortgages but it was hardly high-powered election material.

At about this time the Saskatchewan Government Employees' Union was threatening a strike. The leadership of the union was being openly challenged and the head of the SGEU badly needed a win to survive. He believed he saw his chance on the eve of an election. The NDP were in a difficult position. The last thing they wanted was to be perceived as knuckling under to a union when the economy was in chaos around them, neither did they want a public service strike during the thirty-some days of an election campaign that was no doubt going to center on the administrative skills of Allan Blakeney. If a politician wishes to enrage organized labor, he just has to hint at prohibiting the right to strike. I have advocated eliminating the right to strike for public servants many times, so often in fact that the unions don't even get mad any longer. But when an NDP government does it—even on a limited scale—it is a different story. As Roy Romanow introduced the back-to-work legislation the galleries were full and the watchword was betrayal.

I had a field day with Romanow in the committee stages of his bill. To packed galleries of upset labor leaders and supporters I tore into the NDP for doublecrossing those who had trusted them for so long simply in order to avoid a difficult situation at election time. The applause was so loud and raucous that at one point the Speaker threatened to empty the galleries. The NDP hated it and it showed. The soft hisses that greeted Roy as he got to his feet to respond unnerved him momentarily, but he quickly recovered. The adrenalin was flowing as he came back with a tirade in which he said that he didn't need lectures from someone who would take away the right to strike and had opposed all the progressive labor legislation introduced by his government. He was really worked up and was now talking only to the galleries. He attacked the shortsightedness of the labor movement in looking on a Conservative like me as a friend when his party had shown for forty years who was labor's real ally. It was vintage Romanow and the last time I would see him speak. We passed the bill and went home for the weekend expecting to be on the campaign trail on Monday. We were.

That Saturday evening, at his own nominating convention, Allan Blakeney called a general election in Saskatchewan for April 26. We were ready and the news conference for Grant

Devine to announce the proposed elimination of the gas sales tax was called. In the excitement, there was a minor error in mathematics: the amount of tax was $.29 but it came out as $.40. No problem. It was the thought that counted anyway. Bill McKnight was to prove a superb choice as campaign chairman. He could digest information from the candidates and relate it into the campaign, and he seemed to be able to handle Devine so that the information coming in was used in one form or another almost immediately.

As expected, the NDP reacted strongly to the elimination of the gas tax. They were clearly stung by it and the name calling started right away. But by the time they got around to pointing out the grade three error in mathematics, Devine had held another press conference to announce the mortgage reduction plan, in which all home mortgages would be subsidized down to 13¼ percent regardless of term. The vaunted NDP election machine of 1978 was now nowhere to be seen. Allan Blakeney was no longer the cool, precise administrator, instead he was coming across as uncertain, stumbling, and scrambly. The NDP should have recognized the strategy. After all, they had shown it to us in 1978.

In Thunder Creek it was a breeze. At first I ran into some support for the WCC but they faded after the first ten to twelve days of the campaign. However, I had been around politics too long to take anything for granted and the only way I know how to campaign is hard. At the halfway point of the campaign Devine struck again with the promise of a one-time loan to farmers of $350,000 at 8 percent. With high interest rates ravaging the farm economy the NDP recoiled once more. They were managing to be as bad in 1982 as they had been good in 1978. They began to fight back by making outlandish promises and their credibility dropped every day as their campaign people simply were not able to adjust. In contrast, Bill McKnight had our machine purring and he kept a tight rein on Devine to avoid the misstatement that could turn things back to the NDP. It was over with a week still to go. We had a rally in the Centre of the Arts in Regina that was overwhelming by any standards. The chant "Devine, Devine" seemed to take over all of Regina. It was only a question of how big the win would be.

The NDP seemed to be out of touch with reality. Two days

after our enormous rally in Regina Allan Blakeney wasted the best part of a day in Thunder Creek instead of spending the time somewhere where he could have been of some use. His action typified the type of campaign they had started when they alienated labor on the eve of dropping the writ. The premier had been dogged by placard-waving demonstrators for most of the campaign in protest against the anti-strike legislation and it is doubtful they got the percentage of the labor vote to which they had become accustomed. The NDP machine was in a daze for twenty-eight days.

We went into that campaign with thirty-six seats targeted, with forty-two viewed as the maximum if everything was perfect. Election night saw a majority of fifty-six Conservatives elected to nine NDP. The result was beyond our wildest projections and expectations. We took seats that had never been anything but NDP for forty-five years. Even Attorney General Roy Romanow lost to an unknown former gas-pump jockey who had been the only person willing to run against him. Grant Devine had a mandate unparalleled in Saskatchewan political history. Much will be written in the future on the collapse of the NDP; I do not know what happened but all of a sudden people decided the difficult economy was their doing. Had they gone to the people six months earlier the result could and would have been reversed.

I had mixed feelings on election night. On the one hand, I was ecstatic at my personal high of 61 percent of the popular vote in Thunder Creek and thrilled at finally being part of a government. On the other hand, now that the NDP had been decimated I felt I had nothing left to do in politics and for a time I even considered announcing my retirement at campaign headquarters. I probably should have.

9

Taking Power

In Thunder Creek we do know how to have a party. Our campaign headquarters were jammed to overflowing with supporters. We had a bar downstairs and soon the party had spread onto Main Street. The Moose Jaw City Police must have voted Conservative that day because they were very tolerant until the early morning hours. I recall my next day being a very tough one. Most of it was spent sleeping off the aftereffects of the celebration in my hayloft. I wasn't sure whether I had announced my retirement or not.

Within a few days, a caucus was held in Regina. Despite the huge number of MLAs there was not an abundance of talent. What a contrast to my first caucus as a Liberal years earlier. Every one of those fifteen Liberals would have stood out like a neon light in this crowd of shuffling, jockeying, egotistical amateurs. Eric Berntson and Bob Andrew had been chosen to be the transition team as the Conservative party prepared to assume the reins of government.

After the meeting Devine asked to see me in his office. It was widely assumed I would be the new minister of agriculture; however, my relationship with Devine ranged from frigid to chilly and he now had fifty-six MLAs to choose from. I would not have been surprised had he passed me over, nor would I really have cared. He asked me a few general questions about how my father had proceeded initially, some of which I could answer and some of which I couldn't. We then went on to discuss the cabinet. I suggested he form a cabinet from those he felt could run a department and leave the geographic appointments until next year. Despite my assurances that I would be happy on the back benches he told me they were going to use me and, although he certainly was not specific, I left the meeting with the impression that the cabinet post was agriculture with Sask Tel the Crown.

Three days later my phone rang at 7:30 A.M. and Grant Devine told me he was appointing me the minister of a new department of energy. I was genuinely disappointed and my reaction was negative. Devine said I would be the number three man and I should think it over. I said that I had pretty well decided to decline with thanks but I would call him by noon. On my way out to the ranch I met one of my constituents who asked when I was being named minister of agriculture. I said I was not and would not be part of the cabinet. His reply was, "You take whatever is offered. We've supported you long enough that you owe us a cabinet post." He was right. When I got to the ranch there was a message to call Gary Lane. He was aware of Devine's offer and he came on the line with, "You stupid SOB. You've got two billion dollars to spend in the next four years and you are turning that down!" He had a point too.

I spent the rest of the morning looking at cows with their newborn calves. I had a bad feeling about going to work for Grant Devine. I didn't respect him as a leader and he did not like me personally, which was probably mostly my fault. I had premonitions of a very unhappy experience coming up and I had seen all of those I needed for a while. It would have been much easier if he had passed me over but the lack of available talent had probably forced him to include me. I knew nothing about the portfolio I had been offered nor did I have any great inclination to learn. Agriculture was what I knew inside out but no doubt they were afraid of my right-wing views. I got involved in helping a heifer calve and didn't call Grant Devine until mid-afternoon. When he said his plans still included me, I thanked him for the honor and promised to do the best job I could.

The first thing I did that evening was contact my campaign manager, Chuck Guillaume, and ask him to come to Regina as my executive assistant. I needed someone I could trust to ferret the "reds" out of the department and the Crowns I would be in charge of. I did not want a witch-hunt, but at the same time I was not going to be sandbagged by political appointees from the NDP arsenal of hacks. I wanted the personnel files scrutinized thoroughly and quickly and I would deal with the results. Chuck agreed. I spent the morning at my ranch wondering what an unsworn cabinet minister does the days before he is officially sworn in. I phoned the three Crowns—Saskoil, the Saskatchewan Mining and Development Corporation, and Sask Minerals—and told them I would be their new minister. I arranged to meet with them the following week and told them to bring letters of dismissal for the boards of each corporation for my signature. I was not yet sworn in and I had fired the boards of three Crowns. That was enough for the moment.

The swearing-in ceremony was held the next day at 11:00 A.M. in front of the legislative buildings. It was very ably handled by one of Allan Blakeney's former aides. We let him go later but compared to the clown we brought in to replace him, I have often wondered at the wisdom of that decision. The climax of the ceremony was Premier Grant Devine declaring as his first duty the removal of the gasoline sales tax effective midnight. It was a great start. After the swearing-in I met a secretary who had worked for one of the NDP cabinet ministers. I knew her well and in fact had often quizzed her for any potentially useful information to no avail whatsoever. That kind of closemouthedness appealed to me so I told her to come in on Monday and organize my new office. The office I had arranged to take over was Elwood Cowley's, down in the bowels of the legislature. I was sure Elwood would have left me a bottle of scotch but he must have forgotten. I still had the feeling that the thrill of the day was going to be shortlived.

Monday morning the reins of government were in the hands
of the new premier, Grant Devine. The initial cabinet numbered
sixteen, of which twelve were serious portfolios. Monday afternoon we had our first meeting with two strangers on the new
premier's left. One of them was a defeated federal candidate
named Terry Leier who was notorious in Regina because of
non-payment of taxes on his residential home when he was the
city solicitor. He opened the meeting with a lecture to the new
ministers on protocol and the proper manner in which to conduct a cabinet meeting. This amateur had never been to a cabinet meeting in his life and he was explaining procedures to us
as though he were some form of expert. The other person was
an individual by the name of Derek Bedson who had found his
way here from the Sterling Lyon government via Ontario. To
this day I am unclear of the function he was supposed to have
served. Upon the defeat of the Lyon government, he had somehow landed a position in Toronto at a high salary. When they
woke up, they unloaded him on the unsuspecting new government in Saskatchewan at $85,000 per year. He started out as
cabinet secretary but he was later sent to Vienna where it was
cheaper to open a new office for him than buy him out of his
ironclad contract. Both Leier and Bedson typified what I saw as
Devine's tendency to surround himself with unqualified staff
and then expect very little from them. It was a trait I could
never understand.

Devine laid down the ground rules. He intended to give all
cabinet ministers wide powers of discretion, although he
expected major decisions to go across his desk. He emphasized
this did not mean he wanted to run all departments from his
office but rather he wanted to be informed at all times of what
his government was doing. We were free to select our own
executive assistants but again he wanted to be kept informed.
He described a quick code of conduct that was mostly common
sense. Certainly, what he was saying made sense and was the
way to run a government. However, Grant Devine always
found talk much easier than performance.

You would not believe the deluge of mail, resumes, phone
calls, and whatever else comes to a new government. A new
government means a new order, new contracts, new jobs, and
new programs. My secretary was carrying the stuff in by the

armload saying she had just carried it out as the NDP left power and now she was returning with a fresh batch. If I was getting this volume I could just imagine what the premier was receiving. I hated even to think about it. There were overtures from consultants who were offering to turn anything and everything around, advertising agencies, travel agencies, and enough resumes to fill a room.

Our procedure was to send all resumes up to the office of the transition team, who were to catalog and evaluate them for the different departments. From the point of view of recruitment of quality people for the departments or the Crowns, I thought the transition office was a dead loss. It was annoying when someone I had never heard of before from up there would come down with a potential executive assistant I was expected to hire. I would hit the roof and verbally throw them out of my office. My attitude was that I was accountable for what came out of the department and the Crown corporations so I would make the decisions as to who went in or out. The word spread to stay away from my office and department, and it was also logged that I was uncooperative.

Our first piece of government business was to make one Gary Lane a Queen's Counsel. When I saw the item on the agenda I thought it was a joke. I whispered to Lane, who was sitting next to me, "Has this guy been cleared by the transition team?" He saw no humor in the question. It stands as a monument to political impartiality that Lane awarded this title to himself as the first act of the new cabinet. We were off and running.

I had been a minister for only a few days when Jack Messer, one of my predecessors, took me out for lunch. He said once I was organized, one or two days a week should suffice to keep the office in order. If it took any more time than that then I was not running my department properly. The cardinal sin, he said, was to take work home because then you were a captive of the bureaucracy. That evening I left the buildings with only my car keys. I met Bob Andrew at the door with flow charts, computer printouts, just totally burdened down with documents of all sorts. The bureaucrats really got him good right off the bat.

Eric Berntson, the new minister of agriculture, was no longer the jovial, friendly, and effervescent person of opposition days.

He had withdrawn into himself and there was no question Devine trusted him implicitly. In many respects it appeared Eric was really running the government. Devine and Berntson had a direct hookup from office to office that bypassed both of their secretaries. When I asked Eric why they felt such intimacy was necessary, he denied the connection. His vocabulary remained as foulmouthed as ever but there was a sharp diminishment in his sense of humor. He was obviously doing far too much as evidenced by the disastrous state of the department of agriculture.

I saw very little of Eric Berntson excluding cabinet meetings. He knew I thought he was doing a terrible job at agriculture and I told him on numerous occasions we would one day pay for the poor-quality staff he had chosen. I was told by other ministers that Eric was drinking heavily, although he had always been able to put away a huge volume as long as I had known him and when he wanted to he could always go on the wagon with ease. His tight relationship with Grant Devine was an enigma to all who looked on from the outside—the outside being anyone not in the Andrew-Berntson-Devine trio. Devine never used improper language, in contrast to the foulmouthed Berntson; Devine was always immaculately dressed, whereas Berntson was more often than not a slob; Devine was suave, urbane, and had trouble having a good time anywhere, which was the antithesis of the fun-loving, ebullient Berntson, who, after a few drinks, would take on the world.

The first big personnel decision I had to make was to appoint a deputy minister. By now I had undergone a thorough briefing by the present deputy, Don Moroz. I was impressed with him and he knew it. I was being pressured to give the go-ahead to fire him because of his connection with the NDP government but he was just too bright and talented to be let go and as time went on I was never really to know what his political leanings were. There was no obvious alternative and I feared a change would leave me open to the possibility of having to accept a patronage choice to head a very complex department. Moroz was the invisible bureaucrat extraordinary. He could have worked equally effectively with Attila the Hun or Lenin. I was teased forever after about my "red" deputy; however, if the same criteria that were applied to Don Moroz were used to fire some of the senior civil servants, then we lost some very able people on misinformation. I knew from my father's experience that you cannot handle the bureaucracy unless you understand it, and I did not. Nor did I want to. It was easier to handle the bureaucracy by means of a bureaucrat, and Don Moroz was one who understood the process as well as the politics involved.

The lineup at the political trough was incredible. People I had never heard of were writing and phoning as though they had always been there. New staff were appearing out of thin air bringing down resumes of people they wanted hired. By now most ministers had two or three executive assistants and one even had six. I was still operating with one secretary and one executive assistant. I was naive enough to believe that cabinet ministers are judged on merit. This was a mistake. If it had been that important for me to be a minister, then I should have gone along with the hacks from the transition office and placed the other hacks wherever they wanted. I should have coasted, that is to say initiated nothing, and merely shown up in body to each cabinet and caucus meeting and not have been concerned with any level of contribution. That was what was really wanted from the cabinet. They could not have cared less about performance. All that mattered was that "hardball politics" were played, which meant salaries that boggled the mind and favors to people I was never aware supported the party before.

The huge majority we enjoyed only compounded the problems the new government was experiencing. Grant Devine, to his credit, has always given priority to granting time to his MLAs and listens patiently to their concerns and problems; however, there were almost forty MLAs who had no role to play, and, of course, they were all upset they were not in the cabinet. Some took to prowling the corridors for almost any dirt they could run to the premier with. He was to tell me once, "If you are going to spend the day at your ranch then don't give that information out. I hear about it before you get there." My deputy, Don Moroz, commented once, "It's never the big stuff that gets you, it's the little things that will bring you down." None of us realized Moroz was a prophet.

My first minor personnel problem arose when I instructed Don Moroz to replace a member of my department. When Moroz informed him of the decision to terminate his employment, he sought legal advice and was advised to stay at his desk, which he did. He was now into his second week and I was advised it was having a disruptive effect on the staff. I told Moroz to get him out but he refused to take Moroz's dismissal as effective notice. I turned the matter over to Derek Bedson, clerk of the executive council, who had earned the title of the Lord High Executioner in Manitoba because of his method of dealing with the public service. Several days later, a letter was brought to me for signature which was the notice that the man's employment was terminated. I phoned Bedson and said, "I could have done it this way long ago. Is this the best you can do?" "Sign it, dear boy, and there will be no problems," answered the voice at the other end. The taxpayers were paying $85,000 for this, while those in Ontario who had foisted him onto us were probably still laughing. I signed the letter and never went near him again. The employee in question left upon receipt of the letter.

I would not care to be dismissed myself and I found no joy in the thought of creating discomfort for other people and their families. However, it is the political way and those who go that route for employment have no right to expect clemency from the new party. Why should they? Their jobs in many cases were opened only by dismissing someone else and so the cycle goes on. The cost of settlements to dismissed employees is enormous. When the NDP won in Manitoba they made some extremely high settlements and our lawyers advised us we were now stuck with the Manitoba precedents and there was little point in fighting our employees' claims in court.

As I assumed the portfolio of energy and mines the two priorities facing me were to deliver on the highly publicized heavy oil upgrader and regenerate an industry that had all but abandoned the province because of the repressive policies of the NDP. My job was doubly difficult because the National Energy Policy gave the federal government a hand on the throat of the oil industry under the guise of "what is good for all Canadians" and countermeasures taken by industrialized countries to recent high oil prices had led to a glut on the world market.

Of the three Crowns I had under me, Saskoil gave me the most concern. I had been pleasantly surprised by the efficiency and businesslike attitude of SMDC, and Sask Minerals at Chaplin was small by comparison and was showing a profit. Saskoil was a disaster and an example of government in a business it should not have been in. When Saskoil was placed under me, I assumed my mandate was to whip it into shape and sell it. As Saskoil stood right now, probably little more than 30 percent of invested equity could be recaptured under existing marketing conditions. We had to put it in shape first and then get it on the market.

The president of Saskoil was a likeable individual named Frank Sadler whose background went back to Gulf Oil. I wondered at the start if he was the right person in the job but I decided to sit tight and give him a chance to perform. I told him I had no intention of interfering in day-to-day corporate affairs but Saskoil's honeymoon with the provincial treasury was over and they were going to pay their bills with what came in and they should adjust accordingly. He told me Saskoil anticipated a shortfall of $14 million for that operating year based on present conditions. I suggested they better start cutting costs because if their checks were to bounce I would leave them hanging there. I thought he was going to get ill at that one. Already I had in the back of my mind something drastic for Saskoil, but I wasn't sure what. In the meantime I changed their law firm to MacPherson, Leslie & Tyerman so I would have a better idea of their status when I wanted it.

When I was appointed minister, it was widely assumed by the press that I would be in conflict with the federal energy minister, Marc Lalonde. The National Energy Policy was an undisguised move by Ottawa to bring the western provincial governments to their knees on the resource question. Clearly the target was oil-rich Alberta, and Saskatchewan, although caught up in the conflict, was inconsequential to the federal government. Any attempt to throw our weight around on our own was going to meet with laughter. The decline of the oil industry in Canada was now dawning on the eastern mandarins who were the architects of the NEP and there were signs the program was under reevaluation. I told Don Moroz to quietly inform his counterparts in Ottawa we were under no illusions as to our role and it was our intention to avoid any kind of confrontation. Officially we were to take similar positions to

Alberta. Whatever was good for Alberta was good for us and we had little choice but to let them carry the mail. Our heavy oil upgrader was of no interest to Alberta, but it was out of the question for Saskatchewan without the full support of the federal government. Obviously we had few cards to get heavy with.

The heavy oil upgrader planned for Archydale, in Thunder Creek, was to be a billion-dollar facility capable of refining Saskatchewan crude. Of the consortium of Saskoil, Shell, Gulf, Petro-Canada, and Husky, the project operator was Husky Oil of Calgary, a division of Nova Corporation. Nova was a quasi-government/quasi-private company under the chairmanship of Bob Blair, who, judging from his press clippings, was a dynamic, flamboyant, jet set businessman. His son-in-law, Art Price, was representing Husky and I wanted to talk to him off the record as soon as possible. I was in no position to evaluate the economic worth of the upgrader without a great deal more study and briefing by experts, but the politics I had inherited were tricky.

Art Price was not what I expected at all. He was young, goodlooking, and bright. He spoke cautiously in broad generalities and was obviously as interested in getting a reading on me as I was in getting a reading on him. When I asked him point blank if the Archydale project was viable from his company's point of view he answered in the affirmative without hesitation. However, in the course of our brief meeting it became obvious that very little had actually been done. I was left with an uneasy feeling about the project and decided to meet with the entire consortium immediately.

I arranged for Grant Devine to drop in on the consortium meeting as a symbol of the government's commitment to the project. I was truly hopeful that it would be possible to build the upgrader, but I was getting bad vibes. The Archydale site was not far from my farm and I knew it well. In a year that had any snow, it was a slough. It was a strange choice for the site of an upgrader but that was not my decision nor had I seen the factors leading up to the choice. At the meeting it transpired that little research had been done into the economics of the upgrader and the involvement of the federal government, which was essential, was vague. Yet strangely a contractor had been named for the project—a project that was still only in its conceptual stages—and the president of the company chosen was a well-known bagman for the federal Liberals.

After that meeting, I reported my views to Grant Devine, which were simply that the Archydale project would never go based on what I had seen so far. The NDP government had run a scam. They had foisted a site on the consortium for a project that was mostly fantasyland, but one on which I was expected to deliver. I told Devine I was going out to seek an alternative to the existing consortium in the probable event the present consortium would fail. He agreed and reemphasized we were going to need a megaproject to create employment in the next decade and he wanted all the stops pulled out to get one.

I was rapidly coming to dislike Husky Oil and their tactics. It must have shown because quite soon Bob Blair and Bob Pierce, who had moved into the upper echelons of Nova Corporation after leaving Regina, came down from Calgary. Bob Blair was an executive who had created a mystique around himself. He was an active Liberal and was mentioned as a possible leadership candidate when Pierre Elliott Trudeau stepped down. I was more than interested in meeting this corporate jet-setter who had done so well in Alberta. He was not at all what I expected. He was low key, very casually dressed, and spoke with an inflection that I could not quite place. It was not Irish or Scotch but somewhere in between. He was by no means the dominant person in the room but he was certainly a man in charge of his own people. After the usual fencing was over I was quizzed by Blair and Pierce about my personal views on the project. I confessed to not possessing enough information to have any definite ones, which meant I had doubts. Blair then asked, in the most casual of manners, if the government of Saskatchewan would be willing to look at an alternative proposed by Husky. I was inwardly stunned because this was serious. There were no officials present only Blair, Pierce, and Art Price. It confirmed my worst suspicions. The Archydale project had never been in the real world and now the project operator and the largest member of the consortium was saying in effect, "We want out to do something else." Something else had to be Lloydminster, where Husky already had a facility and the bulk of its wells. The answer to Blair's question had to be yes, and they knew it.

They had us in a box and they knew how to play the political game with the best. Blair had not made his reputation by playing in the minor leagues. The NEP had driven many of the American major league players out of Canada and the federal government's Foreign Investment Review Agency—FIRA—was going to keep them out. When you are looking at billion-dollar projects then you need the major leagues. However, when the major leagues are not allowed in your ball park then you have problems. Caron seemed like it was light years away about then. Husky knew the politics of the upgrader better than we did and fully understood the political ramifications for us if we failed to deliver. They knew they could be tough and push us a long way because we had very few options available. They were the largest heavy oil producers in the province, concentrated mainly in the Lloydminster area. It did not take a great deal of foresight to predict a proposal from Husky for a heavy oil upgrader for Lloydminster in which the federal and provincial governments would put up most of the money and take the bulk of the risk. I couldn't just wait for it. I desperately needed somebody in whom I had confidence to quickly specialize in the heavy oil project. I called Moroz and told him to hurry up—things were happening.

Things certainly change in the way you think and react the longer you are in government. I had liked the ground rules laid down by Grant Devine. To give your ministers a fair amount of latitude, yet expect them to keep you informed and to consult you on the issues of the day was the proper way to administrate in my view. At the start, I took Devine seriously and sent him regular memos either inviting his comments on, or if necessary requesting his approval for, my actions. I soon learned that sending a memo to the premier's office was tantamount to sending it to a dead letter office—there was never a reply. On pressing matters, Devine was good at granting appointments at short notice, but it was impossible to get a decision from him in such situations. From necessity, many ministers, including me, began to minimize the material going to the premier's office and to make many decisions on the spot. It was either do that or do nothing. Politically, the smart thing was to do nothing; however, I was still operating on the foolish notion that someone cared whether you did a good job or a bad one.

The level of our cabinet meetings left a great deal to be desired. The little political games were uppermost and everything would grind to a halt if someone was hired without first being approved by the transition office. At one meeting early in the term, whether a political bloodtest had been done on a girl being hired as clerk II typist got more attention than whether the government of Saskatchewan would proceed on the Nipawin power project of the Saskatchewan Power Corporation. Granted it takes time for a new government to find itself, but a malaise was quickly setting in. The watchword of the government became, "Do nothing while we think about it."

The question of the Crown corporations is a case in point. We had inherited twenty-six Crowns, of which few could be classified as essential utilities. No one in his right mind wanted to sell SGI, or Sask Tel, or Sask Power, or even some of the middle-level Crowns, but all of us wanted to sell some. Our people were demanding it and, more important, we did not need them and the revenue from a sale would have been more than welcome. When I advocated dismantling Saskoil—it did not enjoy any appreciable public support and had a horrible track record—cabinet decided to set up a commission to investigate the role of Crown corporations to be chaired by a Regina accountant who, according to Bob Andrew, would bring down whatever we wanted him to. Devine wanted us to be perceived as taking action but he did not want to do anything hasty. The report was to be merely an excuse for putting off some decisions. I was dumb enough to ask why we didn't just do what we were going to right away rather than play the silly games of a rubberstamp inquiry. Bob Andrew was adamant this was the smart way to go politically because we would now get an independent report advising us to do exactly what we wanted to do and it would appear as though we were listening before acting.

I had invited dialogue with the oil industry and asked them to give us their views on what it would take to revive activity in the province. In the first half of 1982 drillings had been a disaster and the service people, based mostly in Estevan and Swift Current, were literally starving. I made myself and officials available to anyone who had something to say—big or small, private or Crown. We had some excellent presentations and ideas from the industry, the most innovative of which came from Norcean Oil, who suggested a royalty-free, three-year tax holiday on new drillings. As the president of Norcean put it, "You will not lose any revenue because you are not getting any now." That about summed it up and I instructed my department to crunch out some numbers for a proposal. The whole exercise had succeeded in establishing a rapport between the department and those who made the industry tick.

A shrewd and experienced deputy like Don Moroz was essential in transforming the royalty rates in the oil industry. He told me that changes were impossible, regardless of how compelling the case might be, without the cooperation of the all-powerful minister of finance. He suggested I deal with Bob Andrew personally while he would keep the finance bureaucrats informed. We were talking a great deal of money, money we did not have. By now we were all aware of the extent to which the NDP had underestimated expenditures and overrated revenues in their budget and I was now going to try to convince my colleagues we should drastically lower our royalty rates to stimulate a depressed industry. Moroz could get us through the bureaucracy, but I had to get it through the political route. It was not going to be easy and I was giving them a ready-made excuse to fire me if it didn't work out.

Bob Andrew was quiet, articulate, and labeled a "red Tory" —an assessment I never agreed with. He was our version of Elwood Cowley—he ate, slept, and thought politics continually. At the start of our term, Bob Andrew was far and away the most stable part of the government. I viewed him as a captive of his own department but others saw this as an asset. He took hold of the most important department in government and very quickly established himself as the man in charge. He preached fiscal restraint and coupled it with political realities. He kept the bulk of his department intact from the NDP days; however, there was very little doubt he had some capable people. Bob Andrew was smart enough to know talent when he saw it and astute enough to know the proper use of talent makes a minister look good. Part of being smart is knowing your own limitations, and Bob knew his and was adept at keeping others from similar knowledge. He had been one of Devine's original supporters and he had remained loyal at the Kenosee Lake gathering. He enjoyed the complete confidence of the premier.

I always got along well with Bob Andrew and could usually relate to what he was thinking despite our supposed philosophical differences. Politically, he was cautious. He wanted to do something with the Crowns as much as I did. The difference between us was what we believed we could get away with. From the start of my thrust to restructure the royalty rate, I was in constant touch with Bob Andrew and could not have gotten the eventual schedule through cabinet without the unqualified support of finance.

An interesting situation was drawn to my attention in a roundabout manner through the oil industry. The heavy oil company with the fourth largest reserves in the province was an innocuous company known as Canadian Reserve, based in Calgary. They were a subsidiary of Getty Oil of Los Angeles, California and they had a problem. Maybe no one had told Getty Oil when they acquired Canadian Reserve several years earlier about the Federal Investment Review Agency, whose duty it was to guard Canadian interests from the ravages of foreign corporate multinationals, or maybe if they had been told they made a serious error in assessing FIRA's reaction to the deal. It was irrelevant to the Trudeau government that the hated multinationals meant jobs, investment, and a higher standard of living for Canadians. The fact was that most of them were American and anti-Americanism was good politically, hence FIRA. FIRA was originally conceived to protect the antiquated manufacturing industry in central Canada; however, when the Trudeau government made the decision to shut down the western oil industry using the NEP, the body known as FIRA proved useful once again. Getty was caught with a company they had bought but could not assume control of. This situation had been in limbo for almost three years and no one in Canada cared.

My interest in Getty was precipitated by the attitude of Husky Oil. Husky was the largest oil producer in Saskatchewan and the key player in the upgrader game simply by virtue of having the most barrels of crude. They also knew the political game and were going to play it, and rightly so. To my untrained eye there was little doubt we needed a new player and it might as well be a big one.

I met with the man in charge of Getty Oil's Canadian operations and what he told me of his company's position did not make me particularly proud to be a Canadian politician. In effect he was saying, "Why were we not told we were not wanted before we paid our admission to get in?" He was well versed in the politics of the Saskatchewan heavy oil upgrader and very skillfully put the ball in my court: if we wanted Getty Oil, we had to get them through FIRA.

When I got back to my office I asked the department to send me the Getty file. By now I knew that FIRA routinely queried the provincial government on applications before them and I wanted to know what views had been expressed about Getty by the Blakeney government. I found a memo from a senior official in my department recommending to executive council and cabinet that the Getty application be opposed by the government of Saskatchewan. I read the memo carefully to make certain I understood it without question. Logic like that could best serve a socialist government like the federal Liberals or the provincial government in Manitoba, and, not wanting to keep the official from his rightful sphere of influence, I phoned Moroz and told him to get the official out before he gave the disease to someone else.

We will pay the price for the Trudeau years in the form of a reduced standard of living for years. There were some who wondered why we had trouble attracting investment in Saskatchewan. Most of these people seemed to think that Canada is the only place in the world worthy of investment. Believe me, we are not the only country with something to offer foreign investors. As the new government in Saskatchewan took office, eager for outside investment and business, we found ourselves talking to people who likened Canada to a banana republic with a government whose word was not valid and who had no hesitation in changing the rules of the game at a whim. Why should we invest in Canada, they asked, when there are places that really want us? It was a tough one to answer.

I decided to have a study done on SMDC to see how effective they were and to evaluate their corporate decisions past and present. I saw a trace of concern on their faces as I made my announcement and I hastened to explain it was not a patronage study but would be carried out by a group who had no connection to them at all—quite possibly by an American firm. Their faces brightened and their president, Roy Lloyd, said in his typical low-key manner, "I think decisions like Key Lake will stand up to scrutiny." That was a typical Roy Lloyd understatement. Key Lake was a gigantic uranium project in northern Saskatchewan SMDC owned in partnership with Uranerz, a German company, and Eldor Resources, a federal Crown. The mine was the richest in the world in terms of ore quality and could make money at the present depressed world prices, which of course were going to rise. Key Lake was projected to return a billion dollars to the Saskatchewan coffers by 1988.

There were going to have to be some changes in staff at SMDC. We could not keep on NDP activists any more than the NDP would have kept on Tory activists. Joan Duncan's brother-in-law worked in accounting in SMDC and he assisted us with the list of names for dismissal. One name caused me a problem. Allan Blakeney's daughter worked at SMDC and it was assumed she would be the first to go; however, nobody was going to touch her without the word from me. No doubt there was a great deal of adjustment to be made in the Blakeney household already and I was not inclined to rub any salt in the wounds unnecessarily. I told Roy Lloyd we were going to keep her on merit but she should be made aware of her situation and I did not ever want my suspicions aroused on the question of loyalty.

SMDC had their legal work done by the Regina firm of Griffin, Beke & Thorson, which had been Allan Blakeney's old law firm. When I asked them how they rated the quality of the work, they informed me it was excellent. I told them politics would dictate a change and they had best start to terminate with them now. Roy Lloyd was not enthused and carefully pointed out their legal work was perhaps the most exacting of any of the Crowns. Their contracts were international in scope and often were challenged in foreign courts, which made the quality of their legal work very important to them. At the time I probably did not entirely appreciate the significance of what he was saying and assured him whoever the new firm were, they would be interviewed by SMDC before they were given the work. That legal work was to cost me my cabinet position down the road.

I offered the contract to the firm of MacPherson, Leslie & Tyerman, who surprised me by declining. As attorneys for Uranerz, the German company in partnership with SMDC at Key Lake, they viewed the SMDC work as a potential conflict of interest, even though they had a large enough staff to keep the two companies totally distinct from each other. When I had ordered the work removed from Griffin, Beke & Thorson it had not occurred to me that MacPherson, Leslie & Tyerman would turn it down. SMDC needed a law firm immediately. I phoned Harry Baker, MLA Biggar, who was from Saskatoon, and asked him to recommend the most competent Tory law firms in the city. Most of the firms, as it turned out, were too small to handle the SMDC account, which had been known to run as high as $400,000 a year; however, after interviewing the firms on Harry Baker's list, SMDC did find one that was most satis-factory: Sherstobitoff, Hrabinsky, Stromberg & Young. I went through the roof. They were a notorious NDP-orientated firm. In fact, one of the senior partners had been chairman of the labor relations board under the NDP. When I asked Harry Baker why they were on the list, he said that Bob Stromberg was a good Tory but he knew little about the firm. I told him I would be shot by caucus if I were to send the account to a notorious NDP firm, regardless of Stromberg. I decided to leave it up to Harry Baker and the Saskatoon MLAs to find one politically acceptable firm that could also do the quality of legal work involved. The Saskatoon caucus had acquired a reputation as a gathering of "troublemaking lightweights," to quote Eric Berntson. A patronage job would give them something to chew on and solve the problem I had created for myself. Meanwhile, SMDC was in the midst of a computer exchange of yellow cake (uranium oxide) with the Tennessee Valley Authority (TVA), which, although common, was nevertheless very complicated. I was informed SMDC needed the legal ground work on the deal commenced immediately, or it would be in jeopardy. I therefore instructed them to assess the capabilities of Pedersen Norman in Regina.

Yes, Pedersen Norman was Tony Merchant's law firm; and yes, it was Liberal orientated; and yes, Tony Merchant was my personal lawyer. However, the SMDC work was complex and it took a large firm to handle it, and I was not going back to

Griffin, Beke & Thorson after going through the upheaval of terminating them. When SMDC approved Pedersen Norman, I told them to place the TVA contract with them. All nonessential work was to be held in abeyance while the search went on for a final firm. As I said that, I knew I would have to account for the decision some day; however, I felt I was on solid ground. I had tried unsuccessfully to get a Tory law firm and there comes a time when you must stop the political games and get the job done. SMDC had work to do and politics had held things up long enough.

The new cabinet was taking shape. Bob Andrew, while unmistakably a captive of his own department, was going to be a good minister of finance. Eric Berntson, while a good cabinet minister, was a disaster as minister of agriculture. Paul Rousseau was doing a good job in industry and trade. I can't really say whether or not Gary Lane was a good attorney general but in cabinet he gave the appearance of being in control. Graham Taylor was an excellent minister of health and obviously was going to keep getting better. As president of Morris Rod Weeder, newcomer Lorne McLaren brought a great deal of expertise and was a useful link to the business community, but he was uncomfortable in labor from day one. One of the big surprises was George McLeod. In opposition he had bordered on being a dead loss but in government he had found his niche. He had also become quite an orator in contrast to his tongue-tied days in opposition.

The new government of Grant Devine was highly business orientated and made no bones about it. The economy had tightened, yet there were investment dollars out there looking for a home and there was no question Saskatchewan was being appraised by the investment community for stability and indications of our true intentions. Some groups were looking for a way to take an inexperienced government to the cleaners, but others were waiting for a signal. We had to demonstrate we were ready and open for business and this was a new era in Saskatchewan. "Open for business" was Grant Devine's slogan and he wanted to spread the message far and wide. He was a great believer in the theory that talk makes it appear as though something is happening, if there is enough of it.

Devine was fascinated by the dramatic transformation a far-seeing governor had engineered in the state of Georgia, and he invited the governor's right-hand man to Regina to talk to the cabinet. Like Saskatchewan, Georgia had a largely rural base and by means of a series of tax breaks, grants, and innovative ideas, the state of Georgia had built its own industrial sector. The "man from Georgia," as he came to be known, talked about attracting industry, setting up technical schools to provide skilled labor, and using tax incentives today to build a tax revenue base for tomorrow. He advised us to build on our strengths—agriculture and resources—and cabinet was quite taken with his message.

We held a cabinet meeting to discuss what action we should take to show business we were serious. Paul Rousseau, Lorne McLaren, and I felt the time was ripe to introduce right-to-work legislation or, if that was too extreme, at least to freeze the minimum wage for the next couple of years. The proposed industrial strategy got into the hands of the bureaucrats of executive council, however, who were to keep it on the drawing board. Instead of action, it was decided we should talk. We were going to hold an Open for Business conference and tell them rather than show them. It was the old lecture-in-the-classroom trick.

If we were going to build on our strengths, then the resource sector was going to be a key player. As the potash arena was saturated, this left the heavy oil upgrader. Since we had inherited that, it did not have to go to cabinet where it too would have been relegated to the drawing boards of executive council, never to see the light of day again. The industrial strategy, based on the Georgia model, was innovative and possible in Saskatchewan if the political courage was there to carry it through. Grant Devine had thought of it and brought in planners at various stages of his leadership to develop it. However, when in a position to turn a theoretical model into a plan of action he became a captive of the politician's basic instinct to stay in power. In essence then, very quickly Grant Devine made decisions based solely on practical political considerations as he and his inner advisors saw them. And the way they saw it was that it was far safer to do nothing as long as they were perceived by the electorate to be taking action.

Saskoil was a Crown corporation with major problems and I

decided I needed a thorough evaluation by people who knew the corporate structure of the oil industry. By coincidence, I bumped into Jim Whiteside, a former executive assistant to my father who now owned Align Energy, a consulting company in Vancouver. He told me he could get some of the best oil people around to do the study and offered to make a proposal. I told him to put one together and get back to me as soon as possible. Align Energy came back with a proposal to do a study of Saskoil from the ground up. I liked what I heard and hired them for forty thousand dollars of Saskoil's money and told them they had better at least justify their salaries. Harvey Bryant, the soft-spoken Oklahoman in charge, drawled, "If we can't save you a hundred times that we shouldn't be here."

About that time, Paul Rousseau, the minister in charge of the holding company for all the Crowns, called to tell me he was about to fire several heads of Crown corporations. He was assuming Frank Sadler of Saskoil was in that category and wanted to know if Roy Lloyd of SMDC should be included as well. I told him absolutely not on Roy Lloyd and that, although I felt it was coming to that with Frank Sadler, I was not yet certain. I told Rousseau I would prefer to wait for the outcome of the Saskoil report. Paul thought the study was a great idea but said if I wanted Sadler dismissed the time to do it was now, along with the others. I called in Jim Whiteside and Harvey Bryant and asked for a preview of what was going on at Saskoil. Their story confirmed my suspicions. There were too many staff, no sense of direction, and a lack of technical expertise. I decided I would not be doing Sadler a favor by prolonging the inevitable. I called Rousseau back and told him to include Frank Sadler. I was quite happy to have someone else do what I had little stomach for. Paul again queried me about Roy Lloyd and said that according to the transition office, Lloyd was a well-known "red." I replied that being condemned by that group of incompetents was almost a form of recommendation. Paul said that he shared my view of the transition office but reminded me that they had the ear of Grant Devine.

The legislature was not even in session yet and the balance of the MLAs were hovering in the corridors like wolves in search of prey. They were being contacted by the same people who were approaching cabinet ministers' offices with the requests for jobs or consulting work or whatever. They were demanding a say in the appointments to the various boards and commissions, something that was not unreasonable; however, in most cases, what should have been an orderly process usually resulted in a yelling session. It was intense enough that I chose not to appoint a board for the time being for any of the three Crowns under me rather than risk being stuck with some of the geniuses being unloaded onto the various agencies. Patronage is necessary in matters like this and even makes the system work a little better, but the Devine government brought it to a new edge. The question of ability or competency seemed to be of no consideration in an appointment, only whether the person in question was a Tory and a friend of the right minister.

Much of the cabinet agenda was taken up with the subject of how to keep the MLAs happy—an impossible task—and how to make them think they had a role to play. Some were given legislative secretary positions, which gave them some extra salary and a title but nothing of substance as far as being useful was concerned. I was given a new young MLA named Myles Morin, who had won the NDP stronghold of The Battlefords. He was bright, sincere, personable, and, it was assumed, one of the next additions to the cabinet. I really racked my brains to find something for him to do. Any departmental authority would be at the expense of the deputy, and that would not work; and because he was elected and had his own schedule he did not fit into the role of a special assistant. I tried to give him any speaking engagements that came up; however, most groups were insistent on having the minister not the legislative assistant. I felt genuinely guilty about Myles because I viewed him as a real comer—he was not demanding or obnoxious as many of his counterparts were—but I was never successful in finding a proper role for him. Much further down the road, when Myles was passed over for a cabinet post, I was mystified, but then by that time a lot of things did not make any sense.

Don Moroz had found me my upgrader expert in the form of one Jack McPhee. He was a former member of the brain trust of Allan Blakeney's executive council, and it was public knowledge that he had donated to the NDP. I was aware the NDP had put the arm on many public servants for donations and no doubt theirs was a difficult overture to turn down, particularly as they had been a pretty good bet to be around for a good long time. What I expected from my staff, however, was that they should do the job and do it well. As long as there were no breaches of confidence or leaks, I could not have cared less how they had voted in the last election. Jack was a pro and I was never to regret my decision to hire him.

Good people were hard to find and I felt our civil service was far too inbred with University of Saskatchewan degrees. I would have loved to find some diversification, but for the most part it seemed you had to be from Saskatchewan to want to live and work here. The hiring of executive assistants had become almost a status game in the corridors of the legislature and in a twisted fashion a minister was measured by the number of executive assistants he had. And the salaries were outrageous. The ordinary executive assistant off the street with little or no academic background was quickly earning $45,000 to $50,000, usually with a car into the bargain. Good old Dave Tkachuk surfaced as Grant Devine's chief of staff at a trifling $84,000. Dick Collver used to pay him $1,500 per month not all that long ago. The executive assistant I hired from York University with an MBA and some talent in addition came for about $35,000 and thought he was getting the deal of his life. I may have been in another world and perhaps that is why I did not last long in the Devine government. I had two executive assistants and two secretaries to look after a major department and three Crowns. Across the hall in government services, Joan Duncan had more than that for her little department, and upstairs another minister had six executive assistants. Even Jim Garner in highways— a department that ran itself—had more staff than I did. This was one game in which I was the clear loser.

Jack McPhee really jumped into the upgrader project. He reported back to me that the Archydale project was dead and, in fact, had never been alive. He predicted Husky would make a proposal for an upgrader in the Lloydminster area that would incorporate their existing facilities. It was Jack McPhee's view that the entire project was at square one with neither the Alberta provincial government nor the federal government showing much enthusiasm. That was just what I needed. I had inherited something that many assumed was almost at the state of a sod-turning ceremony when in actual fact it had not even reached the drawing board. It was starting to look as though it would never get there either, and guess who was going to be hung for it.

During a progress report on the Saskoil study, Harvey Bryant asked me how committed we were to a heavy oil upgrader. I did not know anything about the technology of an upgrader and the more I listened to Harvey the more depressed I became. In effect he was saying the megaproject was bordering on crazy in terms of risk and potential cost. While evaluating Saskoil, he had of course talked with their upgrader people so he was well versed. According to him, the configuration of the existing pipelines spelled a small upgrader in Regina using the existing Co-op refinery. That refinery was hardly a new one but it had the capabilities to do the job and the project was less than one-third the projected cost of the Archydale upgrader. I called in Jack McPhee and had Harvey brief him. I instructed Jack to go and broach the subject with the Co-op to see if there was any interest on their part. Initially there was not and it seemed things were dead all around.

Bob Andrew was the vice-chairman of Saskoil and had endorsed the Saskoil study. It had always been my expressed intention to see Saskoil sold and Andrew was in private agreement if the deal looked good. By this time Andrew was face to face with stark financial realities and he was desperate for money. I had inherited a white elephant of an upgrader and he had received a budget that was not worth the ink much less the paper.

The study on Saskoil was nearly complete and Jim Whiteside and Harvey Bryant requested a briefing session to discuss the writing of the report. At the start of the meeting Harvey asked about the government's plans for Saskoil. I told him we were awaiting the results of the report on the Crowns before deciding on a course of action. My personal opinion was that it appeared the worth of the company was far less than the invested equity and we would take a bath on any attempted sale. They then asked me how I wanted Saskoil to appear to a potential outside buyer. I replied that I wanted to sell Saskoil as an example that Crowns could be dismantled successfully with public support and I would love a buyer to make cabinet an offer they could not ignore. Harvey then told me about his suspicions. He had looked at the geological maps and surveys and the estimates of reserves and had come to the conclusion the reserves were vastly underestimated. He had no hard evidence, only the instincts he had developed during his forty years in international exploration. The significance of what he was saying was not lost, even on a novice like me.

In Harvey Bryant's opinion, a third-party evaluation should be done now, even if the company were not to be sold, in order to make proper drilling decisions. Harvey and Jim Whiteside told me to prepare for a horror story in the report. The Crown agency had access to all the money it wanted and was expanding far too quickly. Regina was not the center of the oil industry and never would be, and consequently the personnel Saskoil was able to attract were not those who felt they had a bright future in the private sector in Calgary or in Saudi Arabia. Saskoil's drilling techniques in some areas were inefficient and their computer was out of date. The story went on and on. I told Harvey Bryant and Jim Whiteside their report was not going to be made public but they should write it on the assumption it would be, and I asked for a list of independent companies who could give us estimates of Saskoil's reserves.

A few days later, at a fairly lengthy and elaborate planning meeting held in a Regina hotel, cabinet decided to make Dome Advertising the agency of record. The lucrative government contract was a windfall for the little ad agency. They had been with the Tories from the beginning and had often carried the party accounts long beyond a reasonable due date so there was no doubt we owed them a debt of gratitude. However, no one present thought they were anywhere near the best available, yet that evening Dome became the agency of record anyway. That decision should have told me something.

I was committing political suicide over in energy and mines. I cared about being perceived as doing a good job and, in fact, doing it. I cared whether the Crowns under me performed well. I assumed my cabinet future would depend on my performance and I was anticipating being sent to clean up agriculture after Berntson and his new deputy had finally made such a mess that even Grant Devine would not be able to ignore it. Instead, I should have been playing the silly games of those incompetent hacks who came out of the woodwork with their mind-boggling salaries and lists of who was first at the party troughs. I should have shown up for work, gone through the motions, missed few cabinet meetings, and sat in silence at those I did attend. That is the proven formula for longevity in the Tory government in Saskatchewan. However, I had believed Grant Devine's rhetoric—"Give 'er snooze, Bruce"—and I wanted to deliver on promises made to the electorate who had granted us such a massive mandate. I truly believed my job was to find a way to get an economically viable upgrader and to attract the oil industry back to the province. I should have known from this gathering that I was somewhere in left field.

The next item for discussion was the state of Regina drinking water, which had become totally rank with summer now here. It had an impurity content that would have meant condemnation and probably closure in the United States, yet the solutions were almost prohibitive in cost. Water from the South Saskatchewan River, probably from the artificial Lake Diefenbaker created by the Gardiner Dam, had to be brought to the Regina area either by pipeline or by open ditch. IPSCO, a Regina steel firm desperate to avoid layoffs, had offered to provide the pipe necessary at their cost of production.

To me and to many others, the solution was obvious and politically popular—an open ditch down the Thunder Creek basin that could be used for irrigation as well. The federal Prairie Farm Rehabilitation Administration had long been looking at such a project and were enthusiastic backers. This concept tied in with Grant Devine's economic theories of "building on our strengths" and was a means of building up a secondary industrial base through agriculture. The pipeline alternative solved Regina's water problems and little else. We had inherited this political hot potato and caucus was divided on the issue.

This time, the means of postponing a decision was going to be a report on the options available with—if absolutely necessary—a decision at the end. This report was going to solve two things for Grant Devine. It was going to give him some time before he had to face up to the thorny water decision—a decision full of political pitfalls—and provide a job for an MLA. The MLA chosen was Gerald Muirhead from Arm River who, despite having kept the party afloat financially at key times prior to the election, had been passed over for a cabinet post. Gerald had distinguished himself as an expert on water quality in the legislature when he had attempted to throw a glass of water across the chamber at an NDP cabinet minister— missing and soaking George McLeod. With factors like this on his resume, Gerald Muirhead was chosen to make a study of the options available to solve Regina's water problem.

The decision had been made to have a summer session of the legislature, although no one seemed to know why. Moroz and I briefed the premier on our plans for a new royalty schedule for the oil industry and his penetrating cross-examination demonstrated a quick grasp of a complex area. When we left his office, we felt the session had gone well. We were proposing the Norcean plan of a tax-free holiday for three years, along with a drop in royalties on existing production. The royalty drop was not as much as the industry would like to have seen, but most companies were realistic enough to know we could only go so far. We held an expanded meeting complete with officials, charts, graphs—what was known in the trade as a dog and pony show. Bob Andrew was the deciding edge in ultimately procuring the support of Grant Devine, who handled himself like a premier throughout. He called the officials back in once without me present. That gesture made Moroz nervous but I was not offended. A leader has to be certain he is not being snowed by a minister if he is going to run the province.

I received a pleasant surprise when the Co-op asked for a meeting. They were suddenly interested in the possibility of a heavy oil upgrader as a component of their existing refinery. I placed Jack McPhee as our representative and instructed Saskoil to provide them with any relevant data that did not violate any confidences.

I had a meeting scheduled in Saskatoon the next week with federal Energy Minister Marc Lalonde. It was to be more or less a get-acquainted session and an opportunity to get some informal reactions from him about pressing matters such as the heavy oil upgrader, royalty reductions, and the FIRA decision on Getty Oil's purchase of Canadian Reserve, who were still in a state of inoperative limbo. Marc Lalonde was very much in the mold of his close friend and boss, Pierre Elliott Trudeau. He was a charmer and possessed a quick wit and a firm understanding of the relevant issues. How could someone this bright be the architect of a disaster like the NEP? The upgrader at Archydale was a low priority and had never been taken seriously by Ottawa because they never did think it would go. He was unaware of any new project from Husky Oil in the Lloydminster area and doubted if Husky had the resources to go it alone. He knew very little about the Getty Oil situation and said he would find out why they had not been cleared long ago. He understood why we wanted Getty Oil in and he agreed, although he would have preferred Canadian Reserve to find a Canadian partner. I bit my tongue because at that point in Saskatchewan if the check was good, we had no scruples as to its source. We parted on first-name terms and I had an open invitation to call him anytime, bypassing officials. According to Don Moroz, this courtesy was not extended to all provincial ministers.

Out of the blue, my secretary told me she had booked an appointment for a company with a funny name from Redondo Beach, California. The company's name was TRW and they could only come on one specific day and she had taken the liberty of confirming the appointment. I knew of them as a manufacturer of auto parts and sent for a copy of their annual report, which indicated employees numbering ninety-two thousand. For somebody like that, you will be available.

The two gentlemen who presented themselves at my office were a Dr. Norman Petersen and a Dr. Stan Meeker, both from the Los Angeles area. They had flown in from Ottawa and were going to Edmonton upon completion of our meeting. Their business in Ottawa had been with FIRA as they wanted to know in advance what their reception in Canada would be before spending much time getting serious. They told me their meeting with FIRA had been encouraging.

Drs. Petersen and Meeker explained that although TRW manufactured auto parts, the company was also heavily into aerospace. While working on rockets, one of the bright people in their laboratory had discovered a technique they believed could be used to revolutionize enhanced oil recovery. With conventional pumping, only 6 to 10 percent of a reservoir is extracted before a well is considered "pumped out." With some of the new EOR methods, which include pumping steam down to heat the oil, the proportion can rise to as much as 20 to 25 percent. TRW had reason to believe their as-yet-untested process could lead to extraction rates as high as 66 percent. The directors of TRW were suspicious of Canada—a familiar story —and would have preferred to do the pilot project in California; however, the geological formations they needed were in Utah, Saskatchewan, and Alberta. A company the size of TRW had to be confident the process would work or the board would not have sent out their experts; Drs. Petersen and Meeker were not your average, run-of-the-mill people off the street with an idea. I was enthusiastic—I had to be. However, they cautioned me TRW moved very slowly, chose its friends carefully, but was a long-term friend once a relationship had been established. Obviously the attitudes of the governments Petersen and Meeker were talking to would have a significant bearing on the ultimate decision. I assured them the government of Saskatchewan was interested in knowing more about their plans and our people were at their disposal for any technical information or service they might require. We agreed to talk again.

We were now into early summer and many Crowns were still operating with boards of directors appointed by the NDP. According to the attorney general, all the members of a board had to be replaced simultaneously. When I asked offhandedly why the minister in charge of the Crowns in question did not simply dismiss the old board, Gary Lane said that was impossible. I decided not to ask what it meant if the boards had been dismissed before the minister had been sworn in—it just couldn't happen. Many of the Crowns were in difficulty and there was a prevailing mood that a change at the top would solve all the problems. The Saskatchewan Government Insurance Office was a case in point. It was under Paul Rousseau and he fired the president quickly, partly for political reasons and partly because of the financial health of the company. We all knew there were some horror stories in SGI and I suggested to Paul that he bring some insurance experts in to do a thorough analysis of the corporation. Their report could identify problem areas and make recommendations for change, making the job of the new president that much easier. Paul seemed to think an external study was a good idea but suddenly I heard they had a new manager at SGI. The decision not to commission a study was consistent with the thinking that new presidents could be brought in to somehow transform poorly run Crown corporations into models of Tory efficiency. To pretend that somewhere in our little government there was that kind of expertise was not reality.

My relationship with Grant Devine was deteriorating, although not for any particular reason. At no time had it been particularly cordial and he was never to forgive my open opinions of his leadership during opposition days. I did not really care whether he forgave me or not. I had always regarded him as an inept leader of the opposition and my short time as a cabinet minister merely confirmed my view that he was in the same category as a premier. Grant Devine is a fine person committed to his God, his family, and his job, in that order, but an administrator he is not and in an unguarded moment he would most likely agree. A good portion of the blame can be laid on the doorstep of his staff—a group who would not have lasted one day with me. However, the staff were his and he appeared to demand little of them. Matters sent to his office for his approval or authorization were usually never seen or heard of again. Even those marked Personal and Confidential took forever to get a response, if indeed there ever was one. I recall sending him a memo in which I asked if he was satisfied with the level of information I was providing. He did not reply.

I did get a response from Grant Devine when the Tory lawyers started screaming about Pedersen Norman doing work for SMDC. The premier phoned me in the middle of a meeting with the Independent Petroleum Producers and demanded to talk to me right then. I slipped to another office and took the phone, wondering what the emergency was. Grant Devine wanted to know about the Merchant appointment. I told him that it was not an appointment, it was just a temporary solution to SMDC's legal problems. I outlined the events that had led to the present and invited him to find me a law firm that could do the necessary quality of work. He said he was getting a flood of phone calls from federal Tories and lawyers protesting; however, when I asked for specifics, he became vague. Then he said Bob Stromberg was pressuring. I could sympathize with Stromberg's frustration and I told Devine I would give Stromberg's firm the work right away if he wanted me to because SMDC rated them highly; however, I would not defend the appointment of SMDC's legal work to an NDP-orientated firm in caucus. I could appreciate that Devine did not want any more calls on the subject of Tony Merchant and I said I would resolve the question of a legal firm for SMDC as quickly as possible. I found it interesting that such a minute matter could draw the attention of the premier, whereas those of major proportion could not.

10

The Cabinet

The legislature opened—I was still wondering why—in July of 1982 and it was a thrill for me to take a seat on the government benches. When you have been in opposition for what seems like an eternity, it is most difficult to describe the experience when you finally take your seat on the government side. The lopsided effect of the majority had put more government members on the opposition side than official opposition. The NDP, nestled in their little corner of the world, did look like a ragtag army of peasants. All Allan Blakeney had for troops were third and fourth stringers from his days as premier. Dwain Lingenfelter was the best he had but he had always been overshadowed by the Messers and Romanows of this world. Allan Blakeney must have wondered what he had done to deserve this.

The throne speech was innocuous and most trained observers realized this was a session for the backbenchers. There was

nothing pressing and it was really only putting into legislation
what we had already done. Allan Blakeney put up a good front
like the professional he is. I admired the decorum he displayed
during his response to the throne speech. What do you say
when you have been annihilated and have to face the heavy
heckling of new, strutting MLAs? Allan Blakeney, virtually dis-
armed and defenseless from a political point of view, still maintained his dignity. He was a pro.

At the beginning of the legislative session, the NDP were
inept and disorganized and obviously experiencing difficulty in
adapting to their new role. They were choosing very carefully
the ministers they were addressing in question period and were
avoiding me, Lane, Andrew, and, strangely, Grant Devine.
Devine was, after all, a rookie MLA who had yet to answer his
first question and on the first day of regular business he was
visibly nervous. I was certain the NDP would want to give him
a workout. When I finally got an innocent question from Allan
Blakeney I referred to him as the premier throughout the
answer to roars of laughter from the press gallery.

Generally the questions in question period were enough to
send you to sleep. Paul Rousseau had to jar me one day when
my mind was elsewhere. I was being asked by Gerry Hammersmith of Prince Albert whether I had fired anyone personally, to which I replied no. He then asked me to state so
unequivocally and I replied sarcastically—and probably arro-
gantly—that I had done so and if he could not understand a
simple answer he should seek aid of some sort. I knew he was
referring to the departmental official I had instructed Don
Moroz to fire on day one. The next day I was not in the House
and after question period Hammersmith rose and tabled the
letter of dismissal Derek Bedson had drafted for my signature.
Now, it is fair game to grab a point where you can, but you do
not raise questions of privilege when the member in question is
not in his seat. However, the NDP have never had much difficulty in breaking unwritten rules. Hammersmith claimed that I
had deliberately misled the House. The Speaker, Herb Swan,
said he would conduct an investigation.

The next day, I took a real strip off Hammersmith for choosing to raise the issue when I was not in my seat. I then went
through the chronology of events including the instructions to

Moroz, the employee's refusal to leave, and the letter I had signed that confirmed Moroz's verbal firing. I made it clear that I had ordered the firing but had not informed the employee personally. As I sat down, Bob Andrew got up and made a short dissertation on my behalf and Gary Lane then compared my case to similar situations under the NDP and outlined how previous Speakers had ruled. Lane became quite involved in his presentation and was most persuasive. The Speaker said he would rule on the matter after examining the record.

Afterwards I thanked Lane for the way he had become involved as a defense lawyer. He commented dryly that it was time I had a good lawyer—an oblique reference to Tony Merchant, whom Lane despised. Bob Andrew was worried and Lane said, "Prepare for Herb to sandbag you. He doesn't like either one of us." This was very true. Herb Swan was a Christian fundamentalist who made no secret of his disapproval of the rough House tactics of Lane and myself. He disapproved of me because of my marriage breakdown and of Lane because of his lifestyle.

The next day I was in my constituency at two municipal meetings I had previously agreed to attend. Traditionally, no ruling is made when the member is not in his seat; however, that did not stop Herb Swan from ruling I had misled the House. The NDP, of course, were elated and made a production out of the fact I was not in my seat and demanded a vote, which got the bells ringing. I learned of it when I phoned my office on another matter and my secretary told me. I phoned Gary Lane at the caucus lounge, who told me I should get in there and be prepared to eat "crow." I was eighty miles away and had to stop at home to change, but I got in as quickly as I could. The House was reconvened and I apologized even though I had answered Gerry Hammersmith's question truthfully and would answer the same way if he asked it again. The Speaker, benevolently, accepted my apology and the House turned to other business. I scribbled a note for the Speaker that read, "Herb, when I used to get the knife from John Brockelbank, it came from the front." I sent it to the Speaker and left the assembly furious. A gathering of reporters was waiting in the corridors and I repeated my insincere apology. As I was walking away, Joe Ralko of CP asked how John Brockelbank would have ruled. From a distance I shot back, "Brock flashed his knives from the front," and I went home still furious, although not surprised.

Throughout the drive back to Moose Jaw, I thought about what had transpired and got more and more disgusted. Misleading the House sounds far more serious than it really is. I felt Herb Swan had used his position to express his disapproval of my personal affairs and general lifestyle. He had already told my seatmate Gerald Muirhead it was my assertion that I had ordered the firing that had forced his reaction. That was great logic. Who did he think ordered departmental dismissals, the man in the moon?

The next morning I was delayed at the ranch and I came into the cabinet meeting that had been scheduled for that day just as it was winding down. I noticed a scratch pad on which the words "knife" and "Brock" had been jotted down and doodled on. Obviously my comment had been discussed, although you would not have guessed it from the demeanor of the cabinet members. I had no idea of the nature of the discussion and no one was going to clue me in. That is part of the game. You have no true friends in politics; if you are in trouble, you are on your own. The meeting ended and when I got to my office there was a message the premier wanted to see me.

Grant Devine was standing at his window as I entered his office and he opened the conversation with the words, "I want your resignation." I was stunned but said, "If that's what you want, of course, you can have it." When I asked why he said it was over the knife comment I had made to the press. I replied that I could stand to go because I couldn't put an upgrader together or gain the confidence of the oil industry but I found my dismissal hard to take over a nothing like this. He said caucus and cabinet were in an uproar and he had no choice. That was an overstatement but probably reflected the ambitions of the backbenchers, who saw nothing but good for themselves in any cabinet opening. I conceded the knife remark was silly and probably inexcusable. Devine interjected that the note to Herb Swan was equally silly, to which I replied that Swan was just another MLA and the Speaker's hat hardly deified him. Swan really had it in for me if he had run to the premier with my note. I said that I was willing to apologize in the assembly to the Speaker in such a way that there would be no doubt about Devine being in charge. If that was not enough and it was my resignation he wanted, it was his. There was silence. He said, "The only thing that is saving you, and I mean the only thing, is that I can't replace you. You make that apology good." I said I would but I did not want Devine to do me any favors. He said, "Count on it."

When the assembly met, the NDP seemed to think there was blood to be had. In question period Murray Koskie jumped up and directed the lead question to the premier, who turned it to me. I apologized to the Speaker for the remark from one who should have known better and withdrew it unequivocally. Herb Swan said he was satisfied and the matter was over, just like that. A page came by and asked if I wanted any messages delivered; I declined with thanks.

It was pretty obvious after that little encounter that I should not count on a lengthy career as a minister in the Devine government. Fortunately, politics had always been a game with me, one that I had usually enjoyed up until then. Had I ever been faced with a choice between politics and my position at home, I would have walked away without hesitation. As it was, I was close enough to Regina that I could participate and live elsewhere. I disliked government functions and avoided them like the plague. Many of the Tories' real problems arose from their massive majority and total lack of fear of the opposition. No doubt I was not the only minister who was being tattled on to the premier; however, I am sure there was no other minister he would have considered firing for such a triviality. It did not bother me that he disliked me, but I did wonder why he had bothered to put me in the cabinet in the first place. Probably for the same reason he had not fired me today—much as he hated me he needed me for the time being.

I sensed that Grant Devine felt threatened by me and I could not understand why. My personal affairs had long ago removed any leadership aspirations I might have had and no one knew better than he that this was as far as I could go. Indeed, I had no interest in going any further. It seemed to me that in many ways Grant Devine was an insecure, indecisive person. This experience caused me to reflect on my position and how I should play the options open to me. I was miles ahead of any other minister in cleaning out my department and Crowns. In moving quickly and decisively I had made enemies along "hack row" for whom I felt nothing but contempt, and I made little effort to conceal my feelings. I could not have cared less what they did as long as they stayed away from my turf, but no doubt their griping made me appear uncooperative. I had decided that to do your job better than the others was a challenge and to stay ahead of the "ax" could be exciting. My fate was sealed whatever I did, so I decided to be fired—whenever it came to pass—for at least doing a quality job. It must have been obvious that I was doing a good job or I would have been gone long ago.

While the legislature was sitting, a battle royal was going on behind the scenes over the new royalty schedule in the oil industry. We were proposing a royalty-free period of three years on new drilling, as well as reduced rates on existing production. Naively, we hoped the federal government might follow with a reduction on their taxes, a hope that proved to be folly. Leading the battle against the new schedule was Gary Lane and he fought it like a man possessed, claiming we would be labeled as giving $400 million away to the oil industry, who would not respond. As matters stood now, new drillings were down to almost zero so we were not giving away anything because we weren't getting anything. However, it was impossible to get this through Lane's head and he was determined to give the industry no breaks at all. He lobbied everyone who would listen, right down to caucus. Bob Andrew and Berntson were solid allies and I had Devine's very cautious support. Those who had any connection with the oil industry were all supportive. Lane, however, used every trick in the book to delay the changes. We had to go back to the treasury board twice for confirmation of various details, which was all right since we were dealing with a great deal of the taxpayers' money; however, most of the arguments against the new schedule were made out of ignorance.

Finally the schedule passed cabinet. Even though there had been little doubt about the outcome, I was still relieved it was over. Nevertheless, it was still possible for me to be hung out to dry and I was now in the hands of the oil industry. The response to the new schedule was overwhelming and within two weeks drilling activity and general service work started to return to the oil patch. I was safe until the next crisis.

I received a call from Marc Lalonde, who was being shifted to graveyard of federal politics, finance. One of his last acts as energy minister was to facilitate the passage of Getty Oil through FIRA. I thanked him and asked if he had any objections to my informing Getty. He didn't. I phoned the man in charge of Getty's Canadian business to give him the good news and I invited him to study our royalty schedule, which made us the most attractive area in North America. We agreed to meet soon.

Saskatchewan is no Alberta in terms of oil but you take what God gives you and try to do the best you can. We now had one of the world leaders in heavy oil production and we sorely needed them. They were here with bad feelings toward Canada because of FIRA, not to mention the NEP, and it was up to me to make them feel comfortable that further investment in Saskatchewan would be profitable and to assure them that the rules would remain the same. It was difficult to tell what Getty had in mind. No doubt they were used to dealing with screwy governments in their worldwide activities, but they were not exactly ready to write a check for a billion-dollar upgrader yet.

Just because you have won an election does not mean you can perform magic. The euphoria of being part of the government was rapidly being diminished as I became aware of our limitations. As a province, we badly needed a megaproject to stimulate our economy, but they were not that easy to come by. Throughout the seventies big was beautiful but the sobering experiences of an economic slowdown and record high interest rates had taken the luster off formerly glamorous energy projects. While I was not saying so, the Archydale project was in the ashcan, even though it was technically still alive. The Co-op project was a possibility as a backup, but it was small in comparison. When Husky made its proposal, there was little doubt the location would be Lloydminster and it was a fact of life that most of the workers at a new upgrader in that city would chose to live in Alberta with its much lower income tax, no sales tax, and lower municipal taxes. Devine needed something else.

I am not exactly sure who mentioned it first, but by late

summer the idea of a nuclear reactor had surfaced. The subject was political dynamite to put it mildly. The newspapers had been full of Three Mile Island and, more recently, Diablo Canyon, as well as cost overruns and other arguments against nuclear power. Yet, as emotional as the subject was, everyone knew nuclear reactors were the power source of the future. It was fine to talk about the sun, the moon, and tidal power but the sad reality was we were light years away from having the technical expertise to use these sources. The concept, which had received more than passing attention from the NDP, revived as the prospects for an upgrader became dimmer and dimmer. The construction of a nuclear power plant would employ seven thousand people over a ten-year period with probably triple that number employed in support services. It would use our own uranium and it would no longer be necessary to ruin with pollution the few remaining clean rivers and streams we had. One plant would look after our power needs for a generation and beyond and freeze utility rates for years upon completion. We had lots of wide open space to put a reactor where it would not intrude on populated areas.

Besides the politics, the biggest drawback was the enormous capital cost. The per unit cost factor diminished rapidly as the size was increased; however, even the smallest reactor was more than we needed for the foreseeable future. The key was the sale of the surplus power to our American friends, who were usually prepared to buy reasonably priced energy from any source. I took the idea to the premier and he was clearly intrigued. Once Devine had given his approval to investigate the feasibility of the project, I suggested there be no written memos on the subject. The only other people who would know about it would be Don Moroz, Jack McPhee, and George Hill, chairman of the Saskatchewan Power Corporation, which would, of course, be the operator. I don't know whether Devine really expected the project to go anywhere but at least he had no objections to our preliminary investigations into its viability.

The customer I had in mind for the surplus power was the State of California. Their energy requirements and costs had soared, as I knew firsthand from my power bills. The concept of a nuclear power station could fit well into SPC's plans, assuming the sale of power would look after the financing needs.

However, SPC was not the classic picture of financial health most people assumed it to be, and undoubtedly the NDP would oppose the proposal on emotional grounds, despite having seriously considered an almost identical scenario. I believed the concept could still be sold politically on the basis of jobs and cheap power if the proper groundwork was meticulously done. With the sale of excess power, someone else would be providing the essential financial base and we would enjoy the long-term benefits of cheap power. However, if I had a battle on my hands over the royalty schedule, the all-out war over the nuclear reactor would make it pale in comparison.

A prime example of the right hand of government not knowing what the left is doing occurred in the summer months. Don Moroz came flying into my office with a copy of the minutes from a board of directors meeting of the Crown Investments Corporation in which the board had awarded a $500,000 contract to Fluor Construction of Calgary to study the feasibility of a heavy oil upgrader in Saskatchewan. I did not believe it. I phoned CIC chairman Paul Rousseau to ask him if he had any more money around like that and if so why not put it to a more constructive use in Las Vegas. He said his officials had told them we wanted the Fluor consulting contract at energy and mines. It was not that I had anything against Fluor—they were and are a top-of-the-line construction company and would have been my choice to build an upgrader, all things being equal—but the CIC report was absurd and those responsible for it should have been fired. However, it seemed big things did not get you fired in the Devine government and there were little or no consequences for those involved.

Another incident reconfirmed my dislike for Crown corporations and the irresponsible manner in which they operate. Eldorado Nuclear, a federal Crown corporation, purchased the Collins Bay uranium mine and processing operation, using a stockpile of yellow cake at Elliot Lake to pay for the deal.

SMDC were concerned about Eldorado gaining such a significant foothold in the province and drew the deal to my attention. The Elliott Lake stockpile dated back to the fifties when a depressed market was going to force the shutdown of the Elliott Lake uranium mine. Politics became involved in economics and the operation was perpetuated when the federal government bought the surplus production and stockpiled it. The stockpile sat unused in Elliott Lake for years when suddenly it was given outright to Eldorado Nuclear. At this point the NDP government should have fought the transaction far more vigorously than they did; however, their love of Crown corporations clouded their judgment. The sudden inclusion of the stockpile into the marketplace was an unsettling factor in an already depressed market and was an unfair use of the power of the federal government. Eldorado then struck the Collins Bay deal with Gulf Minerals and Uranerz, who owned the processing operation, using the stockpile as payment. Gulf in turn had committed the yellow cake to various utilities in the United States in order to convert the product into cash. The big loser was going to be Saskatchewan in terms of lost production as the stockpile was unfairly injected into the marketplace. The American Senate was considering a bill that could potentially restrict the flow of foreign yellow cake into the country, and the transfer of the entire stockpile to the United States in one gigantic flood was not in our best interest. Most of my knowledge of the transaction was obtained surreptitiously and was denied initially by Eldorado. As far as I was concerned, Eldorado Nuclear was not a good corporate citizen and we would be best off if their presence in Saskatchewan was kept to a minimum.

The deal hinged on a satisfactory provincial environmental impact report to allow expansion at Collins Bay. To this point the report had been months in the making. It was a potential weapon of last resort, but a dangerous one because of the precedents that would be set. However, I saw nothing wrong with discussing the matter with Environment Minister Neal Hardy and in the course of our conversation I suggested the interests of the province would not necessarily be served by a hasty investigation. Neal agreed and the environmental impact study was for all practical purposes lost in the bureaucracy of the department of the environment.

I then called the president of Gulf Minerals in Denver. My surreptitious source predicted the call would send some shock waves through Gulf and, sure enough, Mr. Zagnoli of Gulf Minerals was in my office within days. He was a charming man whose manner emanated integrity. He had known my father quite well and had obviously been well briefed on me. I got to the point quickly, asking Gulf Minerals to stay. I gave him all the clichés as to why they should and assured him a new era was dawning in Saskatchewan. Although he would not confirm a contract had been signed, he did say that the deal with Eldorado Nuclear had gone too far to be stopped. He indicated that Gulf Minerals had taken the message seriously that foreign companies were no longer welcome in Canada. The NDP had made life as miserable as possible for them and that treatment, coupled with the NEP, had caused the board of directors to give instructions to liquidate. Zagnoli went on to say it was unfortunate we were not elected sooner; things might not have happened this way. In essence, he was saying that Gulf was not going to stay where it was not wanted. How can you argue with that?

Mr. Zagnoli and I parted on a friendly note knowing it was not possible to do anything else at that stage. I told him I had to do everything possible to block the deal, to which he replied that if something were to happen that would cause Gulf to continue in operation at Collins Bay, he would look forward to another era of doing business with the province. I recall sitting at my desk after he left reflecting on how warped our thinking had become. Here was a top-quality man representing a company that had established itself as a good corporate citizen in Saskatchewan and had practically been invited to leave by both the federal and provincial governments. The replacement company was not a good corporate citizen—the reverse if you considered their track record in Saskatchewan—and had been less than candid with department people here. I called in Don Moroz to discuss our options. We could, of course, talk to Eldorado and ask them to stay out; however, it was unlikely they would, since they were a federal Crown and they believed they could walk on water. The other option was to pressure Uranerz, the German company. Moroz suggested an audit by the department, which would surely convey the message we were unhappy. I agreed and the wheels were put in motion.

I was visited shortly afterwards by senior people from Fluor, one of the largest construction companies in the world, which had offices in Calgary. Fluor was based in southern California and had vast experience in energy megaprojects around the world. The people who came to see me were very astute and were playing the political game well. They knew the upgrader concept was in trouble and had doubts that Husky could pull off their proposed upgrader alone. For whatever reason they were on the outs with Husky and had come to me well aware that the provincial government would have a say in the choice of a general contractor for any upgrader to be built in Saskatchewan. In their presentation they emphasized the use of Sakatchewan labor and firms and they dropped a broad hint that they had people at their head office who specialized in making projects go. I indicated a real interest in talking to them. As we were about to break off, I asked casually if they had ever built a nuclear power plant. I must not have been casual enough because they picked up on it right away. They said they had a concept they had never tried that they could make most attractive to a customer. I did not pursue the matter, but I knew they had twigged immediately.

Align completed their report on Saskoil and presented it to me in the early fall. It was a condemnation of government going into a business it did not understand without a clear idea of what it wished to achieve. We had inherited a ten-thousand-barrel-per-day company that had been staffed and organized to carry out the functions of a fifty-thousand-barrel-per-day company, with a research and development capacity of a one-hundred-thousand-barrel-per-day company. The top management people were not profit orientated nor entrepreneurial in their approach. Over half the people in the company were engaged in staff or support activities instead of production, hardly typical of oil companies of this size. The corporation's strategic plan, which had been approved by the NDP government, was going to cause the company to lose money until 1990.

There was some good news in Align's report. They rated the field operations and drilling as first rate and noted the exploration department was managed by good people with solid experience. Their recommendation? To get rid of Saskoil as quickly and quietly as possible after a careful audit of their reserves. The report emphasized drastic measures must be taken internally to make the company an attractive investment for potential buyers. I did not think Saskoil had the proper people to accomplish this objective, but then it was going to be difficult enough to recruit a new president for Saskoil without giving him the additional mandate of selling the company he was being hired to clean up. I spent some time discussing this problem with Jim Whiteside and Harvey Bryant and my executive assistants and someone suggested we hire an external team to run the company. I had heard of such procedures in the private sector but I doubted it had ever been done in a Crown. It made a great deal of sense in many ways and I told my executive assistants to get me a list of people who were in that business.

When Terry Leier dropped in with the jolly little band of the premier's friends who were engaged in the process of "finding good people" to suggest the name of a potential president for Saskoil, I ran the concept of a management team by him, stressing the cost-saving aspects. One of Leier's roles was arriving at settlements with terminated employees so he knew better than anyone just what the true costs of fringe benefits were. There was no question it was less costly to hire on a contract basis if at all possible. He seemed to like the idea and, as he was one of the resident tattletales, I knew the subject would be discussed with the premier within days so he would have thought about it by the time I brought the proposal to him.

At this point, I was feeling guilty about what was happening to my home area of Moose Jaw, which had been plagued by economic setbacks as far back as I could remember. My father did his darndest to get some industry for Moose Jaw by offering incentives that were not available elsewhere, but companies were not tempted to set up shop in the small city with its unskilled labor force and limited industrial tax base. The NDP had perpetrated a cruel political joke on Moose Jaw with the Archydale upgrader, which had never been anything but a bureaucrat's pipe dream. Now it was clearly in my lap and I was going to be blessed with the mission of destroying the economic hopes of my hometown.

Moose Jaw had elected two Conservative MLAs whose futures were probably tied to our success with the heavy oil upgrader. As it became obvious to any observer that the project was dying, they were not on my case; they assumed I was doing my best and, unlike most other back bench MLAs, there was not the usual griping and complaining. They were so good about it, I was feeling even worse. So much of the provincial government's business was concentrated in Regina that there was little to send elsewhere. I had the legal and accounting work from Sask Minerals at Chaplin sent to Moose Jaw firms— the accounting work previously having been done in Swift Current. It wasn't much but I was keeping my eyes open for any government business that could be done in Moose Jaw.

My office received a phone call from an irate minister of social services, Pat Smith, over the loss of the Sask Minerals account. The Swift Current firm had gone screaming to their MLA over the loss of the twenty-thousand-dollar account. I was not in the office when she called, "squawking like a banshee" according to one of my executive assistants. "I'm phoning the premier," she kept squawking. Pat Smith was a former head of the Saskatchewan School Trustees' Association who had retained the Swift Current seat for the Tories after the trauma of Dennis Ham and his flirtation with the Collver Unionist party. She came highly rated; however, I felt she and Joan Duncan had been placed in the cabinet at the expense of better qualified men. In this age of equal rights it seems men are often discriminated against. Pat Smith was far from the bright light she was supposed to be, but she was not the weakest cabinet member either. Her nickname among the backbenchers was "the bitch." I called her back to suggest she replace the lost twenty-thousand-dollar account with one of the dozens of agencies that came under the umbrella of her department. Better yet, I would return the accounting to Swift Current if she would send some of her departmental business into Moose Jaw. I acquired an instant understanding of how she had earned her nickname and was treated to a rendition of "squawking like a banshee," as my executive assistant termed it. I was on weak ground since the changing of an accounting firm should have been a board decision, but at this point in time Sask Minerals did not have a board. I returned the business to Swift Current and told Sask Minerals to do a tender call on all aspects of their business, including accounting, for discussion at a board meeting.

The premier had decided it was time to proclaim to the world that Saskatchewan was truly open for business with a government-sponsored Open for Business conference in Regina in the fall. We were going to invite everyone and anyone who might possibly be interested in doing business in the province in a gigantic public relations' move to demonstrate clearly that the purveyors of doom and gloom—the NDP—were safely shut away and would not be in a position to impede business for decades to come. By now a malaise was setting in on cabinet and it was almost appearing as though Grant Devine was becoming weary of being the premier of Saskatchewan. He was withdrawing more and more into his small circle and becoming increasingly inaccessible on government matters. He loved politics and public relations but he did not enjoy the drudgery of administration. Certainly, he wanted to be kept informed, yet only if that meant he did not have to render a decision. His executive council was a mess and it was the talk of the bureaucracy. Because of my frigid relationship with Devine, it was not my place to tell him what was happening or how it appeared and I am not sure he would have cared. By now he was isolated to the point it was impossible to tell who carried weight with him. I still assumed it was Berntson and Andrew, but they would always deny it and say his wife and his father carried more weight than anyone. In cabinet, Devine continued to refer to government reorganization, but for some reason things still looked the same.

I received a call from TRW in Redondo Beach that turned out to be a pleasant surprise. They had completed their geological evaluations and were interested in a $12-million joint venture in the province. I was delighted to hear we were still on their list and that things were moving along more quickly than anticipated. We met in Palm Springs and I suggested they team up with Saskoil because of their extensive research facility—the one the Align report had suggested was a luxury we could ill afford. The $12-million investment seemed a minimal risk compared to the potential benefits. If the TRW process worked, the production potential of the province's reserves would increase dramatically. Drs. Peterson and Meeker suggested a game of golf with their chairman at some future date. Apparently, if you were a golfer you had credibility and if you could putt then you really had some merit. I had hoped we could have gone further but it was a useful session anyway and I invited them to our Open for Business conference in the hope they would like what they saw.

Upon returning home I had one of my rare meetings with

Grant Devine in which I brought him up to date on what we were doing at energy and mines. In a move designed to put pressure on us, Husky Oil had served notice to the consortium that they were withdrawing. The resulting publicity made Devine nervous, even though he had expected the move. The consortium was going to hold together for a time and Petro-Canada would become the project operator. Emphasis was being shifted to the Co-op project, which was now making more and more sense in every respect. I was enthusiastic about the interest TRW was showing in the province. It was for others to evaluate the merit of the project but I felt strongly we should pursue it to the end because of its limitless potential in Saskatchewan. I presented Devine with a copy of Align's report on Saskoil and raised the question of a management team. He wanted to wait for the report he had commissioned on Crown corporations before taking any action. He really did not seem to care much about anything we were discussing and the meeting ended on a most inconclusive note. I may as well have talked to his desk.

The response to our new royalty structure was beyond our wildest dreams. Companies who had indicated little interest in the immediate future were entering the province way ahead of schedule. Norcean, for example, had indicated that regardless of our new royalty schedule, they would not put us on their drilling program for at least a year. They were already in and drilling. The first two months of the new royalty schedule had seen drillings that equaled the first six months of the previous year. The industry had responded in the most dramatic manner available to them—with cash. I could not have been happier with the results of my work as minister. If I did not accomplish anything else, I had at least left a model for consultation between the private sector and the government. However, I was well aware the success of the program would merely cause the backbiters to bite harder.

My relations with the press had always been tenuous. I neither liked them nor respected them nor did I make any pretense that I did. I had seen too many reporters come and go, many barely out of high school with little or no understanding of the issues they were reporting. I used to tolerate them as a necessary evil; however, after we assumed government, I found them even more difficult to deal with. At the start I was accessible to anyone, particularly to out-of-town reporters from the smaller centers and I would try to give them copy. On a particularly busy day, a John Price of CHAB Moose Jaw phoned about the upgrader. I was in between meetings and took the call although I was really pressed for time. The reporter knew nothing about the upgrader and did not even know what questions he wanted to ask. I brusquely told him to call back when he knew what he wanted, and hung up. Price then phoned the premier, who in turn phoned me. Devine was very gentle but said Price had played the tape to him and, while he understood my frustration, that was no excuse to be rude to the media. He was right. After that I hired a press secretary.

Liz MacDonald was very astute and her experience in the old Clark government had tuned her in politically. She was far and away the best press secretary in the building and fitted in well. The press secretaries met once a week to exchange ideas and catch up on what was happening around the buildings. She drew my attention to a survey that had been done on the public's perception of the various ministers. When I asked her who had put out the survey she said she was not supposed to know anything about it. Apparently it had ruffled some feathers when my recognition factor was as high as Devine's and the third-place minister was not even in hailing distance. What had concerned Liz was that I was seen as the best minister but I was not particularly popular. In short, they were checking the wind before they cut my throat.

The Open for Business conference was held in Regina the middle of October and I found myself one of the keynote speakers. There were no major announcements to be made and I really thought we were going to be seen as a group of windbags by the hard-nosed business people we had invited. When it was my turn to speak I decided to announce that from now on mining ventures in northern Saskatchewan no longer had to offer 50 percent of the operation to SMDC, as had been the case under the NDP. In other words, SMDC had enjoyed the luxury of an automatic right of first refusal. I removed the privilege without any consultation but, of course, pretended it was a collective decision. It was the only solid announcement of the whole conference and in passing the premier whispered, "Good job." For all I knew when he leaned over he was going to say, "You're fired."

As the number of drillings increased, the more difficult I thought it would be to fire me. After all, the premier had yet to make a decision on anything, so firing me was going to be the first thing he had made up his mind on. Husky Oil made their proposal for an upgrader in Lloydminster and it was much as expected. Husky would put up very little cash and throw in their existing assets at an inflated price. The taxpayers would take the risk in the $2-billion venture. The key was the federal government, who had to take the most onerous risk, and the unofficial word was they were not interested. The proposal was elaborately made and we exchanged pleasantries and turned it over to officials for further negotiation. Jack McPhee, my upgrader expert, said he had been told by his counterpart in Edmonton there was no way the Alberta government would ever go for this one. The only way the feds could ever be enticed would be to play on federal Energy Minister Jean Chrétien's leadership ambitions and convince him of western support for the leadership when Pierre Elliott stepped down. Quite a task for a Conservative.

Jean Chrétien was a gentleman, as well as a very able, articulate minister. I met him in Ottawa in his office and I found him to be charming and a straight shooter. In the dealings I was to have with him, I found him very affable, reasonable, and willing to consider both sides of an issue. When he was able to help us, I made a point of saying so in any subsequent press release, which I always made certain found its way to his office. I received criticism in cabinet for this but federal politicians must live too, and to steal credit when it should be shared is a dangerous thing. With the awesome power of the federal government, I always chose to share the credit rather than risk having that power turned against me. One had to remember, we were not the big players in energy and you had to steal the crumbs where you could, so when Jean Chrétien did us a favor I was always grateful because he didn't have to.

I had another meeting with the Fluor people at their Irvine headquarters. The Husky project had not generated much enthusiasm from the governments involved, we still needed an upgrader, and Fluor had some unique and interesting ideas. It was difficult to put together a billion-dollar project for a product that was in oversupply worldwide and when the only way the project could possibly succeed was with the cooperation of the federal government. Getty Oil had to come into the picture but they were still deciding how they were going to operate Canadian Reserve.

During the meeting I broached the subject of a nuclear power plant. It seemed Fluor had been waiting for that one. They had a reactor that had never been used and they were dying to try it. However, they were quick to say they could not compete with the federal government's Candu reactor. They were perceptive enough to know that if it was our intent to export power to the United States, the federal government could make it easy for us or complicate the deal to the point where it was out of the question. To use one of the federal government's own reactors would no doubt facilitate matters. Fluor was interested in building the power plant either way and were ready to help in any details. I asked if they could arrange an appointment with Southern California Edison soon to discuss the sale of the surplus power.

When I got home Dave Tkachuk came to see me about the SMDC legal work. I confessed I had not solved the problem yet and asked for his suggestions. To Tkachuk it was simple: give the work to a Tory firm and forget it. He said Stromberg was considering leaving his present firm and forming a partnership with former MLA Harold Lane if they could be certain of the SMDC account. I said it was a great idea but I could not guarantee the account until the firm had shown it could do the work. Tkachuk said they had to have the guarantee first; they would buy the necessary expertise if they had to. I knew an appointment had to be made soon and if Stromberg and Lane could put together a firm with the necessary qualifications, that would certainly solve my problem. My meeting with Tkachuk ended on that note. The sooner the matter was resolved the better. By now, SMDC wanted to stay with Pedersen Norman.

Things had calmed in the Crown corporations and it was now safe to appoint a board of directors for the three Crowns under me. Saskoil came out with a particularly strong board, which I found encouraging. At our first briefing meeting I broached the subject of a management team to turn the company around. Bob Andrew opposed the idea because the report on Crown corporations had not been completed yet; I disputed the validity of that argument since the management team would be a short-term appointment only. The board was enthusiastic and wanted to talk to some of the potential management teams. The Align team that had done the original report on Saskoil was one of the applicants. Almost apologetically Jim Whiteside said, "We didn't do this to recommend us a job." The entrance of Align upset Bob Andrew, who had taken a strong dislike to Jim Whiteside even though he hardly knew him. Ultimately, the board hired Align on a unanimous vote when Andrew was not present. They were hired to run Saskoil at $25,000 a month for a six-month period. Their mandate was simple: make an oil company about to lose $6 million show a profit, and fast. While this board decision was to play a major role in my downfall, it was a major reason why Saskoil turned around so dramatically and in fact showed a profit far more quickly than I had dared hope for. Some real oil people were finally in control. Harvey Bryant knew the oil business and Jim Whiteside knew politics. They paid their entire way in two weeks, although Bob Andrew would never admit it.

Fluor arranged a meeting for me with the vice-president of the gigantic power utility Southern California Edison. I had come to have complete faith in the abilities of Jack McPhee and I took him with me to California. At this level the executives made their time count and we got to the purpose of the meeting quickly. I told the vice-president we were considering a nuclear reactor but we needed a buyer for the excess power. He asked some technical questions and then I was stunned when he said, "You could build a plant that size every year for fifteen years and we would take all you could sell us." That is an amount of power almost beyond comprehension. I had expected delivery to be a major problem. It was not. They would take delivery at the border and, via a series of exchanges with other power companies en route, power generated in Saskatchewan would have little difficulty ending up in southern California. It was a natural deal of benefit to both sides. Their purchase of surplus power would finance the reactor and freeze power rates in Saskatchewan and they would get a long-term arrangement. I designated Jack McPhee to follow up at our end.

When we got back to Saskatchewan I called George Hill and reported verbally to the premier. There was no question Devine was interested although he was skeptical about the delivery of the power. He had a friend in Alberta who was supposed to have some expertise in this area and he had told Devine the logistics of delivery were complex and almost impossible. I bit my tongue and suggested Southern California Edison had some experience in the field; they seemed to feel it could be done and they were the ones who were going to do it. Devine said to "keep going" but to be "careful."

We went into the fall session of the legislature and broke the bad news to the public about the financial mess we had inherited from the NDP. The mess was an actual deficit of more than $150 million. The session was an easy one for me. The oil industry was surging: the number of drillings had soared and we had just completed the biggest land sale in three years to the oil companies. My department introduced legislation that simplified the existing legislation and made our royalty schedule much easier to understand. I was hardly even quizzed. The estimates of the department went through in a breeze. The board of directors of Sask Minerals met and made various changes—among them was a change of accounting firms from Burroughs, Weber, Gross, Downs & Heppner in Swift Current to Hagan Van Iderstine in Moose Jaw as the result of a tender call.

As Christmas approached, if I was in any political trouble with anyone, it was difficult to perceive. I was in demand as a speaker, although I turned down most engagements, and all areas I was in charge of were doing well. In many respects things were going too well and something had to happen. I was to accompany Devine to Vancouver for a fund-raising effort but I was forced to cancel the trip for family reasons. If he was upset, he did not show it and my place was taken by Lorne McLaren. I was taking my family to Palm Springs for Christmas and had some business appointments during the time I was there. Paul Rousseau was also going to be in Palm Springs and was going to accompany me on a visit to TRW in Redondo Beach. The premier held a Christmas party for the cabinet and it was one of the few cabinet functions I attended. It was to be my last.

My family and I left for Palm Springs and spent the holidays there. I was in daily touch with my office but very little was happening and I was able to deal with the few matters that did arise over the phone. Paul Rousseau and I toured TRW's Redondo Beach site and viewed the experimental laboratory where the ultrasecret process was being tested. Rousseau was impressed and both of us gaped in wonderment as we were taken through the area where the space communication satellites were being meticulously constructed. Regina seemed a million miles away about then. Rousseau, as minister of industry, carried weight with TRW and there was little doubt they were looking favorably at Saskatchewan. Rousseau agreed these people were the major leagues and we should not let them get away easily. TRW moved slowly and it appeared they were happy with the manner in which the day had gone. Rousseau and I thought we were on the verge of a real breakthrough.

I returned home in early January and, after checking things at the ranch, went to my office in Regina. The Co-op and the remnants of the consortium were coming in next week to make a proposal for a mini-upgrader and they wanted me to accompany them to Ottawa for a presentation to Jean Chrétien. Harvey Bryant and Jim Whiteside briefed me on Saskoil. They were happy with the progress there and had started an audit of the reserves. Harvey still maintained they were vastly undervalued and the audit would dramatically raise the value of Saskoil. Don Moroz came for a briefing from the department and everything appeared normal. A call came in and I was informed the premier wanted to see me at five. His office gave me to understand Devine wished to discuss the upgrader business so a call went to Jack McPhee to get up here and brief me on anything that should be passed on to the premier.

I went to Devine's office at five and the look on his face and the dead silence meant trouble. I waited for him to begin, having no idea now what was on his mind. Finally he said, "There are two letters of resignation on that desk and one of them is yours." I was stunned even though I had known a day like this was inevitable. I asked why. He said I had stirred up trouble with another minister—meaning Pat Smith—and she was threatening to resign over the change of accounting firms at Sask Minerals. The backbiters had really been at it. I told

Devine the change was a board decision based on a tender call in which five firms had submitted proposals. The decision was unanimous and one of the other board members was cabinet minister Bob Pickering. When Devine replied that I had orchestrated the board decision after the mixup last summer, I invited him to review the proposal call. He then brought up the name of Tony Merchant and said I had assured him Merchant was not doing anything permanent for SMDC. I told him that was true and the situation had not changed since I had talked to him. The Pedersen Norman firm was doing pressing legal work only as far as I knew. I repeated the sequence of events in the SMDC legal work saga. He said his information was they had received $500,000 worth of work, a figure I said was impossible. He wanted answers right away and I said he would have them in the morning.

Devine was leaving for Toronto at noon the next day so I was back in his office early and presented him with the proposal call for the Sask Minerals account and the best information I had on the status of SMDC's legal work. SMDC had already paid Pedersen Norman $2,000 in legal fees, and their estimate of the total fee so far was $78,000, although they had not yet been billed for that amount. I thought the matter would now be settled—I had refuted the claim that Pedersen Norman had received $500,000 in fees and Devine had always known they were only a temporary appointment—but it soon became obvious it was not. Devine said he was getting calls from everywhere over the use of Tony Merchant, although when I asked for names or sources they were not forthcoming—probably because there weren't any other than a few Tory lawyers who wanted in on the gravy train. When I asked him if he had heard any complaints about their work he said it didn't matter whether their work was good or bad. Our meeting ended and Devine left for Toronto. I returned to my office and took a call from SMDC. Eric Berntson was in their office asking for copies of their legal billings. They wanted to know if they should give them to him. I said yes. Later Roy Lloyd phoned. He was in the East and had been summoned to meet with Devine that evening in Toronto. I told him he would most likely be asked about SMDC's legal work and he should tell it exactly the way it was.

I knew at this point my cabinet days were over but I did not know why. Certainly it was not over the accounting contract. As much as Devine disliked me he was not going to trade me for a lightweight like Pat Smith, and the legal fees to Pedersen Norman were minute compared to what was being trifled away all around us. Besides, in SMDC's opinion the Pedersen Norman work was of excellent quality and would stand up to scrutiny and Devine knew it. It was something else, it had to be. It must have come up recently but I had no idea what it was. I had talked to Devine by phone from California just before Christmas and, apart from the usual coolness, everything had appeared to be normal.

Cabinet the following day was held up until afternoon as we awaited Devine's return from Toronto. I had previously scheduled meetings with a couple of oil companies in Regina. I knew I was finished and had not decided whether or not to go to my last cabinet meeting. The decision was made for me when Larry Martin from the premier's office came down to let me know Devine was not back from Toronto. He told me Devine wanted me to skip this meeting because "he had a couple of things he had to straighten with one or two ministers." He then added, "They are acting like kids." I did not ask who "they" were, but it didn't matter. If there was any doubt it was all over, Martin had eliminated it. I went through the motions that afternoon and I was now feeling pretty low. I had been knifed and I did not know why. I had done my job, done it better than anyone else, and the results were—and still are—there to support that statement. I had nothing to be ashamed of as a minister, in fact quite the reverse, yet it was game over.

I met with Devine that Thursday afternoon and he said he wanted my resignation. You have no real defense when you are in this sort of situation. If you are not wanted by the leader or the premier, you must leave. You do not have the right to dispute his decision or to air any laundry in public. He is the dictator and a minister is there at his pleasure or gone at his whim. If it was my resignation he wanted, he could have it, but I felt I was owed an explanation. He said I had misled him on the Merchant matter with SMDC, which I denied heatedly. He said there were stories circulating that I had used SMDC to pay Merchant for my divorce. I didn't know whether to laugh or cry—the preposterousness of it. How do you defend yourself against an outright lie? I told him he owed it to me to tell me the source of the allegation but once again he was giving no answers. The subject shifted to the Saskoil management team he said I had installed at a waste of $25,000 a month. I replied that bringing in a management team was a board decision that only Andrew had opposed and Align was doing an incredible job. He referred to them as "Liberal hacks." Staunch Republican Harvey Bryant a Liberal hack! It was so absurd it was beyond belief. "They have no credibility in the industry," said Devine. I asked him if he had ever talked to them and if not who had told him that. Again, he wouldn't say. "I'm tired of defending you," he said wearily. I commented that I could imagine the kind of defense I would get from him. He said Berntson and Andrew would not sit in the same room with me and he didn't need that. I was even more mystified now and I could not believe that was true from Berntson. When I said I wanted to talk to him Devine replied, "He won't talk to you and he doesn't want anything to do with you." I said I wanted to hear that from him and I left to find him. On my way out I signed the letter of resignation without even reading it.

I found Berntson in the halls and we went to his office where I asked him what this was all about. "Grant has made up his mind," he said. I told him Devine had said it was because of him and I wanted to know why. Just then the phone rang and Berntson answered with, "Yeah, he's here now." He got off the phone and said, "It's up to Grant. I don't care one way or the other. I'll talk to him and get back to you." Translated that meant, "Please leave." I did not know whether to call the staff in or not. I decided to wait until tomorrow until I met again with Devine.

It was afternoon when I met with Grant Devine for the last time. He was going to hold an 8:00 A.M. press conference on Monday to announce the news and then he was leaving for a week in the States. I said I had a lot of things on the go and, while I accepted the inevitability of the dismissal, perhaps it would be wise to give me time to try to clean some of them up. He said he couldn't afford to leave me around while he was away because "I had no credibility left in the oil industry." I felt better after that comment because I knew it wasn't true and, more important, he knew it too.

I returned to my office and called my staff in and told them. Don Moroz joined us because I wanted him to know it from me. We had a few drinks and sat around and reminisced for a while. The others decided to go for dinner but I wished to return to Moose Jaw and I left the buildings for the last time as a cabinet minister. One week later, almost to the hour, the nightmare began.